D0391357

GAME DAY

THE BLUE JAYS
AT SKYDOME

MARTIN & SEAN O'MALLEY

VIKING

Viking
Published by the Penguin Group
Penguin Books Canada Ltd, 10 Alcorn Avenue, Toronto, Ontario,
Canada M4V 3B2
Penguin Books Ltd, 27 Wrights Lane, London W8 5TZ, England
Viking Penguin, a division of Penguin Books USA Inc., 375 Hudson
Street, New York, New York 10014, U.S.A.
Penguin Books Australia Ltd, Ringwood, Victoria, Australia
Penguin Books (NZ) Ltd, 182-190 Wairau Road, Auckland 10, New
Zealand

Penguin Books Ltd, Registered Offices: Harmondsworth, Middlesex,
England

First published 1994

10 9 8 7 6 5 4 3 2 1

Printed and bound in Canada on acid free paper ⊗

Canadian Cataloguing in Publication Data

O'Malley, Martin
Game day

ISBN 0-670-85026-8

1. Toronto Blue Jays (Baseball team). 2. SkyDome (Toronto, Ont.).
I. O'Malley, Sean, 1965–   . II.Title.

GV875.T6705 1994   796.357'64'09713541   C94-930000-4

To the women
in our lives:
CAROLE, HUGHENA, KATHLEEN,
MARGARET, MICHELLE and WENDY

and to
BRAD BUJOLD,
who loved his job
and did it so well

Contents

PART ONE GAME PLAN

PART TWO   GAME DAY

GAME
DAY

PART ONE
GAME PLAN

=== 1 ===

Travels at SkyDome (1)

The first time we went together to the SkyDome was on
Father's Day, 1989, two weeks after it opened. We had
arranged seats at Windows on SkyDome. This is a restaurant
overlooking the field, which for a traditional baseball fan,
whatever that means, is an odd place to watch baseball.

Odd it may have been, but watching the game amid the
glitter and technology of the SkyDome, the possibilities of
tugging the curtain aside to reveal what goes on behind the
scenes were fascinating. Such a great commotion is made
about a Broadway opening—weeks of rehearsal, revisions,
songs deleted and songs added, cast changes, the wardrobe,
the props, the publicity, then the play hits the road for a pre-
Broadway tour, all of which inexorably leads to Opening
Night and a scrubbed theatre packed with an audience of, oh,
a couple of thousand.

What about this place? They don't even call it a Stadium,
or a Park, or a Field; they call it The World's Greatest Entertainment Centre. As anyone who has not been living on the
moon knows, the SkyDome—that's right: cap S, cap D—has
a roof that opens and closes, which makes a great deal of sense
for a playing field in Canada, but which, for a variety of reasons, upsets baseball traditionalists.

GAME PLAN

Windows on SkyDome may be an odd place to watch baseball, but baseball is an odd game. The foul lines proceed into infinity, the game can go on forever—blah, blah, blah. We know that, we are weary of restating it. It is odd, too, because the fans take such a proprietary interest in their game, and make no mistake, they regard it as their game even if they have never caught a fly ball or experienced the mesmerizing impact of a liner heading directly at their foreheads. Baseball fans are the world's greatest second-guessers because it is a game made for second-guessing. Of all professional team sports, baseball also attracts a disproportionate number of female fans, perhaps because of its deceptively gentle outward rhythms, possibly because the tight double-knits make even ordinary male bums look rather fetching, more likely because both sexes played it as kids when the buzzer sounded for recess. Baseball has an inherent snob appeal, which translates as *Your knowledge of the game is horsehit.* (Worth noting, too, that *horseshit* is a baseball word—a scout's word—and it is a noun; *bullshit* is not a baseball word—no more than *piss* or *damn*—but when it is used in baseball it is a verb.)

When they can no longer play the game, baseball players suddenly become more interesting, more rounded persons, less obsessed with the myopic quotidian demands that propelled them in their primes. The truth is, baseball players do not reach the major leagues and remain there unless they have a whopping dose of self-centred obsession, which tends to make them act like pricks. Not all of them—and not if you could plumb the depths of what songwriter Jacques Brel called their "nighttime fears"—but some of them sure can act like pricks.

One of the joys of following the Blue Jays of 1992 and 1993 is that the team contained a disproportionate number of what scouts call "character players." We do not mean character as in "flake" or "jackass," but character as in "integrity" or "mensch." In 1992 there was Dave Winfield, to name only one. Having much success with Winfield as their dominant character player in 1992—he certainly had a public-relations

2

flair for playing the part—the Blue Jays went out in 1993 and replaced him with another, even better one: Paul Molitor. They also added pitcher Dave Stewart, one of the classiest individuals in major league baseball. And they already had John Olerud, who came into his own in 1993, fulfilling the bravest of brave predictions for the sweet-swinging first baseman who will not say two words when one will do. When he was general manager of the San Diego Padres, Joe McIlvaine said, "Ability can take you to the major leagues, on the periphery. But what you have inside decides who becomes the fringe player, the average player, the star....When you get down to comparisons of *average* major-leaguers, what really separates them is what they've got in their guts and their hearts."

Character players have a ripple effect on a team, adding a lot of positives that seem to have an exponential impact, just as bad-ass players have a ripple effect that produces a lot of negatives. The Blue Jays of Damaso Garcia and George Bell demonstrated the bad-ass effect in the 1980s, as the New York Mets of Vince Coleman did in 1993 when they achieved the questionable distinction of becoming the all-time Team Ugly.

The roof was closed at the SkyDome that Father's Day afternoon. There was the tinkle of glass and cutlery, people ordered beef Wellington with a half litre of house red, then examined the dessert list trying to choose between strawberry cheesecake and *crème parfait avec Pernod*. It was an odd place to watch baseball.

Many years earlier, when the Blue Jays played their games at Exhibition Stadium—essentially two large concrete slabs by Lake Ontario, unarguably the worst stadium in major league baseball—Martin helped organize a grass-roots group called "Friends of Outdoor Baseball." The "Friends" were against a domed stadium, and they were fighting mad. Thanks to a weekly column in *The Globe and Mail,* Martin was able regularly to heap abuse on local officials determined to build a domed stadium for baseball. This was when "domed" meant fully enclosed, non-retractable, a roofed stadium of the sort in

Houston, Seattle and Minneapolis. One column was an open letter to Paul Godfrey when he was chairman of Metro Council, Toronto's non-elected "Supermayor," and one of the prime movers in the campaign to build a domed stadium.

"Paul, Paul, Paul," the column began, "is there no way to stop this madness, this bonehead march to oblivion, this juggernaut you have helped set in motion that appears to be grinding its awful way to—a domed stadium?"

To give Godfrey credit, and Martin always gave him a lot of credit, he was also a prime mover in the original campaign to bring major league baseball to Toronto. Without him it might have taken another five years, or ten years; without Godfrey Toronto still might not have a major league baseball team. The man loves the city, and baseball, but in the early 1980s he was caught in a strange time warp that equated domed stadiums with major-leagueness—or, worse, with "putting Toronto on the map." The pop novelist Tom Wolfe used to call this "square-hip," a stinging epithet he reserved for only the squarest of squares.

The column ended: "There are outdoor games and there are indoor games, Paul. Basketball, hockey, bowling, curling, snooker, bridge, poker and sex are indoor games. Golf, yachting, horse racing and, most assuredly, baseball, are outdoor games. The weather is part of it. You want to get a sunburn. You want to watch an outfielder circling dizzily under a high, wind-blown fly ball. If you want to spend $140 million on a roof, Paul, why not for the people who don't have one over their heads?"

Things have changed in ten years.

Who would have suspected back then that a hole in the sky would allow sunlight, which used to be regarded as the healthiest thing imaginable, to attack us with murderous cancers? As for dizzying fly balls, one night in 1993 Shane Mack, an outfielder for the Minnesota Twins, staggered in short left trying to find a John Olerud pop-up that had disappeared against the white Teflon roof of the Metrodome in Minneapolis. Eventually the ball plopped like a ripe apple several feet behind Mack as Olerud watched from second base, having smacked his third double in three at-bats.

The roof at the Metrodome is only 186 feet high—compared to the SkyDome's 282 feet, as high as a 31-storey building—and balls that hit speakers dangling from the roof of the Metrodome are deemed to be in play. Dave Kingman of the Oakland Athletics once hit a ball that sailed through a hole in the roof of the Metrodome. The Twins' infielders watched and watched, but the ball never came down. Kingman's shot through the roof was ruled a double, which provoked an angry outburst from the Athletics, who thought, because the ball went out of the park, it should have been a home run.

Great fun.

As for the $140-million roof, it is to laugh at. SkyDome ended up costing nearly $600 million, and in 1993 the debt remained at an intractable $350 million. It's not that SkyDome doesn't make money; it does—lots. In 1992 its operating profit was $34 million, making SkyDome the most profitable stadium in North America. The problem was interest on the debt ($26.9 million), taxes ($10.6 million) and depreciation ($18 million), which created $21.5 million in red ink. In 1993 SkyDome was expected to hold 245 "event days," which would surpass Madison Square Garden as the busiest sporting facility on the continent.

The baseball Fogies prefer real grass, a more contemplative atmosphere and a keener sense of baseball on the part of the customers, and who's to begrudge them their preferences? Knowledgeable baseball fans do come to SkyDome, and they are growing, but they are vastly outnumbered by SkyDome fans and JumboTron fans and fun-loving vacuum-heads who jump up to The Wave fast as you can chant 3...2...1.... There could be a no-hitter in the works, a tense 2–1 pitchers' duel, but—3...2...1...and the low-boredomers high over centre field start another Wave. They usually boo fans behind the dugouts and home plate—people like scouts and owners and former players—for not knowing enough about baseball to keep the Wave going.

Toronto fans may never be as deeply informed as their counterparts in New York, Boston and Chicago, but they are developing a sense of perspective. Early in the 1993 season, pitcher Scott Brow, just up from Double A, tossed four innings of no-hit ball in his major-league debut, a remarkable feat. When he yielded a single to start off the fifth, the fans greeted him with warm applause. Next day, Juan Guzman pitched four no-hit innings before allowing a leadoff single in the fifth. This time the fans barely reacted, knowing that Guzman's feat had been excellent, but hardly noteworthy. Also early in the 1993 season, Paul Molitor observed that Toronto fans have improved immeasurably since the days when they wildly cheered any medium fly ball to the outfield. One time at the SkyDome Molitor watched a Blue Jay ground out, second to first, moving a runner on second to third with one out, and some of the crowd actually applauded. They are getting better.

The Fogies could do without the massive, Big Brother JumboTron in centre field. The Fogies prefer real grass. The Fogies prefer the roof open, except when it is raining or snowing or cold enough to cause an earache. After attending more than five consecutive games with the roof closed, one does experience a *weltschmerz*, something like March in Winnipeg, or learning you are being audited by Revenue Canada. We call it "Dome Flu."

The retractable dome lets in summer evenings and autumn afternoons, though the original operating premise has been completely reversed. It used to be regarded as an open stadium unless the weather was terrible; now it is a closed stadium unless the weather is wonderful. That it can be opened at all is a victory for Martin's ragtag "Friends of Outdoor Baseball" of the early 1980s. At least they got them thinking.

And the baseball, of course, has been marvellous. For nearly a decade, every season has brought a pennant race. The Blue Jays have been in postseason contention five times— 1985, 1989, 1991, 1992, 1993—and they were achingly close some other times. Tell it to the suffering fans of the Seattle

Mariners, who came out of the gate the same year as the Blue Jays, in 1977, and only began to make a serious run at the Crown in 1994.

In 1977 Seattle won sixty-four and lost ninety-eight, earning a smattering of polite applause for doing rather well for an expansion team. Seattle had to do rather well, because their fans had experienced major league baseball before, with a team of sorts called the Seattle Pilots. Just bringing major league baseball back to Seattle wasn't enough. The fans wanted recognizable major-league *players,* so they went out and bought some. The Blue Jays had no such pressure on them. The fans were happy just to be in the big leagues, being able to munch popcorn and watch the New York Yankees, Boston Red Sox, Baltimore Orioles and Detroit Tigers.

Knowing that nothing but showing up was expected of them, the Blue Jay brain trust rooted around at the Double A and Triple A levels, scooping up other teams' minor-league prospects. The first year, the Jays won only 54 games, losing 107, but they prevailed over Seattle where it counted most— attendance. In 1977 the fledgling Jays drew 1,701,052 fans, while the Mariners drew 1,338,511. The Jays have been prevailing over Seattle, and everyone else, ever since.

Memories are always "old" memories. Lest we forget, even venerable Fenway Park in Boston was newfangled and suspiciously modern when it opened in 1912, the same week the *Titanic* sank. When they added the Green Monster at Fenway, after the dead-ball era for which Fenway's dimensions made sense, the Fogies of the day must surely have complained, "They're turning baseball into a pinball game!"

In ten, twenty years, people will look back to the early 1990s as the golden age of baseball in Toronto. SkyDome transformed the neighbourhood, changed the city, moved Toronto's downtown heart from Nathan Phillips Square at City Hall to the bright lights of the theatre district. The debt on the SkyDome may be $350 million, but the spinoff benefits are incalculable. After being in two successive World Series, people all over North America are as familiar with

Toronto and the SkyDome neighbourhood as any resident of Cabbagetown or The Annex.

Some of the spinoff benefits are calculable. A study completed in the summer of 1993 by the Metropolitan Toronto Convention and Visitors Association determined that, debt or no debt, the SkyDome generated an annual $264.8 million in goods and services in Metro Toronto, and $351.9 million to the province of Ontario. SkyDome also generates about $60 million in tax revenue for Metro Toronto, $70 million to the province.

This does not include new eateries and drinkeries that have sprung up along the streets heading to and from the stadium. At every home game, hot-dog stands are parked on sidewalks, rickshaw drivers hustle customers over the streetcar tracks, and nosy, cap-hatted baseball crowds exiting from SkyDome mix with the patrons in tuxedos and ankle-length gowns coming out of Roy Thomson Hall, the Royal Alexandra Theatre and the new Princess of Wales Theatre, where *Miss Saigon* was playing. The crowds were electrifying, the baseball excellent.

SkyDome needs to grow a little nostalgia to soften the edges. There is that monstrous JumboTron, the hyper recroom ambience, computerized sound effects, modern music, the hyperkinetic pop culture. No more "Give Me Five Minutes More," not even "Take Me Out to the Ball Game." Whether by design or accident, the SkyDome makes welcome those who feel comfortable in a video game arcade, which is the ambience of the 1990s. It is a cultural phenomenon, and the Fogies don't get it, which is a pity because the likes of SkyDome may turn out to be the saviour of professional baseball.

Writing in the New York *Times*, television producer Thad Mumford explains:

A generation of young men and women weaned on the helter skelter of music videos and remote control are hardly in sync with a sport that celebrates amiable meanderings of timeless grace. Our bottom-line pop culture

8

exalts product but has lost patience with process. Feelings of youthful alienation that in previous times expressed themselves in turgid, melodramatic ballads are now nurtured by the often myopic hopelessness and cynicism of today's music and language.

This translates into a kind of generational restlessness that lends itself more to the primordial violence of football or the in-your-face machismo of basketball. The vernacular of the pop culture, once peppered with baseball terminology, is now liberally sprinkled with words like "slam dunk" and "blitz."

Aiding and abetting the cultural estrangement from baseball is the video game. Instead of taking their boundless energy outdoors, playing sports and developing athletic skills, kids now plant themselves in front of computer screens, becoming passively seduced in the process. Can you imagine Mantle, Mays or Snider saying, "I can't come out right now. I'm playing Mindsweeper."

It makes perfect sense to a generation of fans for whom television is as natural as breathing in and breathing out. They were fiddling with video joysticks when they were barely out of diapers. They have grown up with malls and microwave ovens and ghetto-blasters and twenty-four-hour rock television channels. When they hear the Fogies sigh and whisper "real grass" and "breezes" and "Honus Wagner," Generation X shrugs and looks right past them. Their parents have always been telling them to "Turn it down!" Or, "Can't you read a book?"

Yeah, sure.

The players are of the same generation, and most of them enjoy baseball in SkyDome. George Brett of Kansas City may be a little older than most active players, but he is not yet a Fogie who automatically rejects something as newfangled as the SkyDome. He has said he would like to finish his career there, if circumstances permitted. Al Newman, who used to play for the Texas Rangers and now is an advance scout for the Minnesota Twins, scratched his head one evening at SkyDome and said, "I never really thought of this place as a domed stadium." Most games he remembered the roof was open, and even when it was closed it didn't feel like a dome. "It's because the ceiling is so high," Newman said. "It's not anything like the domes in Seattle and Minneapolis." Beeston himself regards SkyDome as a "selling tool" for attracting some of the biggest stars to Toronto. Were it not for SkyDome, he believes, the Blue Jays would not have obtained, or retained, Joe Carter, Jack Morris and John Olerud, to name only three. As for all-star second baseman Roberto Alomar, he literally eats, sleeps and plays there, living in a comfortable city-facing room in the SkyDome Hotel.

To get an idea of the generational cleavage, one day Alomar brought a toy truck to the field and, using remote controls, gleefully zipped it around his teammates' feet near the batting cage. When the game was over, multimillionaire Alomar took his toy truck home, which was an elevator ride away at the SkyDome Hotel. Some nights he stopped at SkyDome's Hard Rock Cafe on the way. Like *Playboy*'s Hugh Hefner, it was entirely possible Alomar could go for weeks at a time without leaving home and still be famous.

Love it or loathe it, SkyDome captures and reflects Toronto more accurately than other stadiums capture and reflect their cities. SkyDome may be a bit brassy and glitzy, but in its way it is more honest than the instant-antiqued look of Camden Yards in Baltimore, where the Fogies go to swoon. The Fogies love Camden Yards—and Tiger Stadium, Wrigley Field, Fenway Park and Pilot Field—but they reflect Baltimore, Detroit, Chicago, Boston and Buffalo the way Disneyland reflects southcentral Los Angeles. Sigh all you want at these restful oases; just don't park too far away, and keep your money in a moneybelt, and walk quickly.

Say what you will, SkyDome *is* Toronto: big, quiet, immaculate, technically brilliant and stinking in debt. What's the point of being cynical? It is an architectural and engineering wonder. It works, it's here and it ain't gonna change. It attracts more than fifty thousand fans a game, more than four million fans a season, and that's just for baseball. For the sixth game of the 1992 World Series, when the Blue Jays were playing in Atlanta, forty thousand fans trekked into SkyDome to watch the game *on television.* If only Marshall McLuhan were alive.

They built it, and they came. One simply can't fight it anymore. The Fogies have lost.

On a rainy afternoon on the last day of July, 1992, Martin drove to the SkyDome in Toronto to meet Paul Beeston, president of the Toronto Blue Jays. Over the past ten years he had met Beeston many times—in Toronto, Florida, California. He did not know Beeston that well, but they kept bumping into each other. He used to say that Beeston is one of those fellows who always makes a great first impression.

Beeston is a cheerful chipmunk of a man with an infectious love of life and work. He puffs long, expensive Monte Cristos, strolls sockless in his shoes and looks ten years younger than his age, which in the summer of 1992 was fifty. He is always saying he has the best job in the world, and, for his time and purpose under heaven, he probably does. How many people can leave their office, brush by a set of golf clubs resting against the wall, walk along a corridor, open a door, step into a luxuriously appointed suite, order a pitcher of martinis and watch the Yankees and Blue Jays at play? (We are imagining the martinis, but if Beeston wanted they would be at his elbow in seconds.)

Martin entered a ramp at SkyDome and drove into a bewildering, colour-coded underground garage. About two days later he nosed his car into an empty space in an area marked Sun Zone, a dank concrete bin where the sun never shines.

You get used to this stuff at SkyDome.

He took an elevator to the third floor and walked through two large doors to the Blue Jays' administration office. The lobby is carpeted, with indirect lighting, comfy chairs and glass-topped side tables. The receptionist asked him if he would like coffee, and a steaming cup was on his side table in less than a minute. Somewhere nearby there were chalk lines, a green carpet, dirt and a pitcher's mound, but the lobby at the Blue Jay brain trust felt like the head office of a Scandinavian import-export company.

Pat Gillick, executive vice-president of the Blue Jays—the guy who makes the big deals, the big trades—entered the lobby and said hello. He wore an open-necked sports shirt and looked relaxed and ten years younger than his age, which is fifty-two. What is it with baseball executives?

After saying hello, Gillick asked Martin if he was still living in Tampa.

Martin was shocked. How could he make a mistake like that?

Gillick has a remarkable phographic memory. In his book *Ballpark Figures: The Blue Jays and the Business of Baseball,* Larry Millson says of Gillick: "His memory is the stuff of legend, earning him the nickname 'Wolley Segap' ('yellow pages' spelled backwards) because of his recall of telephone numbers."

Sports writer Trent Frayne was in Florida in 1986 when Bobby Doerr, who had served as a batting instructor for the Blue Jays, had been elected to the Hall of Fame. Frayne wanted to talk to Doerr so he could write a column on him that day. But how to reach him? Frayne noticed Gillick in the stands so he worked his way through the crowd and asked him if he knew where he could get Doerr's phone number. Gillick said, "Sure." Then he recited a ten-digit number, which included the area code for Oregon. "That's his home," Gillick told Frayne. "If he's not there, you could try a lumber camp where he's often at." Then he recited *that* number, all ten digits. Curious, Frayne asked Gillick when he had last called Doerr. Gillick said sometime over the winter, two or three months earlier.

As Gillick prepared to step into the elevator in the Blue Jay lobby, Martin said, "I've never lived in Tampa, Pat."

This time Gillick looked shocked, as if he had forgotten his own phone number.

After some small talk, he left, using the executive elevator, which probably took him down to the dugout or the bullpen or up to the executive SkyBox. Just before he stepped into the elevator he turned and said, "I'm sure it was Tampa," then the doors clunked shut.

Waiting, Martin realized Gillick must have meant "Napa." The last time they had spoken was in Oakland, when the Blue Jays were playing the Athletics in the 1989 American League Championship Series. At the time Martin lived in the Napa Valley. They talked for only a few minutes after the game that day and Martin figures he must have told Gillick he had come down from the Napa and somehow that stuck in Gillick's febrile mind as Tampa.

Martin remained impressed.

Soon Beeston sauntered into the lobby, wearing an open-necked shirt, sockless in his shoes. He beckoned Martin to follow him to his office down the corridor.

Beeston's office overlooks Lake Ontario. There was a bag of golf clubs leaning against a wall by the door. There was a box of Monte Cristos on his desk. Just outside his door, his secretary, a tall woman in a bright red dress, was standing at her desk talking to someone on the telephone. "I'm sorry," they heard her say in soothing executive-secretary tones, "Mr. Beeston is busy."

"Don't you *love* that?" Beeston remarked. "'Mr. Beeston is *busy*.'"

He sounded like a kid who had won a contest to be president of the Blue Jays for a day.

It was the day after a trade. Rob Ducey, the perennial "only Canadian Blue Jay," and catcher Greg Myers had been sent to the California Angels in exchange for Mark Eichhorn, an effective junk-ball reliever who had toiled for the Blue Jays in the 1980s. Eichhorn's nickname is "Popeye," for his admirable imitation of the cartoon character.

Baseball executives are always energized and happy any

time there is a trade. They enjoy trades more than wins, more than grand slams, more than championships. They affect suitably mournful expressions when they explain what a sad thing it is to lose ol' Whojamacallit, or what a shame it is that George Whatshisname will be pumping gas for the rest of his life in Des Moines, but secretly they enjoy the wheeling and dealing. It is because in their youth they always lost the straw-haired beauty to the captain of the football team and now's their chance to get even.

Beeston talked about the umpires, whose company he enjoys. One of his favourites is Marty Springstead, now umpire-in-chief for the American League, based in New York. Springstead is loquacious and funny and profane and during his time on the field was one of the best umpires in baseball.

"He's one of the few who admits mistakes," Beeston says. "Umpires do get things wrong. They make more right calls than wrong calls, but they make more wrong calls than most people realize."

This was the beginning of the second half of the 1992 season, right after the All-Star break, when the team was regrouping for the run to the wire. Many of the Blue Jays who were not selected for the All-Star Game used the off days for a quick visit home. One of them was Derek Bell, the hotshot rookie outfielder, who flew home to Tampa to visit his old neighbourhood. Bell was one of Beeston's favourite players, for reasons that are not immediately obvious—unless opposites do indeed attract.

Beeston is a white chartered accountant who grew up in Welland, Ontario, where his boyhood was filled with the excitement of watching the locks open and close at the Welland Canal. (When talk of a retractable dome began in the early 1980s, Beeston knew instinctively it could be done, remembering the railway-track technology that opened and closed the huge seaway locks.) Bell is an immensely talented, flaky black dude who grew up in a Boyz-in-the-Hood section of Tampa. Whenever Beeston and Bell encountered one another they slapped hands and twisted fingers and slid palms in what has become a modern tribal ritual for a greeting in certain North American neighbourhoods. (They can't do it anymore, however, as Bell was shifted off to San Diego before the 1993 season in a reform move to rid the team of eccentrics and concentrate on players who wipe their cleats before entering the clubhouse, say "Excuse me" after farting and never lead trump.)

"Derek told me he visited his old neighbourhood when he went home," Beeston said. "He told me he took along a 'piece'..."

A gun?

"...just to be safe."

Martin wondered if Rob Ducey ever took home a "piece" when he returned home to London, Ontario, and worked at the local McDonald's. Beeston looked across at Martin, sensed maybe his hyperbole had gone too far, then retreated to a shucks, boys-will-be-boys explanation and shift-ed to the business at hand.

"What can I do for you today?"

Martin explained that we would like to write about a day in the life of the Blue Jays, the orchestration and choreography of a baseball game at SkyDome. What makes it tick? Why is it so successful? What gives? We want to go behind the scenes, find out about the grounds crew, the official scorers, the umpires, the man who sets off the fireworks high about centre field. We want to know more about you and Gillick. And a few of the coaches and players, like hitting instructor Larry Hisle, and sweet-swinging John Olerud, maybe Paul Molitor, and a wide-eyed rookie....

"Will it have pictures in it?" Beeston asked.

"We could try to arrange that," Martin told him.

=2=

Baseball Begins in Florida

Be through my lips to unawakened earth
The trumpet of a prophecy! O, Wind
If Winter comes, can Spring be far behind?

Percy Bysshe Shelley was a baseball fan. When he was studying at Oxford in 1810, Alexander Cartwright had not yet invented baseball, but young Shelley was shagging flies, probably a pickup game of rounders, baseball's precursor. As a poet, outdoorsman and purist, he railed against the atrocities of plastic turf ("unawakened earth") and every year got caught up in the annual rite of predictions ("trumpet of prophecy").

Shelley would have loved spring training.

No other sport makes such a fetish of preseason training. Every March people haul their Winnebagos from Sault Ste. Marie to Florida to watch grown men throw and hit and hawk chewing tobacco. It is inconceivable to imagine Floridians driving to Toronto to watch the Maple Leafs practise hockey.

One of baseball's attractions is that it allows the mind to wander. Let the mind wander in hockey and you might miss something, or get conked. You might get conked in baseball, too—someone gets conked at every game—but in baseball

16

you can let your mind wander and still pay attention. You can carry on a conversation, read a book, plan a vacation, compare what is happening in front of you to other times and places. And there are so many games in a baseball schedule, so much time, that it does not matter if you miss chunks of it. That is why baseball has scorecards, so people can have a record of the game to read later, when their minds have stopped wandering. Even in dainty games like tennis or volleyball or bridge, let your mind wander and you will get snarled or hissed at.

Not baseball. Baseball is for people whose minds wander all over the place. That's why baseball devised its own jargon, called "chatter." The purpose of chatter—"Hum, chuck…hey batter-batter-batter!"—is to allow the mind to wander without actually allowing it to fall asleep.

Spring training started nearly a hundred years ago when the Chicago Cubs set out in March for Hot Springs, Arizona, to prepare for the regular summer season. John McGraw then took his New York Giants to southern California for a springtime workout. Then Branch Rickey discovered Florida and realized there was a market of retired folks anxious to relax in the sun and actually pay to watch meaningless exhibition baseball games.

The debate rages on as to how useful this spring training ritual is. Do baseball players really need six weeks of conditioning in the semi-tropics to prepare for a 162-game schedule? Think of how much teams could save if they just showed up in April with their spikes and gloves for the home openers. But Percy Bysshe Shelley would tell you there would be no poetry to the sport if spring training were abandoned.

No advance publicity, either.

We pulled up at the Silver Dollar Saloon in east Tampa on the last Saturday of March, 1993. Inside, we sat at the bar, Martin holding a vial of Lorazepam in one hand and a cold Budweiser in the other. He called the Lorazepam his "heebie-jeebie" pills.

GAME PLAN

The jukebox played a sad Garth Brooks song.

We were in Florida for the last week of spring training to do our literary stretching exercises. The last week is when the lollygagging is over, so they say, and the team tries on its game face for the season.

Before we left Toronto the doctor had prescribed some chemical comfort for Martin because another woman had walked out of his life. It is becoming a pattern. "They all grow up and leave home," he said. Driving to the aiport in Toronto, trying to cheer him up, Sean said, "Maybe we'll see a bumper sticker that says, 'Honk if you've walked out of Martin O'Malley's life.'"

"That's funny," Martin said.

Lorazepam is a mild sedative, but so's a Bud. The problem is, you are not supposed to mix them. What to do? He chose the Bud—and baseball, and the sweet warmth of Florida.

It had always worked before.

For the next two hours at the Silver Dollar Saloon we held the eight-ball table against all comers until we were trounced by a Louisiana trucker and a horse buyer from Australia.

For twenty years baseball has been the fly-fishing bond in our life version of *A River Runs Through It*. When Sean was seven he was the batboy for a fastball team Martin played for in the early 1970s. When the Toronto franchise opened its first season on that cold, snowy afternoon at Exhibition Stadium in April, 1977, when Sean was eleven years old, Martin took him out of school to attend the game. They did not need Grandmother's funeral as an excuse; any father would have told any principal that baseball is its own excuse.

Martin concedes Sean is a better student of the game. He studies the anatomy charts, reads Bill James, knows there are 360,880 ways to arrange the lineup (and only one is the right one). When he was fourteen years old he won the APBA Canadian Baseball Championship Tournament, which uses a computer-assisted board baseball game. He won it using the 1961 Yankees. For Martin, baseball is an escape from life. He

18

does not believe there is any serious kinship between baseball and life. It does not, as some hyper-romantic baseball writers would like us to believe, imitate life. Baseball is better than life.

In his early fifties, Martin was still playing slo-pitch ball, staying in the game. His undistinguished playing career began in Little League, when he pitched for a team known as the Pirates, which finished last, in no small measure because of Martin's looping "fastball." He progressed through midget, juvenile and junior baseball, eventually earning a spot in the rotation for Columbus Club, a junior team sponsored by the Knights of Columbus in Winnipeg. The team wore grey uniforms with green pinstripes, with a white shamrock on the cap. That was the pinnacle of his baseball career, pulling on that uniform and standing in front of a full-length mirror in his bedroom. The pinnacle of his baseball career might also have come at the age of nineteen, when he was asked to throw batting practice for the Winnipeg Goldeyes, a Class D affiliate of the St. Louis Cardinals. Martin sagaciously declined, however, knowing that off-duty cops and street crossing guards had also been asked to be fodder for the Class D batters of the Northern League in the late 1950s (one of whom happened to be Hank Aaron of the Eau Claire Braves).

If he searches for anything, Martin's quest is for baseball's elusive G-spot. His knowledge of the game is marred by moments of numbing ignorance. For instance, after forty-five years of watching, playing, reading and writing about baseball, he is still not exactly sure if it is absolutely necessary for baserunners to tag up after every pitch. He doesn't think it is, but maybe there is a rule (Section XXIV, subsection iii, subsection F) that says, "It is absolutely necessary for baserunners to tag up after every pitch."

It has persisted so long he is afraid to ask. It is like living next door to a fellow whose name you always thought was Fred Briggs, but, after forty years, there is a niggle of doubt that it might be Frank Briggs.

If they don't have to, why do baserunners tag up after

19

every pitch? They walk back and stand on the bag or give it a little tap with their toe. They do it all the time, even during a time out. There he was at Grant Field, rubbing shoulders with Rich Garcia, the veteran major-league umpire, and Neil MacCarl, the veteran sports writer and official major-league scorer, and he couldn't sidle up and say, "Um, Rich, something I've been meaning to ask you…"

Martin's father used to read a little item in *The Saturday Evening Post* called, "So You Think You Know Baseball?" One time it explained that it is against the rules for anyone to touch a runner rounding third base heading home, even on a home run. Until he died, he remained convinced that runners smacked on the butt rounding third should be called out, even in the final game of the 1960 World Series when Bill Mazeroski hit the game-winning homer for Dad's beloved Pittsburgh Pirates.

Maybe the rule remains, buried in subsections and agate type. Maybe some day it will be called, the way Billy Martin questioned the height of pine tar on George Brett's bat, or the way hockey managers sometimes ask the referee to measure the curve in a hockey stick.

Baseball is not a game of inches; it is a game of rules. But even Sean acknowledges moments when baseball transcends the rules. Back in 1985, when he was studying at Dalhousie University in Halifax, Sean fell in love with a German-born intellectual, a Ph.D. candidate who knew much about *Sturm und Drang* but absolutely nothing about baseball. During the playoff series between the Blue Jays and Kansas City Royals, Sean explained the game and its intricacies as gently as he could. When the Blue Jays lost the seventh game, Sean fell into a dark Irish funk, which lasted most of the weekend.

"I can't believe you're actually upset by this," the intellectual remarked. Things were never really the same after that. Next spring, after he had left her, she sent him a note with a clipping of U. S. President Ronald Reagan tossing out the first pitch on opening day. "As you can see," she wrote, "baseball is a game for morons."

Up early next morning for the drive across the causeway to Dunedin, where the Blue Jays were playing Sparky Anderson's Detroit Tigers.

In the press room at Grant Field, we sat at a table with Dave Perkins of *The Toronto Star*, Larry Millson of *The Globe and Mail* and Steve Milton of *The Hamilton Spectator*. The discussion was grass, specifically the challenge of growing grass under a roof. Milton said a baseball person in Kansas City told him it could be done by sliding out racks of growing grass on game days. But what's the point? If four million people flock to the SkyDome to watch games on artificial grass under a roof, why go to the trouble and expense of growing grass on racks? "Only twelve fans would appreciate it," Perkins declared. The discussion was over.

At Grant Field we sat in the empty Jay dugout listening to the clink-boink-crack of batting practice. A ball hippety-hopped over the grass, trickled into the concrete bunker and Sean picked it up.

Across the way, standing behind the batting cage, thick black arms propped on the padded bars, was Larry Hisle, the hitting coach of the Blue Jays. He is a big, chunky man with an avuncular face and a voice gentle as a prayer. He played for the Philadelphia Phillies, Minnesota Twins and Milwaukee Brewers. His best years were 1977 with the Twins (.302, 28 home runs, 119 RBIs) and 1978 with the Brewers (.290, 34 home runs, 115 RBIs). Twice he was named to the All-Star team.

At one time, at the end of the 1977 season, Hisle had one of the largest contracts in major league baseball: $3.155 million over five years, which came to about $623,000 a year. Not much by the standards of 1993, but Hisle had earned only $47,200 the season before. In 1979 he ripped the rotator cuff on his right arm and was never the same again. By 1982 he was out of baseball. In his book *Nine Innings*, author Daniel Okrent details Hisle's travails in 1982. "Less than six weeks into the new season, the godawful pain came back, and Brewers general manager Harry Dalton placed Hisle on the disabled list for the fourth, and obviously last, time. At 35, his bearlike body still hard as stone, his legs powerful, his wrists quick, his career was through. Just as the reality of it became clear, he got a call from a friend in the organization. On the phone, Hisle cried."

It was the start of Hisle's second year as hitting coach for the Blue Jays. The first was a smashing success—can't do better than win the World Series—but in the spring of 1993 Hisle's task looked decidedly uphill. (He also nearly died, which we will get to in a moment.) The Jays had unloaded Dave Winfield, Candy Maldonado and Kelly Gruber, who had combined the year before for 57 home runs and 217 RBIs. In spring training the stark reality set in that the Blue Jays had unloaded no less than five of the nine players who had started the final game of the World Series in Atlanta.

Preseason evaluations had the new Blue Jays diagnosed as a team that would have to hustle more than hit. They would have to outrun, outplay and out*think* their opponents this season. Their pitching had suffered, as well. They had lost stopper Tom Henke to the Texas Rangers, David Cone to the Kansas City Royals and Jimmy Key, the brilliant southpaw, to the New York Yankees—and a couple more were about to jump ship (or be pushed). The Blue Jays would be an entirely different team this season, playing an entirely different kind of baseball.

Hisle knew what he had to do: teach the youngsters and the bottom of the lineup how to go with the pitch, hit the opposite way, advance runners and sometimes actually lay down a bunt. He was not concerned with the *top* of the order. The Blue Jays may have lost Winfield, who returned to his home town in Minnesota to play for the Twins, but they had gained Paul Molitor and his lifetime .303 average (over fifteen seasons, all with the Brewers). It was a blockbuster acquisition, one that made grown men and women weep in the streets of Milwaukee.

Hisle also had Devon White back, and Devo was performing exceptionally well in spring training (he would end up hitting .367). And he had Joe Carter back, the major-league RBI machine, who was not performing exceptionally well in spring training. In truth, Carter was performing abysmally, hitting .167, without a single home run. He had a sore wrist, but Carter is one of those reliable producers who does not believe he has to prove anything at dress rehearsal. "They don't put spring-training stats on bubble-gum cards," he said.

Before an afternoon game at Grant Field, Carter and National League umpire Frank Pulli were swapping game stories as they loitered in the sun on the soft grass by the left-field sidelines.

"I can't wait to go north," Carter mused.

"I don't blame you," Pulli said.

"Why's that?"

"Because you can't hit for shit down here."

Carter laughed, then bear-hugged Pulli. One of the pleasures of being an umpire in spring training is that you can say things like that without getting socked in the mouth.

Hisle also had John Olerud back, who would probably be hitting fifth in the order. Only twenty-four years old, Olerud had already logged three years in the majors. He had hit .284 in 1992, with 16 home runs and 66 RBIs. He had enjoyed a wonderful postseason. In November Olerud had married his high school sweetheart, Kelly Plaisted, then later in the winter got a raise of $1,100,000 (U.S. funds, of course). That means he was now making $1,487,500, a nice boost from the $387,500 he earned in 1992.

At a glance, it is hard to imagine two men as different from one another as Larry Hisle and John Olerud. Hisle is thick, compact and black; Olerud is tall, lean and white. Hisle is built like a football lineman, Olerud like a patrician basketball centre. Hisle was forty-six, Olerud only twenty-four. Hisle grew up in Ohio, lost both his parents by the time he was ten years old and was raised an orphan by Orville and Kathlee Ferguson, a kindly black couple in Hisle's home town of Portsmouth, Ohio. Olerud was born in Seattle, the son of

23

a wealthy and prominent dermatologist who had been an All-American catcher in college and made it to Triple A in professional baseball. Hisle came up the hard way, earning his baseball stripes riding the buses in the boonies—Huron, Tidewater, Eugene, Albuquerque. Olerud might as well have stepped out of a limo at SkyDome. He went directly from college baseball to the major leagues, becoming only the fifth player since the start of the amateur draft in 1965 to make his professional debut in the bigs and never spend an inning in the minors.

Only in close proximity do these apparent foils display remarkable similarities. First, they are both exceptionally decent, polite, likeable people—no small thing in a playpen world of arrogant, self-obsessed jerks. As players, they speak softly and carry big sticks. They both approach the art of hitting methodically, cerebrally. They enjoy the *study* of hitting. They also share a deeply personal perspective on baseball, and life, because each man came very close to losing both.

On the morning of January 11, 1989, when he was a twenty-year-old junior at Washington State University, John Olerud collapsed after a workout at the fieldhouse. A few days after he collapsed, Olerud was playing again, as if nothing had happened. His father, however—he was known as "Doc Oly"—insisted on tests, just in case. The tests revealed an aneurism at the base of the brain, which was clipped in an operation on February 27. If the aneurism had not been found and treated, another occurrence could have been fatal. Olerud does not know what caused the aneurism, but he has been told his chances of having another are the same as for someone who never had one. The experience affected him profoundly. He will take no chances, however; he wears a batting helmet even when he is playing first base.

"It helped put a lot of things in perspective, and not just baseball," he said. "When you're going through a rough time, you can sit back and think about it and say, 'Hey, this really isn't a big deal.' You are thankful you're here. You think about the good things."

24

Olerud was the star of the WSU baseball team as a pitcher the season before. He was a murderously effective southpaw with fifteen wins and no losses, but the scouts were more impressed with his hitting: .464 batting average, 108 hits, 23 home runs, 204 total bases, .876 slugging percentage, 22-game hit streak—all Washington State records. *Baseball America* named him NCAA Player of the Year for 1987–88.

For Hisle, it happened the previous winter, after the Blue Jays won the World Series. He was operated on for repairs to his shoulder, but serious complications developed when he was in hospital. He suffered a pulmonary embolism, two blood clots in his lungs, then one of his lungs collapsed and he could hardly breathe. At the worst of it, he had intravenous lines in both arms, was being administered oxygen, his temperature reached 104.2 and his blood pressure felt like someone in the next apartment was bouncing soccer balls off the wall. He was so out of it that he did not know the Blue Jays had signed Dick Schofield as their everyday shortstop until Paul Molitor mentioned it in a telephone conversation just prior to spring training. Whatever, Hisle certainly *felt* like he was dying. At the batting cage, he was still having trouble breathing, which he blamed on the soggy heat of Florida.

"It's a struggle today," he said as he watched Derek Bell taking cuts inside the batting cage. Gene Tenace, the Blue Jays' bench coach, was throwing from behind the screen in front of the mound.

"Beautiful, young man," Hisle said as Bell rocked a liner the opposite way, to the right of second base. Hisle's voice rises barely above a whisper, as if the batting cage were a confessional. He concentrates on attitude, confidence and self-esteem, and his soothing narrative has the texture of butterscotch.

"All you have to do is put the ball in play." Hisle spoke to Bell.

"Concentrate, concentrate, concentrate...."

"You and the ball, you and the ball. Only two things exist, young man, you and the ball...."

Bell never turned to acknowledge his mentor, but he was listening. He cracked another liner, this one a hard shot directly over second.

"Beautiful!" Hisle exclaimed (if the verb is not too strong). "Can't be done any better than that."

When batting practice ended, the cage was dragged away and the grounds crew moved in to prepare the field for the afternoon game. It was getting hot. Hisle walked over to the dugout and sat in the shade. he wore a light warm-up jacket, uniform pants and chunky blue-and-white baseball cleats. He has big feet and big hands, which he clenched and unclenched as he talked about his boyhood, his baseball career, his parents and his adopted parents.

Early in 1979, with the Milwaukee Brewers, Hisle tore the rotator cuff in his throwing arm on a hard throw to the infield in a game against the Orioles in Baltimore on April 20, less than a month into the new season. After an all-star season in 1978, he never fully recovered from that throw to the infield. Three years later he was out of baseball, looking for a job. He loved the game so much that at first he could not bring hmself to watch baseball on television, let alone go to a game. The sense of loss was too great.

When Hisle got the phone call from the Brewers' manager telling him it was all over, he cried on the phone. "I thought I had always prepared for that moment," Hisle said. "But when it happened it was difficult—extremely difficult. I remember sharing it with my son, Larry, on his tenth birthday. Even though he was young, I felt it was a conversation that had to take place because it had a bearing on myself and how I look at things.

"I told him about my family, my growing up. My father died when I was five, so he never saw me play baseball. My mother lived long enough to see me play one year of Little League baseball. It was my mother and I trying to make it."

Hisle's mother died when he was ten, the same age as his son Larry when they had their conversation about life and baseball and family.

26

"I have had the pleasure of meeting presidents, CEOs of some of the largest companies in the world, but none of them could add up to my mother. She was the most caring, under-standing, hard-working person I've ever met. When I was talking to my son, I told him that I hope I'm around for a long time, but if it doesn't happen, it doesn't mean *you're* not supposed to go on."

When his playing career ended, Hisle spent two years with the Brewers as an outfield coach, then he left baseball altogether to work in the construction business. His adopted father was vice-president of a construction company in Ohio and he had often taken young Hisle with him when he visited construction sites. At school, Hisle had enjoyed math and had done so well at it that his new dad had often asked him to help him prepare bids. Much later, when he was playing base-ball, Hisle had earned a degree in mathematics from Ohio University during the off-seasons.

"When I lost my mother I told myself, there's nothing that could ever happen that I'm not prepared for, that could hurt me more than that. I can't think of anything in this world—nothing! If I lost both arms and both legs, it might come close, but it wouldn't be worse."

Hisle wanted to talk about John Olerud, a player who keeps attracting contrary nicknames. Playing college ball he was "Cheetah," for his absence of speed. With the Blue Jays he is "Gabby," for his tendency not to say much. Some nick-names are not contrary at all, as in "Hobbsy," for Roy Hobbs, the hero of *The Natural*. It is because of his swing, which is as close to perfection as baseball gets. Don Mattingly of the New York Yankees thinks major league baseball should make a video of Olerud's swing to be distributed to everyone seri-ously considering hitting as a career. The Olerud swing has been compared to Stan Musial's and Ted Williams's and a dozen other legends of the game. Olerud's boyhood hitting model actually was George Brett. In his first three years with the Jays, Olerud tended to start slowly, tentatively, hitting in the low .200s in April and May, then gradually building through the season until he reached a steady .300-plus clip, which lifted his final season average to a respectable .265 or .284.

At spring training this year, Olerud was hitting the shit out of the ball, to all fields and over the fences, finishing tops in the grapefruit circuit with a .433 average.

"You mentioned John and I started to smile about it. His quietness," Hisle said. "I remember trying to strike up a conversation with him and really not getting very far, until I mentioned computers...."

Hisle has been working on a computer program for the Blue Jays, one he hoped would predict pitching patterns and sequences of opposing teams. It was an ambitious program, but Hisle has never been afraid of hard work. Before he took on the job of hitting coach, he requested ninety-minute videotapes of every Blue Jay hitter. He also studies videotapes of selected minor-league players.

Briefly—it is difficult to briefly describe anything Hisle sets out to accomplish—Hisle wanted to chart every pitcher his hitters would be facing in the American League. He had broken down the strike zone into 780 component parts. He would record the temperature at game time, the wind, whether it was the first or second game of a doubleheader, the speed of the pitch, the sequence of pitches, the hitters' success with different counts, whether there were runners on base, where the runners were, whether it was a home or road game—and what happened.

"Everything I believe is important I included," Hisle explained, taking a deep breath. "This is the most difficult challenge I've ever undertaken. The big problem now is accessing the information."

Let's deal with the count. Hisle did a special search to see how Olerud did with an 0–0 count (no balls, no strikes). In 1992 he discovered that Olerud was taking far too many first pitches. He encouraged Olerud to be more aggressive, and this spring it looked to be paying off, with Olerud's .400-plus average.

"It's all in there, somewhere, but I can't always retrieve it," Hisle apologized. "That hurts the players, and it hurts the team."

He promised he would take us into his video room during the season and explain the program in greater detail. He still had lots of work to do.

On flights with the team the year before, Hisle would always be working on his laptop, and he got many of the players interested in computers. Most of the players bought laptops to play children's video games, though some used software for bridge and chess. Olerud bought a laptop because he wanted to learn about computers. He thought he might gain an edge.

In the dugout Hisle said, "I know John *loves* computers. So if I want to talk to him about hitting, my first words are, 'John, last night I was working on my computer, and there's this concept that really intrigues me...' John's eyes would light up, and we talked about computers, then from computers we would go to baseball. He is a very studious young man. You can almost see his brain working every time he steps in the batter's box."

By this time, two men were hauling an organ up one of the aisles, preparing for the game. It was warm and sunny, with a soft breeze. They set the organ behind a row of seats behind home plate as fans trickled into the 6,000-seat stadium. A woman in a floppy, wide-brimmed, wine-coloured hat, wearing a white blouse and baggy red shorts, sat down at the keyboard and played "I'm Looking Over a Four-Leaf Clover." In the early 1980s, the same cucumber-sandwich music was piped in during batting practice. Back then, the Kansas City Royals used to bus in from Fort Myers, way down in the south of Florida. It was a long, hot trip. One morning, in the batting cage, Willie Wilson of the Royals could stand it no longer. "What the mothafucka music is that?" he yelled between swings. Next came a tinkling rendition of "Raindrops Are Falling on My Head." Wilson stepped out of the box and shouted up at the press box, "Turn that shit off!"

Game Plan

In the game against the Tigers, Derek Bell got picked off second after a lazy pop-up to third base. The third baseman noticed Bell dawdling off second base and fired to the bag to complete a 5–4 double play. It was embarrassing.

Cito Gaston, manager of the Blue Jays, was furious. Bell was loaded with talent and potential. In 1991, playing for the Triple A Syracuse Chiefs, he hit .346 and was named *Baseball America*'s Minor League Player of the Year. But his insouciance on the base paths that afternoon was the last straw.

The vogue word this spring was "styling," as in "showing off," as in "putting on the dog." It might be an unwarranted swagger, too-cool purple sunglasses, or acting like an accomplished veteran when you are still very much a rookie. That was Bell's sin, and it was grievous. After the game, the usually mild-mannered Gaston ripped into Bell and two days later Bell was on a plane to San Diego, a Blue Jay no more. He was traded to the San Diego Padres for an outfielder named Darrin Jackson. Jackson was supposed to have a better "attitude," which is another vogue word this spring.

When we talked in the dugout, Hisle seemed to have a premonition about young Bell, whom he liked as a person and admired as a skilled baseball player.

"This game can be such a blessing," he said. "But it can be the most uncaring profession ever. If a person hits .320 every year, drives in 100 runs, hits 30 home runs, people will tolerate all his actions. Derek Bell is an extremely young man, entering a profession that can destroy a person's life at the drop of a hat, in the split of a second. It does cause players to worry, causes them to agonize over problems that would never be part of their lives had they not chosen this profession."

As Hisle talked, sunlight spilled into the dugout, and the morning heat raised a film of perspiration on his face.

"I told Derek yesterday we were going to work on specific parts of his game to enable him to become the best player possible. It would mean extra time on base-stealing, on defence, on getting jumps on the ball, rounding bases, hitting

30

to the point where you won't have any time to do anything but think about the game. If he doesn't succeed, then it's not his fault. It's *my* fault.

"Last night I was telling my wife about working with Derek. I've been through all this. I've had ups and downs in my career. I know what young players are going through and there's a certain point as a coach I have to say, 'That's my fault. It's not his fault. He's too young to understand what life is about, what this game is about.'"

Is he too big for his britches, acting like a star before he's earned it?

"That's a valid point. When I was Derek's age there was a code of ethics, a strict code that as a rookie you said very little, did what you were told and played the game by the book. I now see rookies come to camp and their actions are equal to a ten-year veteran. For example, when I played I would never have worn sunglasses as a rookie during warm-ups and drills."

Why no sunglasses?

"It presents an air of, 'Look at me. I'm good.' I know people should wear sunglasses to protect their eyes, but sometimes the sunglasses they wear are more for show. When I worked in the minor-league system I knew my job was more than hitting instructor. I had to find out about the personalities of these young men because personality has a big bearing on performance. A certain amount of cockiness is important, but when I played I would never tell anyone I was going to perform at a certain level. When I stepped in the batter's box I believed I was the best player on the planet, but I kept it to myself. You train the mind by repetitive positive thinking, meditation, whatever it takes to get to the point where you honestly believe it."

It took Hisle a long time to get the hang of it. Early in his career he lacked confidence and was self-deprecating to the point of paralysis. In Hisle's first season with the Philadelphia Phillies in 1969 he had excellent rookie numbers: .266, 20 home runs, 56 RBIs, 18 stolen bases. But he didn't believe in himself. "In all honesty, I don't know how I did it," he once told *The Toronto Star.* "It must have been pure physical ability because I didn't have the right mental approach."

Back then, he used to visit Al Oliver, who had grown up in the same neighbourhood of Portsmouth, Ohio. Oliver has a major-league career average of .305 over seventeen seasons. One day during the off-season, Hisle pestered Oliver with questions about what pitchers gave him the most problems. Oliver said he couldn't think of any, but Hisle trudged home, sat down and dutifully compiled a list of twenty-five pitchers that gave him problems. Next season he hit a woeful .205. "My confidence went from low to non-existent," he said. "I played as poorly as anyone in history."

During the next off-season he took a psychology course, where he learned how to visualize success. He began writing notes to himself, saying he was the best in the game. Eventually, he started waking up in the morning believing it. "Most of the players here are technically sound to a degree where they have the chance to be successful," Hisle said. "The difference is their mental toughness."

It was time to get ready for the game, but before heading to the clubhouse under the stands Hisle returned to the topic of the lineup and the new team the Blue Jays would be in 1993. "We're really blessed," he said, meaning, again, the *top* of the lineup: Devon White, Roberto Alomar, Paul Molitor, Joe Carter, John Olerud. At this stage, judging by the way they were playing—Hisle knew Carter would come around— the top five hitters in the lineup looked stacked. (By midseason they would be dubbed the WAMCO, using the first letters of their surnames, and all five would be selected to the American League All-Star team.)

It was the bottom of the lineup that concerned Hisle. "What makes this game exciting, especially with a team like ours, is getting production from the sixth, seventh, eighth and ninth hitters. Going the opposite way, advancing runners, bunting. If their production diminishes over the course of the year, we're in trouble. We're in deep trouble."

The mood was different this year.

With the Blue Jays world champions, everyone seems vindicated. There is a swagger and savvy among the players, coaches, even the media and fans, and most of all Cito Gaston. After all the second-guessing and Cito-bashing, what can you say about a manager who brings home a World Series winner?

"Shoulda taken him out in the seventh...."

Yeah, but we won it all.

"Shoulda laid down a bunt to move 'im to second...."

Yeah, but we won it all.

We were at Baseball City, near Orlando, for a game against the Kansas City Royals. It has been spring training home for the Royals since 1988, when they moved from Fort Myers way down the Gulf Coast. Baseball City started out as an ambitious theme park, a Disneyworld of baseball. The stadium has 8,000 seats and cost $18 million. There is also a 2,500-seat auxiliary stadium, indoor and outdoor batting cages, forty pitching mounds and a $3-million players' residence. The problem is, Baseball City is land-locked, like Kansas itself. No sand, no surf, no ocean, only parched fields and scrub trees beyond the outfield and the whirring highway between Tampa and Orlando. Now it looks like Baseball City may be going down the tubes. What do the kids do when daddy's puffing around the bases at a menopausal fantasy-league camp?

Spring training was coming to an end, but the Blue Jays had a lacklustre record, having lost twice as many games as they had won (...*but we won it all*). They had been working on the basics—hitting the cutoff man, pitcher-to-first plays, grooming players in unfamiliar positions, trying out the rookies. It was important now to show a little competitiveness, not to sell more tickets back home, which is the goal for any cellar-dwelling expansion franchise and it means something to beat the Yankees in spring training, but to get used to winning before Opening Day.

In the Blue Jay dugout during batting practice, a gathering of writers, broadcasters, television people and assorted hangers-on formed around Gaston. It was a friendly gathering. Gaston is much more relaxed and at ease with himself this year. His back isn't bothering him anymore. He smiles more easily, laughs more easily, has an easier time exercising his authority, which means he can allow himself to be testy. He is as soft-spoken as ever, but his quiet demeanour now has *presence.*

Spring must be sweet for him.

People were telling stories of nasty fans. It started the day before in Dunedin when Ken Carson, the Blue Jays' director of minor-league business operations, received some severe abuse from two fans after the game at Grant Field. Carson was walking behind the backstop, a walkie-talkie in his hip pocket, flipping a game ball from hand to hand.

"Hey you!" one of the fans shouted. "Give the kid the ball."

The two men were standing in an aisle behind home plate, motioning to Carson to give the ball to a small boy behind the visitors' dugout. Carson, thinking they were playful kibitzers, smiled at them.

"Think you're a big shot with your walkie-talkie?" one of the men bellowed. "C'mon, give the kid the ball! You with the bald spot."

"Hey—*baldy*!" the other man shouted.

Several players around the backstop, and coach Bob Bailor, instinctively removed their caps and rubbed their fingers on their heads.

Carson flipped the ball toward the mound. "There, feel better?" he said. "Why don't you go to the concession and buy the kid a ball?"

Boston fans are the nastiest in both leagues, Gaston said, eating sunflower seeds in the dugout. One time when the Jays were at Fenway, a fan called out to Rob Ducey, the Canadian-born outfielder. The Boston fan told Ducey he could not understand why the Jays didn't play him more. "You're better than most of the regulars," the fan said. Pleased, Ducey wandered over to the fence to meet his admirer, who asked him if he would mind signing one of those balls lying on the ground.

"No problem," Ducey said, picking up one of the batting-practice balls, signing his name on it, then handing it to the fan.

As Ducey walked back toward the batting cage, the Boston fan shouted after him, "You suck! You don't deserve to be playing."

Philadelphia can be tough, too. Gaston once watched a fan beating up a security guard at Veterans Stadium. At this point a radio guy, sitting on the dugout steps, said he thought the toughest fans were in Pittsburgh. During one game, a fan had a heart attack and a nurse in the crowd came to his aid, administering mouth-to-mouth resuscitation.

"Then this guy opens his fly and takes a leak on her," he said.

There was silence in the dugout.

"On the nurse."

There was silence in the dugout.

"I can't substantiate it," he said, "but that's what happened."

Gaston popped a sunflower seed into his mouth and looked out at the field.

In a game at Clearwater, where the Philadelphia Phillies play, Brian Williams was talking about the Bell-for-Jackson trade. Williams was in Florida for some stretching exercises himself, preparing to do telecasts for CBC television. As a television announcer, Williams has roamed the world covering the Olympics and most other crucial global summits ranging from international hockey to Grand Prix motor racing. Baseball, however, was a serious challenge for him at this stage of his career.

Several times, in a booth in the press box, Williams would be calling a game without a microphone, watching the play on the field and on a small monitor in the booth. "Alomar to his left...a 4–3 groundout...the Cardinals go down one, two, three...." He was practising.

At Jack Russell Stadium in Clearwater, Williams heard that not only had Bell been traded, but the Blue Jays had traded pitcher Bob MacDonald to the Detroit Tigers and given pitcher David Wells his unconditional release. Gaston wanted him in the bullpen, Wells considered himself a starter, and for Wells that meant an abrupt goodbye from the world champs. Wells and Gaston had had some run-ins the year before and Wells did not advance his case when he reported to camp ten pounds overweight, then stuffed four more pounds onto his already pear-shaped frame under the palms of Florida.

As we talked, Dave Perkins of *The Toronto Star* came up the aisle, heading to the press box. "Talk about an Excedrin trade," he said. "They got rid of two headaches in one afternoon." He meant Bell and Wells; Perkins had no quibble with MacDonald, a twenty-seven-year-old lefty reliever who had won four games over three major-league seasons. MacDonald had been sold to the Tigers, which pleased him because his pregnant wife, Monique, comes from Sault Ste. Marie, a short day's drive from Detroit.

Williams left Jack Russell Stadium and hustled back to nearby Dunedin and the Blue Jays' clubhouse at Grant Field. Bell and MacDonald had already cleared out, but big "Boomer" Wells was at his locker, packing, nearly in tears. Wells was making about $2 million a year with the Jays, and his unconditional release meant that unless he was picked up by another team, he would suffer a $1.7-million pay cut. When Al Leiter, another pitcher, approached Wells, Wells mentioned the move, and Leiter said, "Yeah, well, we expected it."

The look on Wells's face was pain and incredulity. "You *expected* it?" he asked. Leiter had meant the Derek Bell trade; he had no idea of what had happened to his pal Wells. "Bullshit," he told Wells. "I can't believe it." Wells convinced Leiter it was true only by producing the documents detailing his unconditional release. With Wells gone, however, it meant that Leiter, the lefty obtained from the Yankees in 1989 for strong-armed outfielder Jesse Barfield, might finally make the starting rotation for the Blue Jays in 1993. Bad news, good news.

Williams, meanwhile, was absorbing it all, anticipating his first telecast in Detroit in June when he would be able to reflect back on that day in Clearwater when Bob MacDonald became a Tiger. "That's good material for a baseball telecast," Williams said. "When you're doing a baseball game, you tell stories." He shaped his voice into the felicitous telecast modulations and, two months ahead of himself, rehearsed, "Remember that afternoon in Clearwater, Tommy? [Talking to broadcast sidekick Tommy Hutton.] The day they sacked Wells and traded young MacDonald to Detroit? Well, MacDonald wasn't unhappy that day. You see, his wife, Monique, was pregnant, and she lives…"

After the game in Clearwater, Pat Gillick stood on the sidelines in front of the visitors' dugout, surrounded by a scrum of reporters peppering him with questions on the day's manoeuvres. Willams was there, notebook at the ready. "Tell me, Pat, would you call the Bell-for-Jackson trade a 'character trade'?"

Gillick didn't hesitate. "We'll take an asshole, too," he said, "if he can hit."

In the movie *Bull Durham*, the world-weary catcher instructs the rookie fireballer on apropriate clichés to use when he gets to The Show. Fortunately, most rookies do not have world-weary catchers as cliché mentors, so when they reach the major leagues they are ingenuous enough to regard an interview as something like a normal conversation.

That was what it was like when we met Rob Butler in Plant City, a few miles east down the highway from Tampa. The Blue Jays were playing the Cincinnati Reds. Butler looked like a rookie out of central casting—fresh face, shock of black hair, Tom Cruise looks.

He also wore his uniform the old way, showing lots of sock and stirrup, lots of calf. In the early 1990s, the fashion is for baseball trousers to be stretched nearly to the ankles, showing almost no sock at all. That is cool, like purple-tinted sunglasses, though it makes baseball players look like high school phys-ed instructors.

Spring training was ending and both teams were trying on their game faces for the new season. Despite this, there was an interesting addition to the Blue Jay lineup: batting leadoff was Butler, a twenty-three-year-old Canadian who had spent all of his spring training at the minor-league complex at the other end of town.

The night before, Mel Queen, director of player development for the Blue Jays, had told Butler he would be suiting up for the game against the Reds. "I was in total shock," Butler would recall later. "I hardly slept that night."

Next morning it got worse. That was when Butler discovered he would be facing Jose Rijo, one of the toughest starters in the National League, a powerful veteran with a hard slider and a wicked forkball. Butler learned this as he was stepping into the batting cage for his pregame cuts.

"Rijo," he muttered to himself. "Oh, nooo."

In his first at-bat, Butler worked the count to 3–2. "I don't know how I ever got to a full count. I was so anxious," he said. His patience paid off, as he cracked a double to right centre, then scored on Darnell Coles's double. He got three more hits that day to go 4-for-5.

"After the game I was on cloud nine," Butler said. "There was an amazing feeling coming over me. I just wanted to be there, in that situation. I wanted the moment to last."

The summer before, Butler played for the Dunedin Blue Jays of the Florida State League. Playing centre field, batting from the left side, he hit an impressive .358, with nineteen stolen bases.

He grew up in Toronto, playing many of his early games at Talbot Park in Leaside, down the street from where we used to live. On many summer evenings Sean and I watched from the rickety stands behind the third-base line, sipping homemade lemonade prepared by the players' mothers and sold at the canteen behind home plate. Butler played for the

East York side that won the annual midsummer midget tournament at Talbot Park in 1987. Back then, Butler used to
pitch and play the outfield, but the scouts liked the way he
could hit.

Bob Prentice, director of scouting in Canada for the Blue
Jays, often watched Butler from the grassy hill in the shade of
the McDonald's restaurant at Bayview and Eglinton. "He had
all kinds of ability and an outstanding attitude," Prentice said.
"He was a pull hitter, so I worked with him in the batting
cage under the stands at SkyDome, getting him to spray the
ball, hit to the opposite field. I wanted him to learn how to
bunt, too, because he's got decent speed. Drag bunts, push
bunts.

"'Go for average, use your speed, make things happen,' I
used to tell him. 'Forget about power. You'll hit four or five
home runs by accident.'"

The next day in Florida, Butler batted leadoff again, this
time against the St. Louis Cardinals at Grant Field in
Dunedin. As if to prove his effort against Rijo wasn't a fluke,
he walked, singled twice to the opposite field and beat out an
infield grounder for his third hit of the game. In two games
he had seven hits in ten at-bats, then reported for the team
that would play in Syracuse.

In the clubhouse after the second game, Butler sat on a
stool at his locker in full uniform long after most of the other
players had stripped and showered. "I just want it to last," he
said again. Not a word about giving 110 percent or playing
one game at a time. That was when Darnell Coles, naked
from the showers, walked by and said to Butler, "Don't
change a thing, man. Don't change *anything.*"

Butler said, "Thank you."

The writer E. B. White once wrote an essay called "The
Ring of Time," about a young woman riding barefoot on a
horse in a circus tent. It was a practice run, she was in her
early teens, wearing a bathing suit, her feet smudged with
dirt, but for ten minutes she performed with a graceful insouciance in the nearly empty tent. White wrote, "She will never

be as beautiful as that again... She is at that enviable moment in life when she believes she can go once more around the ring, make one complete circuit, and at the end be exactly the same age as at the start."

It is like that with rookies.

Spring training was over, at least for Florida. After the game against St. Louis, the Blue Jays headed to the airport for a succession of flights that would take them to Vancouver for two more exhibition games, then the season would begin in Seattle.

We would catch up to them when they returned to SkyDome for Opening Day.

=== 3 ===

The Home Opener

Friday, April 9, 1993.

The roof was closed: no snow, no sleet, no rain, no wind, no cold. We were blowing on our hands walking across the bridge over the railway tracks to the SkyDome, marvelling again at how un-Canadian the neighbourhood had become—pennant vendors, peanut vendors, hot-dog vendors, musicians playing hot jazz, scalpers hawking fistfuls of tickets.

"Tickets to sell!"

"Tickets to buy!"

"Anybody, tickets!"

This did not feel like the city of churches, the city of clean streets. This was loud, expectant, exuberant, clamorous, brassy—the world champs are back, here we go again. There is a big-league hustle to the SkyDome neighbourhood that bears no resemblance whatsoever to other neighbourhoods in Toronto—The Beaches, Nathan Phillips Square, North Toronto, Parkdale, Mount Pleasant, The Annex, Moore Park. Even the fans trekking to the SkyDome seemed to have acquired a swagger over the winter ("...we won it all").

After their exhibition games in Vancouver, the last games of spring training, the Blue Jays flew down to Seattle to open

41

the 1993 season and immediately got clobbered by the Mariners, 8–1. Manager Cito Gaston made a curious decision when he assembled the lineup for that game. He sat out hot-hitting John Olerud, replacing him at first base with rookie Domingo Martinez. Odd enough that Gaston would sit down someone who led the majors in hitting in spring training with an average of .433, but Seattle also happened to be Olerud's home town and he had arranged tickets for busloads of family and friends. It was as if Gaston knew the treasure he had in Olerud this year, and, as if it were made of antique porcelain, he did not want it cracked in the first game of the season. The starting pitcher for the Mariners was Randy Johnson, a long-haired, string-bean giant (6'10", 225 pounds) with a ninety-six-mile-an-hour fastball that often goes menacingly awry. Johnson was also a lefty, defying the stereotype of the "nifty little southpaw." Gaston did not want a lefty–lefty con-frontation between Olerud and Johnson.

Olerud continued to be Larry Hisle's pet project. He wanted him to handle inside pitches better. He wanted him to be more aggressive, to go after first pitches. But this was just tinkering. Mostly, Hisle stood back and admired the nat-ural ability of Olerud. "John is not a mistake hitter," Hisle said. "He hits good pitches. He's the kind of hitter who scares pitchers. They never are sure what to throw John. He hits for average and power, and he hits their best pitches."

Another Hisle project was to convince Dick Schofield, the new starting shortstop the Blue Jays had acquired over the winter, to quit hitting fly balls and concentrate on driving the ball to all parts of the field. He came upon this plan after studying Schofield's statistics, before he actually watched Schofield at the plate. This was when Hisle was recovering in hospital, after he nearly died from blood clots on the lung. Propped up in his hospital bed, Hisle examined Schofield's numbers, which were delivered to him by the Blue Jays. He noticed that Schofield's fly-ball to ground-ball ratio was near-ly the same as Joe Carter's. Something is wrong here, he thought, something out of kilter. It made no sense because

42

Carter, being bigger and stronger, could send many of his fly balls over the fence, while most of Schofield's fly balls were outs. Hisle wanted Schofield's ratio to be more like Roberto Alomar's. Alomar hit two ground balls for every fly ball, while Carter and Schofield were hitting roughly two fly balls for every ground ball. This season, Hisle would work on Schofield's swing. He wanted to level it so he could go for liners and gappers and opposite-field shots.

Another thing, the Blue Jays seemed to be having difficulty against left-handed pitching (which would become more apparent during the season). Hisle's explanation was that the Blue Jays are an aggressive, free-swinging, offensive team, and most of the left-handed pitchers they face in the American League are control pitchers, pitchers who can baffle hitters with pinpoint location. Jimmy Key, for one. Being aggressive and free-swinging, the Blue Jays simply fared better against power pitchers, whether coming in from the left or right. Hisle was more interested in left-handed *batters*. If he were starting over again, he would work at becoming a switch-hitter, or, better, make himself into a pure left-handed hitter. In his playing days, Hisle did more than okay as a right-handed hitter—he was an all-star selection—but because there are so many more right-handed pitchers than left-handed pitchers he is convinced he might have won batting titles if he had been swinging from the left side. Most of the great hitters of the game were, and still are, left-handed hitters: Babe Ruth, Ted Williams, Lou Gehrig, Rod Carew...Wade Boggs, Brett Butler, Len Dykstra, John Olerud.

Jack Morris started for the Blue Jays in Seattle, lasted into the fifth inning and gave up seven runs on ten hits to begin the season of 1993 with a 14.54 earned run average (which would get fatter during the rest of April). The Jays won the next day, 2–0, behind the two-hit pitching of Al Leiter. This time Olerud played first base, got one of the five Toronto hits and began what would be for him a season of dreams.

Arriving well before the first pitch, we took a window

table at Café on the Green, the restaurant in the SkyDome
Hotel that overlooks the field. We ordered coffee and went
over our notes, watching the teams warming up, preparing for
batting practice. With the roof closed, two colours predomi-
nate inside the SkyDome, blue and green, creating a cool,
watery, aquamarine effect. Unlike the raucous neighbourhood
outside, in here Canadians display their usual reticent polite-
ness and good manners. It is as though the sheer wonder of
the innards of SkyDome somehow intimidates and inhibits
them and they revert to form. People wandered in, stood by
the window, looking down on the field.

"Wow!"

"This is wonderful!"

"Oh, my!"

And inevitably, to one of the waitresses, "Can we sit here
and have a drink?"

It is a restaurant. There are waiters and waitresses and bartenders and menus and a kitchen. And empty tables. And
they wonder if they can actually sit down and use their
money to buy a drink. More people come in.

"Can we sit here?"

"Of course."

"Really?"

In the SkyDome, in the press box high over home plate,
there was the familiar voice of Howard Starkman, the Blue
Jays' director of public relations. He sits at a microphone at
the west end of the press box, front row. Starkman has been
with the team since its inception in 1977. He is always working. It is rumoured he gets eighteen hours off a year, between
Christmas Eve and Boxing Day, providing no trades have
been made. Starkman has a calm, monosyllabic voice, with
just enough of an edge to carry nicely over the intercom.
The voice is familiar, reassuring. If Starkman were on the
public address system of a torpedoed ship, nobody would
panic. "Ship has been hit, starboard side. Outside temperature
twenty degrees Celsius, sixty-eight degrees Fahrenheit, winds
eighteen miles an hour, waters choppy. Lifeboats on port side

for men, starboard for women and children."

The Cleveland Indians were in town to play the Blue Jays in a three-game series. Starting for the Indians was Jose Mesa, for the Blue Jays Juan Guzman. Guzman and Galen Cisco, the pitching coach, walked out through a door in the left-field bullpen and strolled toward the Blue Jay dugout, Cisco looking like a high school principal with his valedictorian. The two men conversed as they walked, Guzman carrying his shiny blue jacket, one of the sleeves dragging along the bright green turf. As the fans recognized Guzman they appreciated the significance of the occasion and a ripple of applause began from the third-base side of the field, building to a polite crescendo as Guzman reached the orange warning track by the dugout.

There were the anthems, then the presentation of World Series rings, no fewer than 232 of them. The Blue Jays had commissioned Tiffany & Co. to design the fourteen-carat gold championship rings. The design displayed the team logo over a baseball, the eye of the Blue Jay set with a solitaire diamond, surrounded by sixteen diamonds representing each year of the team's history. Each player's name and jersey number is engraved on one side of the ring. It also has the 1992 World Series logo set in a maple leaf, with the inscription "Canada's 1st," meaning the first Canadian-based team ever to win a World Series. It also has the American League logo, below which is the number "4,028,318," for the league attendance record the Blue Jays set in 1992. It is a busy ring.

Members of the 1992 Blue Jays assembled on the field to accept the rings, which came in a small blue box. Rance Mulliniks, now no longer with the team, wore a brown double-breasted suit, looking more than ever like the bank teller he always looked like as a player. When it was Mulliniks's turn to receive his ring, the crowd gave him a loud cheer, then Pat Gillick walked up and administered an affectionate bearhug.

Sean asked Mulliniks after the ceremony if it felt strange to be on the field with his old teammates, the only one in a civilian suit and tie. "I don't miss playing," Mulliniks said.

"My skills had started to diminish and I was losing the desire to play hard. Baseball wasn't as much fun. What I miss is the clubhouse atmosphere and the friends I have in baseball." Sean then asked if he could remember his last at-bat as a Blue Jay. No, he couldn't remember it that well, Mulliniks said, only that it was the previous September, in a game against the Texas Rangers, in the bottom of the eighth, pinch-hitting for Winfield, against a left-handed pitcher, when he lined one over the infield for a base hit to left field. "That's all I remember about it," he apologized.

A sad note to Opening Day 1993: a "Media Advisory" asks the media to refrain from questions about Cleveland pitchers Steve Olin and Tim Crews, who were killed in a weird and tragic boating accident in Florida during spring training. A third pitcher, Bob Ojeda, survived, but was badly injured. It was a cruel blow to the Indians, who were assembling an interesting and competitive team, which Cleveland hoped would be a contender when the new Cleveland stadium opened in 1994.

Joe Sawchuk was the official scorer of the home opener. He sat in the front row of the baseball press box, beside Starkman, directly over home plate on the third level of the SkyDome. Sawchuk had worked all his adult life for Ontario Hydro, mainly to subsidize his abiding love of baseball. He is a short, bald, wiry man in his fifties, with skin that has the look and texture of football leather. He is one of four official scorers the Blue Jays used for their home games in 1993. The others were Louis Cauz and Neil MacCarl, two former sports writers, and Doug Hobbs, an automobile salesman in St. Catharines. One does not take a course on how to become an official scorer. One simply has to have grown up with baseball and absorbed its countless eccentricities and nuances as if through the pores of one's body.

Sawchuk was a scrappy sandlot third baseman when he was growing up in Toronto. He started playing baseball at the age of ten for a team called St. Peters in a Catholic Youth

Organization League that played many of its games at Christie Pits, a park in a downtown neighbourhood of Toronto where fans watch from steep green hills. He played amateur baseball until he was in his mid-twenties, then become an amateur umpire, the best in the city. The instincts that make someone a good official scorer apply also to making a good umpire. Knowing the rules helps, but just knowing the rules is not enough.

"I had the judgment and that's what umpiring's all about," Sawchuk said. "The prerequisite to umpiring is having judgment—ball, strike, out, safe. Some know all the rules and don't have the judgment and they're terrible umpires."

Sawchuk was such a good umpire that when major-league umpires threatened to go on strike in 1978, Sawchuk was the man the Blue Jays called to round up a crew of amateur umpires, just in case. Sawchuk called two friends, Rich Panas and Al Contant, two umpires he had known over many summers on the sandlots of Toronto. He knew they were good enough to handle major league baseball.

On August 25, 1978, Sawchuk received a call from Bob Prentice, the director of Canadian player development for the Blue Jays. The call came at 10:50 A.M., to his office at Ontario Hydro. Could he bring his umpiring crew to Exhibition Stadium for a game between the Minnesota Twins and Blue Jays starting at one o'clock in the afternoon? Sawchuk agreed, left his office, took a taxi home to pick up his umpiring equipment, only to discover his wife was out shopping in the family car and his umpiring equipment was in the trunk. He knew he did not have much time, and it would be difficult because he would have to get to the stadium and work his way through the crowds attending the Canadian National Exhibition.

Sawchuk called another taxi and drove to Talbot Park in Leaside, where he knew he could obtain the umpiring equipment he needed. Approaching the Canadian National Exhibition grounds, his taxi got snarled in traffic, so Sawchuk got out and worked his way through the crowds, carrying his cleats, mask, whisk, counter, cap, chest protector and uniform. A policeman stopped him as he was entering the stadium.

"Where are you going, sir?" he asked Sawchuk.

"I'm going to umpire the ball game," Sawchuk told him. "I'm on the dish." The dish is what the umpires call home plate. Sawchuk, as the senior umpire of the amateur crew, would be the crew chief and he would be calling balls and strikes that afternoon.

"That's a good story," the policeman said. "You might as well keep going."

He managed to find Al Contant, who worked for Coca-Cola and happened to be delivering a truckload of pop to the Canadian National Exhibition. He did not have any luck reaching Rich Panas, however. The game had already started when Panas heard over the radio that he was needed, and he did not arrive at the stadium until the third inning. The game started with Sawchuk umpiring behind the plate, Contant at first base, Sam Ewing of the Blue Jays umpiring at second base and a player from the Twins at third. When Panas finally arrived he had to push his way into the stadium, then he jumped over a fence by the sideline bullpen and ran onto the field, pursued by security guards.

As for the pressure of umpiring a major-league game, Sawchuk remembers the toughest part was calling balls and strikes. "You had to be really fine with the strike zone," he said. "On the sandlots you're always a pitcher's umpire because the pitchers tend to be wild and don't find the strike zone that often. Games would last four, five hours if we were too fine with the strike zone. That was the most difficult, changing that philosophy. In the major leagues it actually has to be a strike."

Sawchuk's crew was the only replacement umpiring crew that did a rotation whereby the umpires go clockwise around the field from game to game, the plate umpire moving to third next day, then second, then first, then back to home plate. Some professional umpires from the minor leagues who arrived for games in Toronto were impressed that Sawchuk's umpires did a rotation. One of them told Sawchuk he had called twelve consecutive games in Cleveland behind the plate. As fill-ins, Sawchuk and his crew each received $250 a game, paid in U.S. funds. "It was pretty good pocket money," he said. "I took a vacation from Ontario Hydro and umpired in about twenty-five games that year."

Sawchuk began scoring games in 1980. Before that, local baseball writers often scored the games, among them Neil MacCarl, a longtime baseball writer for *The Toronto Star*. It had been decided that covering and scoring a game constituted a conflict of interest, so the Blue Jays advertised for official scorers, Sawchuk applied, and his application was accepted. For each game he was paid $50 U.S., which had risen to $75 U.S. when the 1993 season rolled around. MacCarl, incidentally, became an official scorer again in 1993 after he retired from the *Star*.

The play-by-play of the game was fed into the auxiliary box, and there was another familiar, reassuring voice: Tom Cheek. He had covered the Blue Jays on radio since the first game in 1977, and since 1982 with booth sidekick Jerry Howarth. In the final game of the 1992 World Series in Atlanta, Cheek was in the radio booth calling the game in the bottom of the eleventh inning. Normally it would have been Howarth's turn. Instead of calling every inning together, they take turns, with Cheek calling the first, second, fifth, sixth, ninth and tenth, if necessary. Howarth called the top of the eleventh, including Dave Winfield's two-out, two-run double down the third-base line to score White and Alomar, but he had stepped aside to let Cheek call the bottom half in case the Blue Jays held on to win for their first World Series championship.

In his book *Road to Glory*, Cheek admits he was embarrassed at his performance in 1985 when the Blue Jays won their first American League division title. "When George Bell sank to his knees in left field at Exhibition Stadium with the final out of that ballgame, I found myself sort of croaking the details to the audience because I had a cantaloupe-sized lump in my throat," Cheek wrote. He called it "one of the most embarrassing and unprofessional moments of my career." He did not want to mush again, with the Blue Jays leading and pitcher Mike Timlin on the mound. In his book, Cheek quotes himself: "...to the belt...pitch on the way...and there's a bunted ball...first base side...Timlin [voice rises]...to Carter...and the Blue Jays win it...the Blue Jays are World Series champions!"

Turning over the mike to Cheek was a classy gesture by Howarth, especially considering all the quiet speculation over the years that they could not stand each other. There was something faintly amusing about the idea of two men sitting side by side in little booths all over America 162 games a year, every year, acting like a couple of castaways adrift in a dinghy in the middle of the Pacific Ocean with their backs to each other. For the record they both deny any animosity and Cheek felt compelled to set the record straight in his book. But as sincere as his intentions may have been, the brief tribute to Howarth near the end of the book reads as if Cheek was making a forced confession after being worked over by the cops in a basement holding cell. After spinning yarn upon yarn earlier in the book about Early Wynn, Cheek's fondly remembered sidekick for the first five seasons, Cheek devotes less than a page to his partner for every year since.

> Jerry and I are dissimilar people in physical appearance, personality, and points of view.... The latter did create some problems along the way, though rarely to the extent some chose to believe. Our partnership is in its 12th year—longer than many marriages endure—but there have been a few snags....
>
> When Jerry came to town, he brought a satchel full of notes, enthusiasm, scholastic thoroughness, and a some-times-abrasive single-mindedness....
>
> I'm often asked in passing, "Where's Jerry?" To which I generally reply, "I don't know." Until I see him in the

ballpark...I haven't the foggiest idea where Jerry is at any given moment. Tending to his affairs, as I am mine, I assume.

Not exactly Horatio's "And flights of angels sing thee to thy rest" soliloquy after the death of Hamlet.

Howarth, a devout Christian who was born again in 1987 after a Bible-study meeting with former Blue Jay pitcher Don Gordon, likes to spend time with his family when he is in Toronto and keeps to himself on the road. Cheek, once described by an anonymous Jay in Alison Gordon's book *Foul Balls* as "the tallest groupie in the league," likes to pal around with Gaston and the players. In *Road to Glory*, Cheek explains that he had no small part in how Gaston became manager of the Blue Jays.

Back in 1989, the year Gaston replaced former manager Jimy Williams in midseason, Gaston vowed he would never take the job full time. He enjoyed being the hitting coach, he got along well with the players, and he made it clear he wanted his old job back as soon as a replacement for Williams could be found. This was when the Blue Jays were considering hiring Lou Piniella as manager.

When Williams was fired, the Blue Jays were 12 and 24, and fans and front office were getting restless. With Gaston temporarily in charge, the Blue Jays seemed a lot more relaxed, and they started to win. Soon after the move to SkyDome in 1989, the Blue Jays left on a road trip to Cleveland, where Gaston was summoned to attend a meeting of the Blue Jay magisterium to discuss solidifying Gaston's position as manager. Gaston remained reluctant to take the managing job full time. When Cheek arrived at Municipal Stadium, Gaston invited him to his office.

"What do you think of this whole thing?" he asked Cheek.

Cheek told him, "Cito, sometimes in life opportunity only knocks once, and if you don't answer it may never knock again. If you want to manage this ball club full time, then you better speak up loud and clear, tell them you can do it and you want it badly. Don't put yourself in the position where someone else gets the job and you look yourself in the mirror the next day and say, 'Damn, it could have been me!'"

That evening Gaston sat alone in the hotel bar until last call, Cheek's little speech ringing in his ears. Next morning he awoke early, headed to the airport, sat down with Beeston, Gillick and chairman Peter Hardy and told them he would take the job full time. The rest of the season, the Blue Jays went 77–49 under the avuncular Gaston and won the American League East.

In the auxiliary press box we could hear the piped-in voice of Cheek saying. "Infielders back, outfielders straight away."

The home season had begun.

Martin looked around for Kevin Boland, an old friend who writes a weekly column for *The Financial Post*. Alas, he could not make it to the home opener, as he was finishing some business in Florida. Martin had hoped they could play a little "dirt ball" to set the season off right. Dirt ball is betting on the number of times the ball lands and stays on the dirt pitcher's mound at the end of every half inning. Usually the first baseman or catcher or infielder rolls the ball toward the mound after the third out, and sometimes the ball stays on the dirt and sometimes it rolls off. Sometimes the umpire accepts the ball from an outfielder, then drops the ball on the mound, where it either stays or rolls off. Usually it rolls off, or never reaches the mound, so if you bet on it staying on the mound dirt you get odds.

Boland used to cover baseball for *The Globe and Mail* in the early 1980s, when the players used to call him "Baretta," for a television cop-show character. He had an easy knack of infiltrating, getting along, and he used to play cards with the players in the Blue Jay clubhouse, always with a wad of tobacco sloshing in his mouth. He also wrote books on two players, Dave Stieb (*Tomorrow I'll Be Perfect*) and Kelly Gruber

(*Kelly: At Home on Third*). Stieb never was perfect, but he came awfully close. Once at SkyDome he came within an out of a perfect game. When Stieb pitched his no-hitter in Cleveland on September 2, 1990, after the final out he pointed directly at Boland up in the press box as if to say, "See, I told ya."

After four innings the Blue Jays were up 7–2. After six innings the Indians were up 9–7. Guzman lasted into the top of the sixth, when he was pulled after giving up ten hits, two of them home runs. Of the eight runs he allowed, seven were earned. He looked sharp at the start, striking out five and walking only one. The key to Guzman is his walks-to-strikeouts ratio. Ron Taylor, the former big-leaguer who works as team physician for the Blue Jays, once told Martin about what he called a "pitcher's statistic," which is that half the walks score. "It may not work out mathematically, but that's what a pitcher thinks about when he's on the mound." Some baseball observers say that with a strikeout pitcher like Guzman, two strikeouts nullify one of the walks. With a sinkerball pitcher, two infield groundouts nullify one of the walks. Whatever, by the sixth inning Guzman had lost his edge and was tiring.

Home openers seldom indicate how the season will unfold, but this game encapsulated the 1993 season. The Blue Jays would score a lot of runs, but they would give up a lot of runs, and things would get very interesting. This home opener was one of those untidy games, like a game of work-your-way-up involving the entire neighbourhood, when the team that is ahead when the street lights go on wins.

In the baseball press box, now politically corrected to Media Lounge, statistics were being churned out furiously. After every home run Starkman announced the actual distance the ball travelled. And we were brought up to date on any interesting thing that happened here, there or anywhere. During the home opener, for example, we were told that young Rob Butler had homered in a game in Syracuse. There are statistics for everybody, stacked in slots by the entrance.

GAME PLAN

For runs scored and allowed the previous year, it was not enough to say the Blue Jays scored 780 runs and allowed 682 runs. No, this time we were provided with runs scored and allowed inning by inning over the entire 1992 season:

Blue Jays	93	114	105	75	83	80	80	82	57	6	1	–	4
Opponents	81	79	98	78	89	73	77	55	47	–	4	1	–

A lazy columnist could get a day's work done simply by gazing at these sheets during the pregame meal. Nothing is considered too marginal. There are sheets on individual and team records in day games, night games, turf games, grass games, against left-handed starters, right-handed starters, when the dome is open, when it is closed, when the dome is open in the first inning and closed in the ninth. Both teams also provide special packages of statistics on themselves, detailing injuries, when players were acquired, their birthdays, the names of their wives, children and home towns, their hobbies and awards and who was the last to get hotfooted in the clubhouse. For believers in the power of biorhythms, there are breakdowns on won–loss records for every day of the week. The most startling numbers of all were the preseason ticket purchases. Before the first pitch of 1993, 3,400,000 tickets had been sold, and twenty-eight games were already sold out.

In the third inning Martin wandered over to the regular press box to sit with Dr Ron Taylor, the Blue Jays' team physician. He was sitting beside Dr Allan Gross, a consulting orthopaedic surgeon from Mount Sinai Hospital. They were admiring the new World Series rings. For Taylor, it would be his third, having won two others as a player, first with the St. Louis Cardinals in 1964, then with the Amazin' Mets of 1969.

Taylor was an unusual athlete, one who always kept his priorities in order. He was seventeen years old when he was drafted by the Cleveland Indians as a big, promising Canadian pitcher, having blown away everyone he faced on the sandlots of Leaside, a green and shady neighbourhood in Toronto.

54

Taylor was good enough to persuade the Indians to let him keep up his studies as he played baseball. For five years while he studied electrical engineering at the University of Toronto he reported late to the Indians every spring, after exams, for minor-league assignments in the summer. When he graduated in 1961 as an electrical engineer he turned down more than a dozen lucrative jobs so that he could devote himself entirely to baseball.

As the team physician, the tall, craggy-faced Taylor has the best of both worlds. For a long time as team physician he arrived at the stadium early, pulled on a Blue Jay uniform and pitched batting practice. He has a room under the stands where he often completes notes from his day at his midtown Toronto medical clinic. He keeps up with the game outside by watching it on television, ready for any emergency that should arise.

He took the World Series ring out of the Tiffany box and asked Martin if he'd like to try it on. It was a heavy knuckle-duster, gleaming with small diamonds. Taylor said he often gets calls and letters from people who are interested in any 1969 New York Mets memorabilia, including his team uniform, and the World Series ring. He keeps his Mets and Cardinals rings in a safety deposit box at the bank, but the Mets uniform is in a closet of his house. He's been told he could get $15,000 for it.

Several years earlier, Taylor had invited Martin and his girlfriend to his apartment to watch a World Series game. As Taylor took drink orders, Martin's girlfriend asked Taylor if he especially missed baseball at World Series time. "It must bring back strong memories," she said. "Oh, no," Taylor told her. "I don't even think about baseball anymore. I'm a doctor now. Baseball is all behind me." With that he left the room, only to return later with a tray of drinks, completely outfitted in his New York Mets double-knit uniform, right down to the orange-and-blue AstroTurf cleats.

Martin had met Taylor in 1973, the year after Taylor was released at spring training by the Montreal Expos. It was a hot, dry afternoon in Lethbridge, Alberta, where Taylor was coaching the Lethbridge Lakers of the Alberta Baseball League. He had his priorities in order again. He was waiting to hear from the University of Toronto to see if he had been accepted by the medical school.

In 1983, in his book *Doctors,* Martin wrote about Taylor in a chapter he called "Rookie Doctor." He told of a morning in 1975 when Taylor and his classmates tagged along after a senior doctor, a dermatologist, visiting patients at a downtown Toronto hospital. The dermatologist was a good teacher, but a haughty and arrogant man given to imperious condescension. Taylor and the other students followed him from room to room, nervously anticipating questions about symptoms and diagnoses.

In one of the rooms there was a patient with a violent red rash, which the dermatologist described as "an eruption." He described the colour of the rash by using the proper medical term, *erythematous*, from the Greek. The dermatologist talked with the patient, discussed other medical matters with his students, then abruptly turned to Taylor and asked him to describe the rash.

"Erythematatous," Taylor answered, mispronouncing the word.

"Erythematous!" the senior doctor corrected.

Taylor was flustered, his face turning nearly as red as the rash itself. He was thirty-six years old, by far the oldest student in the first-year class. He was older than some of his professors, and during the first few weeks at medical school some of them had mistaken him for the janitor. The doctor told Taylor that he might benefit from more reading, and not just medical texts. He recited a list of authors, ending with Ernest Hemingway. "You *do* know of Ernest Hemingway?" he asked Taylor, who was still preoccupied with the proper pronunciation of erythematous. Taylor knew what he wanted to say, but he chose not to say anything.

During his baseball career he had travelled to most of the major cities in the United States. And he had been overseas, to Europe and Asia. He often sought out bookstores in his travels because one of his hobbies was collecting rare books. He loved the feel of old books, loved to read and discuss what he had read with people who knew what they were talking about. What delighted him most was discussing books with the people who wrote them. What Taylor wanted to tell the dermatologist was that, yes, he knew of Ernest Hemingway. In a bar called Toots Shor in New York, a young Taylor had once shared a table with Hemingway and spent an afternoon over cold beers talking about books and baseball.

The Blue Jays ended up winning the home opener 13–10, in a game that went three hours and eleven minutes, which would be a common occurrence during the rest of the season. The Blue Jays had too much offence to contain games under two hours. One of the big question marks this season was Ed Sprague, Kelly Gruber's replacement at third base. Sprague booted a grounder early in the game for an error, but he had a splendid day at the plate with four hits, one of them a solo home run, and four runs batted in. It did not take long to forget Gruber.

After the game, in the clubhouse, it quickly became apparent that another replacement, Paul Molitor, would be a presence on and off the field. As the designated hitter, he had a triple and scored twice. In the postgame scrum the writers gathered at Molitor's locker to hear what he had to say, and, just as important, *how* he said it. One of the first questions was, did he think Devon White's two-run triple to put the Jays ahead in the bottom of the seventh was the play of the game. No, he did not, Molitor said. He thought Dick Schofield's bloop single to tie the game in that same inning was more important.

The scrum hung around Molitor, listening to him talk of many things—the growing level of baseball knowledge on the part of Toronto fans, Cleveland's "pesky" offence, how the designated hitter should be confined to the major leagues and not used in college or amateur ball. Out of uniform, stripped down, Molitor displayed hairy arms, hairy chest and an ordinarily trim physique, something like the serious fellow in the office you play squash with once a week. He reads, listens, thinks about a question before he answers, and his replies are unadorned with clichés. The writers were appreciative, and one sensed there would be many more postgame sessions at Molitor's locker this season.

Across the room, the other high-profile free agent acquisition, pitcher Dave Stewart, was showing a box of rings to outfielder Darnell Coles and a few curious writers. There were his World Series championship rings from the 1981 Los Angeles Dodgers and 1989 Oakland A's teams, plus pennant-winning rings from the 1988 and 1990 A's. "They're all nice rings," he said in his high-pitched, raspy voice, as Coles watched in bug-eyed silence. "Those ones [pointing to Alomar's hand two stalls down] are outstanding."

Along the narrow extension in the back corner, near Gaston's office, bullpen coach John Sullivan sat half naked, staring at the new bauble on the fourth finger of his right hand. Gaston peered in, asking Sullivan to see what his ring looked like. "I've waited thirty-five years for this," Sullivan said quietly. "It's damn nice. I'm going to wear it in the shower right now."

Beside him was Larry Hisle, looking around the room at the players from the 1992 team who were acting like kids on Christmas Day. He leaned over to catch a glimpse of Molitor, his teammate fifteen years earlier in Milwaukee when Hisle's career was drawing to a close and Molitor's was just beginning. When Hisle arrived home a few hours later, he said to his wife, "You should have seen the look in his eyes when the other guys were passing their rings around. This year, I want to win one for Paul."

=== 4 ===

Midnight at SkyDome

Above field level the place was silent and still. Most of the seventy hotel rooms facing inside were dark. A few late-nighters lingered at the Hard Rock Cafe on 300 Level. Elsewhere, the building showed no signs of life from the first row of the stands to the top of the roof, 282 feet above where the Toronto Argonauts had defeated the Winnipeg Blue Bombers in an open SkyDome several hours earlier.

Only on the field itself was there activity. It was not even a field anymore. The bright yellow uprights were taken down and stored away. Large patches of bare concrete were exposed as a forklift with two headlights and a long, protruding metal rod prowled the floor of the SkyDome. The rod inserts itself into two-thousand-pound rolls of AstroTurf, then carries them to a storage area under the SkyDome Hotel.

Without the spectacle of a game or even the appearance of a sporting venue, the SkyDome had a feel of enormous emptiness. It looked gutted. When eighteen thousand seats on 100 Level began their nine-minute journey between what will be the first- and third-base lines for baseball, the scene became even more disorienting. It looked as if the entire building was being folded up and stored for the weekend.

The supervisor of the conversion crew is Frank Grespan,

59

thirty-nine. We watched him from the perimeter of what would be left centre field when the outfield wall goes up sometime before morning. Up close, the remaining strips of green turf looked incongruously dainty when contrasted with the solid grey concrete underneath. "Should we take our shoes off?" Martin said as we stepped onto the turf of the deep centre field. Then we remembered that three-hundred-pound nose tackles had been digging their cleats into the stuff all afternoon with no ill effect. We walked across toward what was becoming the baseball infield. Grespan was tinkering with the 6,500-pound roof of the Blue Jay dugout, which at the moment was flush with the ground. The dugout itself must be hoisted from underground with hydraulic lifts.

Grespan was barking out instructions to his seven-person crew, all of whom have university degrees. A handsome man, Grespan has salt-and-pepper hair, wears glasses and a diamond earring in his left ear. He wore faded jeans and a dark blue cotton work shirt—literally a blue-collar guy. We watched the forklift approach another huge roll of AstroTurf, insert the rod into the roll, then trundle off across the outfield. "Looks rather, uh, phallic," Sean suggested.

"Around here we call it 'The Dick,'" Grespan said.

Grespan likes to see himself as a working-class stiff. He told stories of rubbing shoulders with doctors and lawyers at dinner parties and finding it is he who is the centre of attention when he says what he does for a living. "It's the funniest thing. No matter how high people are in the social spectrum, they all want to talk about the dome. I see these people on the tours when I'm here in the mornings. Professors will leave the tour, come down to the field, stand on the mound and try a windup. And they'll stand at home plate and eye the 400 mark in centre field. They love it. It's like all their dreams come to them in one split second." (Brad Bujold, head of the grounds crew, would not be pleased to hear this. No one is supposed to touch the mound. He told *The Toronto Star* once, "Even the Pope had to walk around it when he came here.")

Grespan was working at a leisurely pace. It was only a few

minutes into a Monday morning and the Blue Jays had an off day. Grespan's crew had until noon Tuesday before the grounds crew took over. Grespan did not have to perform his usual all-nighter to get the field converted from football to baseball.

As someone whose job description requires him to work only when the SkyDome is deserted, Grespan was delighted to be interrupted, to have some company. He was in a chatty mood. He started with the story of having been taken to his office at gunpoint when he was spotted wandering the corridors of 000 Level by U.S. Secret Service agents. That was the day of the 1991 All-Star Game at SkyDome, which President George Bush attended. No one was taking any chances. The agents released Grespan only after he managed to convince them he was who he was.

Then there was the time Michael Jordan and the Chicago Bulls came to the SkyDome for an exhibition basketball game and Roberto Alomar came down from his SkyDome Hotel suite to watch. As Grespan tells it, immediately after the game Alomar walked across the polished wood floor of centre court, oblivious to the security personnel trying to keep away the groupies who rush to Alomar whenever he is within rushing range. Alomar was unconcerned about the scene he was creating and insisted he wanted to meet Jordan, who happened to be in a foul mood that day. When Alomar finally nudged his way up to the basketball superstar, Jordan had no time for the little Puerto Rican, thinking he was another autograph hound.

"Not now," Jordan said, then walked away.

We talked about the likelihood that the Blue Jays would once again make it to postseason play, and the effect this would have on Grespan's duties. If Toronto made it to the World Series again, Game Two would be at the SkyDome on Sunday, October 17, the same day the Argonauts were scheduled to play there. If that happened, the Argonauts would be forced to play elsewhere, another in a season of indignities for the beleaguered football team. If the Blue Jays won the World

Series again, Grespan hoped there would not be a repeat of 1992, when forty thousand fans ran amok in the SkyDome after watching the final game on the JumboTron. They did $300,000 worth of damage to the field that night, more than 75 percent of Grespan's annual budget. The fans behaved as if the Berlin Wall had come tumbling down, and the citizenry scrambled for pieces of the rubble, mementoes of history.

"They stormed the field, looking for souvenirs, digging up dirt with their bare hands," Grespan said. "Some of the turf was cut into pieces. It's really tough to do, but they managed to pull it out and rip it up. Some of the strips were twenty feet long. It was incredible. They even cut out the four-hundred-foot marker in centre field. People were walking out with pieces of warning track on their shoulders. The security people were stopping them, asking what they thought they were doing. A week later I saw ads in the paper saying Blue Jays turf for sale—'World Series turf.'"

In 1993 observant fans would have noticed long strips of AstroTurf running to the outfield wall from first, second and third base that were a darker hue of green than the rest of the field. That is the legacy of the night of October 24, 1992. The reason these strips are darker—thicker and springier, too—is that they had to be borrowed from the Argonauts, who have their own turf to accommodate the different dimensions of a football field. Baseball may be a more lackadaisical sport, but the sheer volume of games in a season wears down the artificial turf much more than football, no matter how brutal football may be.

Grespan has been head of the conversion crew since the SkyDome opened in 1989. Asked about his qualifications for the job of overseeing SkyDome chameleonic transformations from a baseball park to rock concert theatre to monster truck dirt pit to Jehovah's Witness baptism pool party, Grespan replied, "Luck. I worked for thirteen years at the University of Toronto's athletic centre, the one they call 'Fort Jock.' It was a multi-purpose facility—basketball, volleyball, track and field, et cetera. But nothing compares to this. I had so many

sleepless nights when I first came here. I was moving furniture
in my sleep. Not a word of a lie. I'd be up, looking around the
apartment with my hands on my hips, wondering what to do
next. My wife would come out and say, 'Get back to bed,
Frank.' I lost fifteen pounds that first year."

His first conversion was from the gala grand opening on
June 3 (the roof opened during a torrential rain storm, soak-
ing the $250-a-ticket crowd) to the Blue Jays' first game at
the SkyDome two days later against the Milwaukee Brewers,
when Paul Molitor got the first-ever hit at the SkyDome (a
first-inning leadoff double off Blue Jay starter Jimmy Key).
Getting ready for that first baseball game was a baptism of fire,
Grespan said. The innards of the SkyDome were still being
assembled the day before the opening ceremony, which meant
that Grespan and his crew did not have the luxury of a dry
run. The first conversion they did was for real, and it took
nearly twenty-four hours of round-the-clock, seat-of-the-
pants manoeuvring. They can now do a complete conversion
in ten to twelve hours. "We made it by the skin of our teeth
that first time," Grespan said. "The paint was still drying
while the players were coming on."

Four years later, changing the field lines from one sport to
another is still one of the most time-consuming aspects of the
conversion. Two Zamboni-like machines take up to ten hours
to do the job, and there are still traces of the football grid in
the baseball outfield after an Argonaut home game. It is not
that the actual football lines are showing through; it is that the
places where the football lines used to be are cleaner than the
unmarked areas around them, like the living-room carpet
after the sofa has been moved. It could be worse. Wayne Sills,
a member of Grespan's crew, has a chemistry degree from the
University of Toronto, and he checks with former faculty
members to find new ways of making the lines easier to erase
and brighter. One way of doing this, he found, was to add
Tide laundry detergent to the lines. This is the common-
sense ingenuity Grespan respects. He gave no quarter to the
high-priced consultants in $800 suits who proliferated when

the SkyDome was being built.

"That was one of the first things I learned in 1989. The draftsmen and the $150-an-hour people could come and say, 'This is how you're going to do it.' Well, they were totally wrong. The workers who helped me most were the ones with tools in their hands who really knew how steel worked. These Portuguese and Italian labourers would ask in their broken English, 'Are you the guy who's going to work with this stuff?' And they'd shake their heads. They pitied me. I asked why and they told me about tolerances and eighth-of-an-inch clearances between the columns and steel beams. It was then I knew I was in trouble."

Grespan was not alone in being sceptical whether the SkyDome could deliver on all its hypertechnological promises. There was a suspicion among many Torontonians that the building, the roof in particular, would be rife with glitches. What if it didn't work at all? Higher foreheads than Grespan said flat out that the SkyDome was a disaster in the making.

David Geiger, who heads a New York engineering firm that had worked on nine domed stadiums, told *The Globe and Mail* before the opening that the SkyDome was making a quantum leap in technology and would suffer for its hubris. "I'm not sure retractable roofs work," Geiger said. "Look what happened in Montreal.... My bet is the roof will take much longer to move [than the twenty minutes predicted] and they will end up leaving it in one place most of the time."

What *The Globe and Mail* failed to mention was that Geiger had presented one of the losing bids to the Ontario government in the competition that eventually selected Toronto architect Rod Robbie and his Ottawa partner and structural engineer Michael Allen. Other than Robbie and Allen, Grespan was one of the first people to know that the retractable roof would work.

"Just prior to the opening, a large Russian delegation came here. The top engineer for Russia—it was the Soviet Union then—came to visit SkyDome with fifteen colleagues. I had prepared this presentation, a media guide, slides, all the bells and whistles. It had to be done through an interpreter. I was feeling pressure. It was all new to me and I was a little wet behind the ears. We're sitting around a boardroom, me and the top engineer in Russia! About three minutes into my presentation, the top guy says, '*Nyet!*'"

Grespan, startled, stopped his presentation and looked at the Russian engineer, who seemed bored by all the charts and diagrams. He looked at the interpreter for help. The interpreter conferred with the engineer, then conveyed his wishes. "He says, 'We go.'"

"I didn't know what was happening," Grespan said.

The interpreter explained. "Roof."

"All right," Grespan said. "You're our guest. Let's go."

It was early February, the wind howling outside, and it was bitterly cold inside the unfinished stadium. Grespan and the Russian delegation trekked up the construction scaffolding. "He left me behind by a good fifty paces," Grespan remembered. "He went to one of the bogie wheels—the driving mechanism for the retractable roof—and he looked at it. After a while I asked, 'Is it going to work?' He said, 'Yes.' This was three months before we moved the roof. The membrane wasn't even on yet."

On a sweltering July afternoon in Toronto last year, we met the man whose design made the Russians marvel. He was on the second floor of a nondescript warehouse building on Soho Street in the Queen Street bar-and-nightclub district, a few steps from a motorcycle hangout. We had to make two trips before we successfully interviewed Roderick Robbie, the architect of the SkyDome.

The first appointment had been scheduled for the end of the afternoon of Friday, July 2, the day after the Canada Day holiday. Robbie had taken an extended long weekend, however, and had forgotten to cancel the appointment. After finding Robbie AWOL, we walked to The Black Bull, the motorcycle hangout, for a beer. It was an island of tough in a sea of effete, existential urban couture. Those among the black lipstick set made sure to tiptoe around the row of Harley-Davidsons lined up outside. While discussing the aborted interview, we listened to a waiter tell us how the owner had stood on the roof of a patron's car a few days earlier and smashed the windshield with a crowbar because the fellow had made a mess of his bar.

When we went back to the car half an hour later it was gone. We walked eight blocks to the waterfront and paid a $175 ticket-and-tow charge to get the car back. We cursed our stupidity as the clerk at the municipal lockup processed the fine. But in our defence, it was not the first time a journey beginning at Rod Robbie's office had ended in a vortex of debt.

When we met Robbie a week later, he directed us to a makeshift boardroom decorated with a travel agent's leftover posters of France on the walls, pigeons nesting on the window ledge, and humid, fetid air inside. The architect who devised a way to let four million baseball fans a year bask in the sunshine on summer afternoons, then enjoy room temperature on cold, rainy nights, did not have air-conditioning in his office.

"Look at this place," Robbie said disgustedly. "We're sitting in these uncomfortable surroundings because we defaulted on the buildings we owned on St. George Street (across from the Royal Canadian Yacht Club). Before SkyDome I never had any debts in my life. Now I have $900,000, which is kind of mind-boggling. That's an appalling amount of money."

Okay, so $175 is not much compared to the losses Robbie incurred building SkyDome. But $900,000 is not much compared to the $350 million in excess of the original $243-million price tag of SkyDome, an overrun the province of Ontario has resigned itself to sucking up. Or, look at it this way: Divide that $350 million among the eight million men, women and children residing in Ontario and you arrive at a per capita SkyDome debt of $43.75. Multiply that by the four members of our immediate family and you end up with an

O'Malley SkyDome debt of $175, which we now would like to consider paid in full.

It was not Robbie's fault that SkyDome ended up costing more than double his initial estimate. Having to squeeze in as an afterthought a 348-room hotel, 62 extra luxury boxes, a fitness club, The Founders Club bar and restaurant, and the state-of-the-art facilities of Dome Productions after the blueprints had been drawn and the numbers crunched through a computer in Ottawa—all this tends to add to expenses. And there was a ten-week construction strike a few months before the official opening.

Most people think the cost of the retractable roof is what made the SkyDome so expensive. It certainly has scared cities around the world from buying the rights to Robbie's design, though a retractable dome stadium is in the works in Taiwan, and another is planned for Saudi Arabia. Robbie insists that the retractability added only 8 percent to the total cost. The most dramatic variance in cost, he says, is between an open-air stadium and a domed stadium, not between a domed stadium and a retractable domed stadium.

Nevertheless, Robbie feels, with the flinty indignation of a Brit, that he has been screwed. And to judge by his warehouse-office, his feelings appear to be entirely justified. He used to share a private box at the SkyDome with eight other architectural firms, but the debts Robbie incurred creating the SkyDome forced him to default his share. "I thought they would have given us a box," he said. "Not one of the prime ones, but a box that could be used as a museum of what we did. We have twenty-five hundred drawings sitting in a locker. We never got any free tickets. We paid $250 each to go to the opening."

The only hint of affluence now was a red Saab parked outside. But even that, as we were informed in a two-page, handwritten fax Robbie sent us the day after we wrote about him and the Saab in our *Globe and Mail* column, has become a money pit on wheels. He signed a four-year lease for a snazzy new silver Saab—silver is wife Enid's favourite colour—in 1989 when SkyDome opened. Robbie thought that having designed what has been called the Eighth Wonder of the World would give him a bit of a comfort zone. He was wrong. When the $17,000 bill came due in 1993, Robbie was so broke he had to roll over the lease and accept a used red Saab in trade. As he explained in the fax, "The red Saab is the last thing left (complete with its own line of debt) from that hopeful SkyDome period."

Robbie's problems started right after construction was completed in 1989, when his company, RAN International, submitted a $36-million invoice to Stadco, the company formed by the province and a thirty-member private consortium to build and operate the SkyDome. Stadco had a minor quibble with the invoice, about $12-million worth of quibble. When the lawyers had finished duking it out, RAN International received only $23.9 million, and had to promise not to bring any more legal action against Stadco.

Robbie accepted the money, even though it was $1.4 million less than his stated costs. He needed the money, fast, because he was teetering on the edge of bankruptcy. Back in 1983, the Robbies had mortgaged their house to raise the money to prepare the winning bid, which took $700,000 and eighteen months of planning, working nights and weekends. When he won the bid, he dropped all his other projects so he could devote himself full time to the SkyDome. In the summer of 1993, Robbie turned sixty-four years old. The irony is that people assumed, because of the remarkable success of the SkyDome, that he had achieved the crowning moment of his career and could retire in luxury for the rest of his life. People had no idea the desperate circumstances he was in.

"They said, 'Take it or sue us.' And they knew we couldn't. Everybody who worked on this project, including the lawyers, got paid as they went along. I would have thought in a civilized society we would have got our costs, plus ten percent. They just fucked us. It's as simple as that."

It was not supposed to end up this way for the British-born architect with the red beard, horn-rimmed glasses and ruddy hands who had designed the Canada Pavilion at Expo '67, itself an impressive architectural triumph. Robbie was an outsider in the clubby world of architecture when his vision of a "secular cathedral" beat out thirty-three bids to win the job of a lifetime in 1983. Unlike some of his competitors, who frequently emphasized their baseball know-how during the bidding, Robbie knew nothing about the game and said so. But he considered his ignorance a virtue because it meant he would have no preconceived ideas about what a baseball park should be. He didn't know anything about molecular biology, either, but that didn't prevent him from designing many successful medical laboratories.

He is an obsessive man, and his obsessions go far beyond architecture. In one stretch of his life he spent fifteen years writing a 777-page, single-spaced manuscript about his philosophy of life, which he titled "Minds." He made sixteen copies for his family and friends. Talking with Adele Freedman, the architecture critic of *The Globe and Mail*, he described it as the work of "a mid-twentieth-century industrial peasant."

"I'm not a baseball fan, I'm an architect, and this was an immense challenge. We did it for the challenge, the honour. The fact of the matter is that if you win the thing...you become part of Canadian architectural history, for good or evil. This is not going to be knocked down in thirty years. It will probably be here two hundred, three hundred years from now."

He even designed it to withstand twenty years of neglect, if that should happen. A small example is the outside of the roof, which washes itself clean after every rainfall. "I know about these things," Robbie said. "I used to work for British Rail."

His partner, Michael Allen, a structural engineer, is the one who invented the technology for the retractable roof. Allen and Robbie would rack their brains over pasta and red wine at La Grolla, a restaurant in north Toronto, then Allen would fly home to Ottawa and work on his computer until he could prove that their latest concept was unworkable, which it always was. The eureka finally happened when Allen was alone on another flight home from Toronto, when he began scribbling and doodling on a notepad on the pull-down tray at his seat. He considered a design with a fixed panel at the north end, with three movable panels that would stack up behind the fixed one when the roof was open, leaving 92 percent of the field in sunshine. Allen spent the next weekend applying all his engineering smarts to the task of proving that it would not work. He failed.

It worked.

"He sent me his stuff and asked me what I thought," Robbie said. "I told him, 'This is a work of fucking genius.' The geometry was pushed to its absolute limit. We were working with eight-inch clearances between the panels."

The word genius is also used liberally in reference to Robbie by just about everybody who came in contact with him during the building of the SkyDome. Even the vice-president of corporate affairs for the SkyDome, David Garrick, whose boss, Richard Peddie, is the purported Darth Vader behind Robbie's financial misfortune, concedes that Robbie is a genius. And why not? In its first four years of operation, the roof had travelled 115 miles opening and closing and had stuck only once, when a transformer blew. Even that resulted in only a slight delay, and the roof soon was operational again, opening and closing in twenty minutes. Think about that the next time you see an escalator in a subway or shopping mall fenced off because of mechanical malfunctions. For each of those four years the SkyDome has been voted Stadium of the Year by *Performance* magazine. The building had a pre-municipal-tax, pre-debt-servicing profit of $30 million in 1992. In 1993 the SkyDome became the busiest stadium in North America in terms of event days, surpassing Madison Square Garden in New York City.

As for Robbie's survival skills and talent for looking out for number one, Peddie is less effusive. In a *Globe and Mail* article, he said the contracts with RAN International never promised to cover Robbie's expenses and profit. "They say we'll pay you X and that's the way those things work," Peddie explained. "We paid him according to our interpretation of the deal, and ultimately he agreed to that."

Paul Beeston is another heavy hitter who is solidly in Robbie's corner. "Rod Robbie is one of the most remarkable people I have every met," he told us. "We would ask him if he could do something and he'd say he didn't know how, but he'd do it. And he did it. He'd always question, always consult. We are either co-authors or co-destroyers of this because we certainly had every opportunity to put our input into it."

Architect Eugene Lyle was Robbie's point man for the baseball end of the design, meeting regularly with Beeston, Gord Ash and Public Relations Director Howard Starkman. He also recruited baseball-writer-turned-mystery-novelist Alison Gordon to fill him in on the lore and beauty of the game. "I found the game peculiar because there weren't strict rules about what shape the field should be," Robbie said. "But we felt there was nothing to learn from other stadiums, except mistakes."

One of the most intriguing concerns was over the field of play. Artificial turf is one of the reasons the SkyDome is considered a mockery of baseball's traditions, but Robbie and his colleagues expended a considerable amount of energy and creativity trying to make real grass inside the SkyDome workable. It had been tried in the first baseball dome, the Astrodome in Houston, but the experiment failed. Robbie thought of a system that involved sliding grass in on huge trays for game days. He consulted experts at the University of Calgary's sports medicine department. He tried experts at a place called The Turf Institute in Guelph. He sent out tenders world-wide to anyone who thought they could figure out a way to maintain a portable grass field for game conditions. There was much interest in the challenge, but no one was willing to put up the $5-million bond Robbie asked for to show they were serious.

In the end, there were four finalists for the field contract, all of them artificial-turf makers. One was an Australian company with the innovative concept of artificial grass that "grew" in four-inch strands out of a sand base. It was used for some cricket fields, and was being considered for tennis. The ideas was that it would behave like grass, complete with bad hops and soft landings. It looked like grass, felt like grass, and fell short only on smelling like grass. Theoretically, it could even be manipulated by devious and clever groundskeepers, the way it has been done in baseball for generations. It could be hardened with added sand for a quicker game, or, when a Rickey Henderson was in town—when he was an intimidating enemy base-stealer—the sand load could be reduced to slow things down. Strands along the lines could be shaved to coax bunted balls fair or foul, infields could be made fast or slow, depending on the age and dexterity of the home team's middle infielders. The only hitch: once it was mowed it would stay mowed, and could only be changed by replacing it.

A man named David Hastings was in charge of the turf question. He got a kick out of the Australian bid, but ultimately it was up to the players to decide, and they wanted the real artificial grass, not the fake sand-fettered grass. Hastings invited the Blue Jays and Argonauts to test the four finalists' stuff in the parking lot at Ontario Place one spring afternoon in 1987. "We pretended we were Chinese scientists and asked them to do different manoeuvres on each strip and rate them from one to five," Hastings said. The football players did tackles and pass patterns. The baseball players did some batting practice and fielded grounders. "We pushed the sand-based one," Hastings said. "We thought it was interesting. Pat Gillick was interested because it played like real grass. The football linemen liked it, too, but the other players looked at it as more of a curiosity."

One of the worries for Robbie was the matter of sabotage and terrorism. "This building had to last for at least a hundred years," Robbie said. "We thought that by the law of averages some lunatic would try to bring it down with explosives, or dive an airplane into it. You have fifty thousand people sitting

72

under this thing. There are a lot of sick people out there and you only need one or two. The day before it opened there was an eight-hour meeting and everybody who attended had to sign off to take responsibility that it was safe to open. We, of course, had the biggest burden. The roof had to be checked and rechecked to see if there were any beer cans up there, or bolts, or wrenches, or ice picks. For instance, somebody left a bolt [on the tracks] when we were testing it, under panel two. The panel came around, rolled up on the bolt and fired it from under the wheel. It lifted the bogie about an inch, but it put an earthquake shock through the building."

Like, *Booooom!*

Robbie deliberately left much of the concrete exposed, as well as the steel latticework under the roof, as a way to emphasize the massiveness of the place. He had considered shapes in nature—lobsters, crayfish, scorpions—that had articulated shells that could be used for inspiration. "Remember the Sydney Opera House [in Australia]?" he said. "It had all these shells. But those shapes were extremely difficult to build because they were not susceptible to direct mathematical analysis. They were artistic shapes that were extraordinarily complex. They figured it out by brute engineering. I thought SkyDome should have a certain organic history to it."

As the session in Robbie's office was winding down, Martin mentioned that one morning when he was driving westward on the Gardiner Expressway, the SkyDome looming ahead, he thought it looked like a gargantuan…igloo. Hearing this, Robbie fingered his moustache and looked intrigued. Then, mostly to himself, he muttered, "An igloo? Hmmm. That never occurred to me. An igloo."

It was approaching seven o'clock and we had a baseball game to go to. The hot, muggy day had given way to a thunderstorm. Robbie himself had not been to the SkyDome for a long time, but he offered to drive us there in his Saab on his way to an Italian restaurant for dinner with his wife. "I don't like going there now," he said as we poked through the crowd

73

of pedestrians rushing to the stadium while the rain continued to pound the windshield of Robbie's car. "Everything
about the experience has been ruinous and SkyDome
reminds me of my problems. I watch baseball a lot at home,
on television. Enid has become a baseball freak. She grew to
like it after I started this."

Walking up the concourse from the street called Blue Jays
Way, nobody in the crowd recognized the man behind the
wheel, though without him there would have been no game
that night.

=== 5 ===

The Grounds Crew

Saturday morning in May at the SkyDome. Outside, it is cool and crisp. Inside, as always, when the roof is closed, twenty degrees Celsius, sixty-eight degrees Fahrenheit. Some of the floodlights are on inside, but streams of sunlight spill in from the street-level entrances to the bars and restaurants above the outfield fence. The emptiness, the quiet and the dominant blue and green inside create a cool, calm effect, like being submerged in a shallow lake. Or in space.

Occasionally the silence is broken by the distant hum of cleaning machines in the stands, where the grounds crew, wearing blue jump suits, steam-blasts the seats to remove all the trace evidence of caramel corn, pop containers, peanut shells and assorted detritus from the night before. From a distance, the spray from the three-foot-tall cylinders looks like flour.

Down on the field, Brad Bujold, head groundskeeper, stands several paces foul of the third-base bag. He is thirty-five, wearing track pants and a blue T-shirt, with a round face and healthy-looking frame that shows the beginnings of a paunch in the middle—like an athlete after his first year of retirement.

"See this?" he says. He is pointing at a brown splotch on

the green artificial turf: chewing-tobacco spit.

"Ed Sprague?" Sean asks.

He shakes his head.

"Rich Hacker?" Hacker is the third-base coach for the Blue Jays.

Bujold shakes his head again.

"The umpire," he replies. "They're the worst."

At least it wasn't bubble gum. Bujold loathes bubble gum. The stuff melts into the turf on sunny days and has to be disintegrated with a chemical spray. He used to have a sign at Exhibition Stadium telling the players to please not spit their gum on the field. He thinks he may have to put up a gentle reminder at the SkyDome.

Bujold is responsible for 142,000 square feet of artificial turf connected by eight miles of zippers, enough for 50,000 pairs of blue jeans. He has kept the playing field of two stadiums up to major-league standards since 1984, five years after he was hired as one of those enthusiastic, raggedy-ass part-timers who run onto the field after the fifth inning to change bases and redraw the chalk lines accompanied by the *William Tell* Overture.

Bujold grew up in Toronto during the baseball void between the demise of the AAA Toronto Maple Leafs and the birth of the Blue Jays. His favourite team was the Cincinnati Reds, the Big Red Machine of the mid-seventies. Johnny Bench. Pete Rose. Dave Concepcion. Bujold's uncle lived in Montreal and he often went to Jarry Park when the Reds were in town. He does not know why he preferred the Reds to the Expos. Another one of those unexplainable love affairs so common in sport.

Bujold was hired by the Blue Jays in 1979 by then head groundskeeper Gord Ash, now the assistant general manager of the Blue Jays. He was thrilled to learn that the director of stadium operations was Terry Barthelmas, who had come to Toronto from the Reds' organization. Fourteen years later Bujold still uses a lot of Barthelmas's techniques, most of which originated in Cincinnati.

Behind the scenes at SkyDome are dozens of people who have accidentally made a career out of the game of baseball, and they make a good life out of it. The players themselves, of course, top the list, as there are no undergraduate courses on how to be a shortstop, or how to hit the cutoff man. No guarantees, either.

Spend enough time around SkyDome and one finds that dedication and job satisfaction are exceedingly common. After a while we stopped asking Blue Jay staffers how they liked their jobs because invariably they were "paid to have fun," or "it beats having a real job." You will find this with all major-league teams—they call it The Show, after all—but the Blue Jays happen to be better than most teams at fostering it. They provide staffers with trips to road games, even during postseason play. They reward them with special service rings. As a result, the staffers are like Japanese salarymen: all that's missing is a company anthem to sing at the beginning of each day (though the catchy "Okay! Blue Jays!" might do). In a feature on the Blue Jays after the 1992 World Series, titled "The Blue Jay Way," *Sports Illustrated* remarked, "No other club in baseball has the front-office continuity of the Blue Jays."

Bujold walks to second base and pulls up the turf where it meets the infield dirt around the bag. To any committed Blue Jay fan, that spot conjures up a vivid memory: all-star short-stop Tony Fernandez lost for the season in the dying days of the 1987 pennant race with Detroit when he broke his elbow after being upended by a charging Tiger. Before that play, the Blue Jays had the best record in all of baseball—with a week to go. They would have been heavily favoured against the Minnesota Twins, who were barely above .500, to go to their first World Series. Instead, with rookie Manny Lee filling in, Toronto lost seven games in a row and finished second.

"That was a total fluke," says Bujold. "You have to hit it exactly on the spot to cause that kind of injury."

The "spot" is a gap the width of a knife edge between the six-inch-wide steel beam where the turf ends and the dirt begins. When the Blue Jays moved from Exhibition Stadium to SkyDome, so did the ghost of Tony Fernandez. Today the steel is protected by a rubber strip, to the great objection of the company that won the contract to install the new turf. They considered it an affront to their ego that their design would be modified in any way. That being said, in 1993 the Blue Jays went out and lost four shortstops to injury before the end of May: Eddie Zosky in spring training, followed for varying lengths of time by Alfredo Griffin, Luis Sojo and Dick Schofield, who broke his arm after a collision during an opponent's steal attempt and, late in May, was expected to be out for the season.

Bujold's job is not as demanding now as it was during his tenure at Exhibition Stadium. The very idea of an artificial turf groundskeeper seems a contradiction in terms, since there is very little "ground" to keep. There is real dirt at home plate, the bases and the pitching mound, but that's it. Nevertheless, Bujold is the Maytag repairman of groundskeepers. He has been relieved of the one variable that keeps every groundskeeper on his toes: weather. That is the purpose of all domes, including the first in Houston in the 1960s, which was built to keep out the heat.

Suddenly, after five years of readiness for anything from rain to wind off Lake Ontario (Jim Clancy was blown off the mound in middelivery after his fifth pitch of the game), to fog (Kelly Gruber hit an inside-the-park home run on a routine fly ball before the game was mercifully called), Bujold does not have to be ready for anything. He is like the crack news reporter in a town where nothing happens.

The field at SkyDome is not even designed to cope with rain. At Exhibition Stadium the outfield had a curved, crown shape for drainage. When Bujold took his customary place at the end of the dugout, where manager Cito Gaston now sits, centre fielder Rick Bosetti was visible only from about midthigh because of the over-the-horizon effect of the field. When it rained, the water flowed off down the sides of the crown. At SkyDome the field is flat; if rain fell unimpeded, the water would form a pond.

Bujold is teased during summer months with open air—but only dry, gently moving open air. Like Tantalus in Hades, surrounded by food that receded when he reached for it, Bujold looks up at the Toronto sky and dreams of menacing cloud formations, rolling thunder, zaps of lightning, only to have the elements taken from him as soon as they appear. Hearing Bujold talk about it, his present duties sound like those of a farmer contemplating a dome over the province of Saskatchewan. Crops would grow under perfectly climate-controlled conditions, hail storms would be a thing of the past, an automated sprinkler system would replace rainfall. Sensible, perhaps, but not as aesthetically pleasing, or professionally satisfying.

One of the only times it rained inside SkyDome during a game was in the inaugural series against the Milwaukee Brewers in June of 1989. During the second game—the first Sean ever saw at SkyDome—a sudden storm blew through Toronto so quickly that George Holm, director of stadium operations, could not get the roof closed before the deluge began. As play stopped and all the players and fans looked up in lock-jawed amazement at the 19 million pounds of concrete and steel moving noiselessly overhead, Bujold and his crew ran around frantically trying to cover the infield with tarps.

"We ran out there, put the base tarps down, then I started yelling at the guys to squeegie the warning track. It didn't click in that, hey, the roof is still moving. It was going to be over in a couple minutes. No sense in sending the guys away when I was just going to be bringing them right back.

"It was a weird feeling. You know it's going to stop raining at second base any minute, so I can take the second-base tarp off. Then it's going to stop raining at first, third and the pitching mound, then home plate."

It was surreal, as if God were taking a piss on home plate, sending a message of displeasure with the architectural hubris of SkyDome. The whole time, Bujold could hear Rich

Garcia, the crew chief umpire, cursing in Spanish.

"I don't have as much to do with the umpires anymore," Bujold says. "That's what I miss the most. I'm not dealing with the weather reports, a rain situation. Sure it makes my job easier, but I feel it's something that's been taken away from me. I used to be the guy who phoned the weather office. Now it's upper management who does that and makes the decision whether the roof is open or not. All I get is a radio report saying 'We're going to be open tonight.' So I miss that part, the rapport I had with the weatherman, the umpires. When everything worked well, and we had the timing of the storm coming in, it made you feel good, like you've done your job.

"Once the game started I had a hot line in the dugout. I'd be relaying updates to the umpires during the game. Now I'm away from it." During games at SkyDome Bujold and his crew sit in a concrete bunker beyond the left-field foul pole, under the stands. "I feel like I've been pushed aside," Bujold says. "I used to worry about everything. I miss that."

Sometimes Bujold feels more like a housekeeper than a major-league groundskeeper, though he still keeps in touch with his peers around the league, including the dean of all sport groundskeepers, George Toma of the Kansas City Royals. Toma has been chosen by the organizers of soccer's World Cup in the United States in 1994 to find a way to lay grass atop the artificial turf at some of the major venues to accommodate international standards. Though he will not use this technique at the World Cup, he discovered while at Kansas City's spring training site at Haines City, Florida, that the artificial turf there naturally sprouted grass if left alone. That was when there was an artificial turf infield and a natural grass outfield.

"We have our own union, so to speak," says Bujold. "We call each other and help each other out. I was told it wasn't like that before. They used to keep their ideas to themselves. It's much more of a fraternity now. We all know what the other guys are doing. Detroit, for example, is well known for fiddling with the field. I went there once and the batter's box was like a beach, a great help to sinkerball pitchers. It was unbelievable. And the grass in the infield was real long so Alan Trammell and Lou Whitaker could get to the ball. We can't do that here.

"Some people think grass people work harder. But unless they work with the artificial turf, they don't realize that we have to sweep the carpet every day. On grass, if you take a divot, it can be easily fixed. Rip the turf out here and you've got to replace it—you've got to sew it together. Things are more noticeable on turf. If you're laying it down and there's something under there, say a small pebble, that little pebble becomes a distinct bump on the field.

"You can hide a lot on a grass field. If it's a rainy day and the players get mud all over their cleats, the mud and dirt get camouflaged by the grass. Do that on artificial turf and you get footprints all over the place. It's like maintaining a carpet, like a woman would do at home in the living room. The kids come in from playing in the sandbox outside, run through the house into the kitchen to the fridge, and you've got footprints all over the living room."

In 1993, for the first time, Bujold went to Florida and met groundskeepers from all levels in the Blue Jay chain—the rookie league in St. Catharines, the AA team in Knoxville, the AAA team in Syracuse. They compared notes to make their procedures as streamlined as possible so there is consistency for players coming through the ranks. Of course, SkyDome is the only facility without grass.

"I love it down in Dunedin," Bujold says. "When you go there first thing in the morning, right after the grass has been cut—that's baseball."

There was one bad time, right after the Jays moved to the SkyDome, when Bujold suffered the worst slump of his groundskeeping career. Ironically, after years of expertly managing chaos at Exhibition Stadium, Bujold's world collapsed soon after he arrived at the comfy confines of the SkyDome. For the first time with the Blue Jays, he was not enjoying his job. He did not leave his worries at the office when he went home at night. He dreaded coming to work the next day.

The problem? The pitching mound, so dependable for a decade at the Ex, crumbled before his eyes almost daily. By the sixth or seventh inning the game would have to be delayed while Bujold trudged out and repaired the mound. It is a groundskeeper's nightmare: public humiliation in front of fifty thousand fans, hundreds of thousands of television viewers and one angry pitcher. Those days, if he had forgotten to put his pants on before going out to the field, he would not have felt more embarrassed.

"It was driving me up the wall. Pitchers on our team were getting on my butt all the time. Jim Acker used to say before the game, 'Well, what inning are you going to come out today? We're having a raffle.'"

Bujold's difficulties were duly noted toward the end of the 1990 season when the players held their annual meeting to vote on how playoff bonus shares should be divided among part-time players and Blue Jay support staff. Non-players have often been voted healthy cuts, even full shares (over $120,000 U.S. for the 1992 and 1993 World Series wins). That year, Bujold did not get a dime of bonus money.

"I had a rough year and it showed when it came to bonus time. The players didn't take care of me and I guess I can accept that. I wasn't doing my job."

Bujold was stumped. He agonized over the problem all winter. He had been using the same New Jersey clay-and-dirt mixture that had worked fine all along. He called New Jersey and was told it was the same stuff they had always sent. He asked the pitchers which American League mounds they liked best. Struggling for a solution, he remembered Tom Henke used to rave about the mound in Chicago.

Bujold called Roger Bossard, his counterpart for the White Sox. Bossard told him he supplemented the Major League Baseball mixture with a clay known as Blue Gumbo from local construction sites. Bossard guessed that Toronto, being a lot like Chicago, should have a similar type of clay under the city.

Bujold figured matters could not get any worse. He gave it a shot.

"I called Gazzola Paving here in Toronto. They were doing some work at the corner of Church and Lombard. They took me there and explained about the layers of shale. I took a load of it and dumped it in the parking lot outside SkyDome. It was even better than the clay in Chicago. The pitchers loved it. We still have a load in the parking lot that will last us for a while."

Once the game starts, the crew has lots of free time, so they either sit in the office/storage area or on the elevated seats behind the outfield wall in left centre, about ten feet from an identical perch where the Blue Jay relievers sit. There were fourteen men on the crew in 1993. They worked only during home games between studies at school or other pursuits. Sometimes, when there are games Friday night and Saturday afternoon, three or four guys stay overnight at SkyDome in a loft above the office area. For cushions they use pieces of padding for the outfield fence. For blankets they use World Series bunting.

Grant Groves, a twenty-six-year-old graduate student at the University of Toronto's Faculty of Education, has worked with the grounds crew four years, so he is one of Bujold's veterans. He sat with Brad and Sean on the bench above the outfield fence during the sixth inning of one game. The view was splendid. They leaned their arms on top of the bench while they talked. The highlights of his days on the crew are the same as any other members who have been around long enough to experience them: the All-Star Game in 1991, when the crew wore tuxedos and were driven onto the field in the fifth inning in a limo, and the 1992 World Series, when they were all flown to Atlanta, at the Blue Jays' expense, for Game Six.

Groves remembered watching Lloyd Moseby hit a game-winning double late against the Baltimore Orioles in the clinching game in 1989. "He hit it right here, right off this fence," he said, pounding the fence top.

Bujold remembered feeling part of one memorable game, sitting like Kilroy over the outfield fence. "I had a great view of Devo's catch," he said. He did not have to explain what catch he was talking about. "I was sitting at the end of the bench there," he continued, pointing to a place about ten metres from the 400 marker in centre field. "We were look-ing, wondering, will he make it? We knew he was close. Then it was instantaneous, the catch and the slam into the wall. We felt the vibration."

The hardest year for Groves was 1989. The team started off poorly and there was the daily grind early on of switching the Jays and Tiger logos on the outfield fence between sixth and seventh place. (It was Alison Gordon, who used to write about baseball for *The Toronto Star* and now writes baseball murder mysteries, who suggested that the circular team logos along the outfield fence be arranged in order of the divisional standings.)

Then there was the nightmarish midseason transition from Exhibition Stadium to SkyDome. Groves worked twen-ty-four hours straight on the last day, and the field was not ready until half an hour before game time.

Though Groves believes there were grounds crew work-ers in the past who idolized the players too much and pestered them for memorabilia, a few players stand out in his mind as having been particularly worthwhile people to know. "Tom Henke always talked to us. I was sad to see him go. He would time us during our fifth-inning sprint to the field. He treated us as equals. He wasn't into the caste system where you have the players, management and us, the lowly workers. David Wells was great, too. He came here earlier this month with Detroit and said the next time he was here on a week-end he'd take us out for a beer. Derek Bell took us out a few times, too. It's interesting that some of the players who don't get along with the media get along fine with us. Maybe it's because they are closer to us in age and maturity. But baseball's supposed to be fun. The team this year is a lot more serious."

Back inside the bunker, Bujold left to answer the phone. Fans sometimes call from a bar asking questions like, "Does the ninety feet from home to first extend to the front or the back of the bag?" (The back.) Or, "How high is the pitching mound?" (Ten inches.)

When they can't think of other things to talk about, the grounds crew talks about Chuck Macaluso, who happened to be away in Europe on vacation. He had been away only two weeks, but had already sent three postcards. The crew has a treasure trove of Chuck Macaluso stories.

He distinguished himself early in his first year in 1988 when he was told to lightly sprinkle the home plate area after a game at Exhibition Stadium. When Bujold arrived, Macaluso was standing on home plate, having drenched the dirt so much he was in the middle of a small moat, trying to find a way off. "Nowhere to go, and he's standing there with the hose in his hand, still spraying," Bujold remembered.

Then there was the time Macaluso heard that if two people tipped the Coke machine forward they could get a free pop. Problem was, one day Macaluso wanted to see if he could do it alone. When the other guys found him, he was pinned under the Coke machine, trying unsuccessfully to bench press it off him. He injured his ankle, but was too embarrassed to tell Bujold how he did it, so he hopped around for the next few days in silent, excruciating pain.

On another occasion he was retouching the third-base foul line when his "looper," the device that parcels out the chalk, broke. Panicking, he ran up to a baffled George Bell in the outfield yelling, "My looper's broken! My looper's broken! What can I do?"

"All you need to know about Chuck," said Bujold, "is that once when he was in charge of making fried chicken fingers at Exhibition Stadium, he put his thumb in the boiling grease to see if it was warm. I was told that after I hired him."

One baseball player has taken a shine to Macaluso: Chicago White Sox reliever Bobby Thigpen, who a few years ago set a major-league record for saves that still stands. Recently, however, he has lost his edge and been relegated to mop-up work. One day when Macaluso was working security around the visitors' bullpen, he and Thigpen started chatting, and they now look each other up whenever the White Sox come to town.

"Nobody here would admit it," said Bujold, back in his office with the crew, "but we're all missing him now. I've told him he's got a job here for life if he wants it."

"Because he can't do anything else," someone hollered. There is another explosion of laughter.

The oldest member of the grounds crew is Paul Eagan. He is fifty years old, which makes him the elder statesman by twenty-four years.

On most nights during the game, while the others are idling or doing odd jobs, Eagan is in the work area adjacent to the office with a wheelbarrow full of dirt and clay for the pitcher's mound. It has become his responsibility, now that Brad Bujold's mound woes are over.

Eagan may be the most educated groundskeeper in baseball. He has three university degrees: B.A. in English, philosophy and religion; M.A. in religious studies (he nearly became a Catholic priest); and a physical education degree. He also has a teacher's certificate.

His varied academic past predates an equally eclectic working life, which has included stints as a teacher for the mentally handicapped, a Toronto Transit Commission driver, a staffer on the volleyball crew at the 1976 Montreal Olympics and a year as a sports writer for a weekly newspaper in Prince George, British Columbia. But rarely has he felt more professionally fulfilled than he does now, working at SkyDome. Eagan has a passion for the game that the players may equal but would have a hard time surpassing. "When Brad offered me the opportunity to look after the mound, I learned as much as I could from the guy who did it last year. Then I talked to the pitchers. Just the other day I told Juan

Guzman, 'If there's a problem, let me know.' I know from my amateur pitching that if you go out on the mound and you're worrying about it, it takes your concentration off. You can't pitch the game you want."

Eagan discusses his mound duties, and baseball in general, with the earnestness of a Guatemalan aid worker.

"I've put together, by luck I suppose, a pretty good mound. I say that in all humility. The younger guys would put the mix [clay, dirt, water] together fast. I can understand that. It's only a part-time job and they can only spend so much time on it. What I started doing is breaking it up and screening it down to powder form. Then, I don't pour all the water on at once, because if you do you get big coagulated chunks and it takes forever to break down. I add a tiny bit of water at a time, like I'm making a sauce. By the time I'm finished it comes out in little beads."

Eagan likes to sing Irish folk songs during quiet moments. When Sean wrote about him in a column for *The Globe and Mail,* he left two long messages on Sean's answering machine to say he "had never felt so honoured my whole life." His only regret, the messages said, was that his parents had not lived to see such kind words about their son in print.

Eagan played organized baseball for three decades, and he had big-league dreams. When he was in his teens, he was a hard-throwing southpaw with excellent control. He played for the St. Stephen St. Croix in New Brunswick in the late 1950s, pitching on several New Brunswick provincial championship teams. He finished his career in Newmarket, a town an hour's drive north of Toronto, relying on off-speed stuff in a sandlot senior league. He hung up his cleats when he was forty-six.

"It was flattering that I was still able to pitch at that time. When I was young I threw the ball very hard, but when I was older I had to adjust. Guys were used to facing good, strong pitching, and I used a lot of change-ups to upset their timing. I would use what I had left of my fastball, then throw junk for strikes—get them out in front. For the most part I was fortunate to get by. Sure, they hit me the odd time, but it was a credit, I guess, that at my age I could still get guys out."

The closest Eagan ever got to the majors was a one-day, all-comers tryout in 1959, held by the Boston Red Sox across the border from New Brunswick in Presque Isle, Maine. He noticed a newspaper advertisement that invited anybody within a two-hundred-mile radius to come out. Reluctantly, wary lest he sound boastful, Eagan elaborated on his three innings of glory.

"They watched me on the side for fifteen minutes or so, then I threw three innings in a game. They praised my control—naturally they would—and my speed, but when they have so many to pick from you have to be unreal. They didn't think my body would take it, the way I relied mainly on my arm to throw the ball. Even in the years I pitched in St. Stephen, as well as I pitched, I had to go to a chiropractor after every game for an hour to get popped out."

Sean wanted to know what his line score was for those three innings.

"It wouldn't be fair to say," Eagan said. "That was thirty-four years ago."

After further prodding, he relented.

"From what I recall, and I may be flattering myself, but I don't think so—I would never do that intentionally—I would say that probably, over the three innings, they didn't hit the ball hard off me at all. They may have got a hit or two, that's all. They didn't hit anything out of the infield.

"I don't regret the fact that I never played professional baseball. I love the game itself so much."

Now, entering his sixth decade on earth, Paul Eagan has finally made it to the majors. Fans who arrive early at SkyDome, three or four hours before game time, can see him shagging flies in right field during batting practice, before the Blue Jay outfielders take to the field.

"They've never said I can't. Maybe they would if they felt I wasn't capable, or if they thought I might get hurt. But then, they've seen me grab a few. I started last year. A lot of times balls would get lost in the lights. In practice, when this happens the players just back away. They figure it's not worth getting injured when they're not in a game. One day when I was out there before a game a ball got lost in the lights and [Blue Jay bench coach] Gene Tenace was standing beside me. I suppose pride and having played the game and always having made an effort to do whatever I can do, instead of shying away and covering my eyes, I just put my glove up where I thought the ball would come out and by luck the ball came out right where I thought it would. I caught it. Tenace looked at me and said, "You're a fool! I would have just run."

It is out there in right field, long before the first fan arrives at SkyDome, that Eagan stands where the big-leaguers will stand a few hours later, and wonders what might have been if the Red Sox had not been so hasty that day in Presque Isle in 1959.

"What usually happens is, from five to six o'clock the players come out to the field. But from four to five just a few guys who want extra hittting will go in the cage. Last year, when Dave Winfield would come out to right field, I would just move out. Brad told me that once the players come out, just move out so you don't create any problems. In the beginning, Winfield looked at me quizzically, as if he was saying, 'Who are you and what are you doing here?' But after he watched me for a few days, he'd just come out to right field, we'd nod at each other and I'd walk off. That was the understood thing.

"Baseball has always been my first love. I always told the guys, when I go I'll either go the traditional way, at sea, or I'll be cremated and have my ashes mixed with the clay for the mound. So if the next guy screws up, I'll come up from the ashes and haunt him."

In his years as head groundskeeper, Bujold says, he has made only two hiring decisions he later regretted. It wasn't that they screwed up, just that they had no passion for what they were doing. "They treated it like a job. All they cared about was whether their time card was right." Bujold gestured to the grounds crew seated around him and said, "Even with you guys, by the end of a seven-game home stand, I'm pretty sick of you. It's like living with someone."

"But you start missing us after two days," one of the crew chirped.

"Yeah," said Bujold.

When management doled out the 232 Tiffany-designed World Series rings to the players, coaches, scouts and full-time support staff, Bujold, being the full-time member of the grounds crew, got one. It was a distinction that at first made him uncomfortable. After spending thousands of hours working side by side with his crew, he felt badly that he was the only one honoured with a World Series ring.

"I felt guilty. But I thought about it for a long time and then I looked at my ring and told myself, 'Hey, it's not just for last year. It's for all the years I've been with this organization. The times by the lake at Exhibition Stadium when I've pulled a tarp in the wind and rain, all those hard times down there."

He remembered one time. It was at Exhibition Stadium the weekend before Opening Day. The crew had worked hard all week getting the field ready. A vicious wind blew in off the lake on Sunday. Bujold got a call at his home—the tarps were starting to blow off. "I was living at my parents' house and my dad and I drove down to the stadium. My dad was helping me put the tarps back on the field. He grabbed an end of the tarp, but he didn't know how to handle it. He was trying to help out, but in the wind the tarp was acting like a sail. It took Dad right into the Blue Jays' dugout. I'm yelling, 'Let go! Let go!' The wind pulled him off the ground. So that came to mind. Those extra efforts."

=== 6 ===
Travels at SkyDome (2)

Before each Blue Jay game, Fred Wootton sits at a table in 000 Level, which in most other buildings would be called the basement. The table is the size of a small card table, and Wootton sits in a chair against a wall, watching the pregame commotion: players arriving, players' wives and children, ushers, security guards, ticket takers, the media, off-duty policemen, plainclothes policemen. Wootton's place looks like a lemonade stand at the side of a busy highway for 000 Level in this part of the SkyDome is a circular concrete roadway that goes completely around the inside of the stadium. When the Blue Jays return from road trips, the truck from the airport drives right inside and stops at their dressing-room door, where the luggage and equipment is unloaded. Some players—like John Olerud and Ed Sprague—wait patiently for their golf clubs, which are always the last items to be removed from the truck. They need their clubs if they want to get an early start the next morning. Somewhere on the other side of the wall behind Wootton is home plate and all the rest of what everyone else knows as SkyDome.

Wootton is head of security, the manager responsible for throwing out drunks, dopeheads and otherwise obstreperous boors—an average of twenty-five fans a game get the heave-ho from the SkyDome—and he is the only staffer at the SkyDome ever to have his photograph in *Playboy* magazine. That was quite a time. It happened at Exhibition Stadium in 1983, the afternoon the gate-crashing, pendulous stripper who calls herself Morgana hurdled a low wall by the visitors' dugout and ran onto the field, grinning and bouncing every which way. In the photograph, Wootton is grinning, too, as he assists Morgana off the field. "She was a very bright girl," Wootton remembers.

In the season of 1993 Wootton turned seventy. He looks like the grandfatherly fellow in the Quaker Oats commercials, with a bushy white moustache concealing his upper lip. He is a big, robust man, certainly no one to tangle with even at the age of seventy. He had come off a bad winter, though. A month after the Blue Jays won the 1992 World Series, Wootton's doctor told him he had lymphatic cancer. He had to undergo chemotherapy, which caused him to lose all the hair on his head and body. Even the thick white moustache under his nose vanished. "I even lost all the hair in my nose. I never thought how important the hair in your nose is, but when it's gone your nose is always dripping." If that was not bad enough, while he was being treated with chemotherapy his immune system weakened to such an extent that he was stricken with a severe case of blood poisoning, which began with a minor cut on one of his fingers. He was still recovering on Opening Day, 1993, but by the All-Star break in July, Wootton was ready to take on the rest of the season. The man has the constitution of a bison.

Wootton joined the Blue Jays staff in 1978, two weeks after he retired from a thirty-eight-year career with the Metro Toronto Police, when he was fifty-five. He and his wife, Audrey, had planned on spending his winters in Florida. When he met her in 1947, he was a World War Two air force veteran and Audrey was a professional singer, performing at the Orchard Park Hotel, near Greenwood Raceway. After his retirement from the police force, Wootton had plans to work the warm-weather months in Toronto in the lawn-spraying business with his son, Barry, who was a captain with the Toronto Fire Department. "Nine to five has never been my style," he said.

Looking back, he regards the days at Exhibition Stadium as much "cozier" that at the SkyDome. He handled security before beer was sold, when not nearly as many fans had to be thrown out. As a baseball stadium, the old Ex might not have been pretty, but it was easier to police because there was only one level all spread out on concrete slabs by the lake. He used to get by with only 19 off-duty policemen, whom he calls "coppers." At SkyDome, Wootton regularly hires as many as 40, and in postseason play as many as 100, all guaranteed a minimum of three hours' work at $38.50 an hour. They always include 6 plainclothes policemen, who prowl the corridors, aisles and washrooms looking for trouble before it happens. The off-duty policemen are in addition to the regular stadium security staff, which Wootton also hires, and which amounts to 140 at SkyDome. He needed only 30 security staff at Exhibition Stadium.

During his last years as a working policeman, Wootton was in charge of 14 Division, which encompassed the neighbourhood of Exhibition Stadium. Naturally, he selected his off-duty coppers from 14 Division, which caused a great deal of resentment from policemen in other divisions, who had to be content making extra money riding escort at funerals or beefing up security at conventions. The Blue Jays, with their eighty-one home games, at $38.50 for a minimum three hours, represented the mother lode of moonlighting. When the Blue Jays started to play their games at the SkyDome, the resentment shifted neighbourhoods because the stadium is in 52 Division. For the sake of fairness, Wootton decided to hire his off-duty coppers from divisions throughout Metro Toronto. He also arranges for someone from the drug squad to talk to the new players every spring about drugs and Canadian gun laws.

Over the years he has become friends with many of the players, among them former pitchers Joey McLaughlin, Jim Gott, Dave Stieb and David Wells, and former bare-armed

93

third baseman Roy Howell. Howell, for his part, thinks Wootton is a genius at crowd control. When Howell was playing third for the Blue Jays at Exhibition Stadium, he was the object of vitriolic, verbal attacks by two women who had season tickets for seats near the Blue Jay dugout. They insulted his fielding ability, his looks, his manhood, and their high-pitched cackles carried over whatever roar might be coming from the crowd. Howell told Wootton that just anticipating the barbs from the two women before a game kept him awake the night before.

One day Wootton got a call from Pat Gillick asking him to come to his office for a meeting. When Wootton arrived he found Gillick seated in his chair and Howell across the desk from him. The attacks had become so bothersome that Howell had asked Gillick if he could do something to stop them, so Gillick had called in Wootton. As Howell was explaining what was happening, Wootton caught a glimpse of Gillick flashing him a conspicuous wink. When Howell left to dress for the game, Gillick said to Wootton not to give it any more thought. "If he can't stand the heat," Gillick said, "then he shouldn't be in the kitchen."

As it turned out, the Blue Jays left the next day on an extended road trip, during which time the two women managed to get better seats, ones directly behind home plate. When the team returned, they continued their harassment, but Howell could not hear them. Wootton had nothing to do with the new seats, but Howell assumed he had arranged it and he was profuse in his gratitude. Years later, long after he had retired from the game, Howell returned with his wife to the SkyDome for the All-Star Game in 1991. He was still grateful. When Howell encountered Wootton at his stand on 000 Level, he introduced his wife to him, and said, "This is the fellow who managed to stop those wicked women from yelling at me."

"It had been on his mind all those years," Wootton said. "Of course, I never told him the real story. I mean, how could I?"

Wootton is not the only employee of SkyDome whose salary is supplemented by Old Age Security cheques. Looking around the place during Blue Jay games gives one the feeling of stepping into the most opulent retirement home in North America. Though the ticket takers at the turnstiles may be, as an American writer said during the 1992 World Series, "Ken and Barbie clones," once inside the building many of the contracted employees look more like Grandma and Grandpa Moses.

"The Blue Jays have no mandatory retirement policy," Wootton said. "If they did, I'd lose half my staff. I have a bunch of old geezers, besides myself, who decided they wanted to stay in the work force instead of sitting on a bench in a plaza somewhere talking about days gone by. Besides, I get more continuity from the older guys. The younger ones work for a summer and then take off."

Elder statesman among the geezers is Roy Railey, who turned eighty-two during the 1993 season. His job is to keep the bleacher bums at bay when Dennis Eckersley and the rest of the visiting relievers are warming up in the bullpen near the right-field foul pole. Railey has his own chair there, which he can be seen sitting on quietly most games, a portable radio in his breast pocket and a set of earphones around his neck so he can keep track of what the cheering or booing is all about. His view of the field is impeded by the right-field wall, and he thinks standing tippy-toe on his chair to take a peek would be undignified. He also does not like to vacate his post during his shift, so he brings a bag lunch and sets it up on a fold-up tray.

"Don't call me Pop or Grandpa," he said one warm September night when the roof was open and the Blue Jays were playing under the stars. "If you remember my name, you're a great guy."

To get from his home in suburban Scarborough, Railey pedals his one-speed Eaton Glider, which he bought in 1925. Estimated round-trip distance: thirty miles. (Railey has never thought in kilometres.) "It's mostly downhill coming here. I used to be able to do it in under an hour." Railey smiled when he said this and his eyes nearly disappeared in folds of soft skin. "Now it takes me a little longer. With a good head wind, I can do it in about an hour and five minutes." Biking back home uphill along the Lakeshore is a tougher go, about ninety minutes door to door. When the Blue Jays are on the road, Railey swims five times a week. He would bike in the winter if he could, but he does not have skid chains.

"Riding is a pleasure. Work is a pleasure. After six weeks of retirement [from his job as a driver for IBM] I was climbing the walls. All I did was walk back and forth between the fridge and the living room. You have to love what you do. I know some people who retired and after a few weeks they go to their doctors and say, 'Give me some pills, I'm depressed.' When I was working I used to look forward to Mondays."

After being forced to retire when he turned sixty-five, Railey did odd jobs, delivering goods for drugstores and pizza parlours, anything to pass the time of day and make himself feel useful. He has not missed many shifts since he started at Gate 12 at Exhibition Stadium in 1986, keeping the drunks in line. "My pension isn't indexed. It's still in 1976 dollars."

While we were kibitzing with Railey, Special Security Supervisor John Fogg sidled up beside us. Fogg is only seventy-four, another of Wootton's policeman buddies. In 1993 he was recuperating from double knee surgery, performed by Dr. Allan Gross, the Blue Jays' consulting orthopaedic surgeon. Fogg used to live around the corner from Railey in Toronto's east end, near Danforth and Pape, when he was growing up in the 1930s. That was when Railey played big band music with Jack Kent Cooke, who was wildly successful running the Toronto Maple Leafs AAA baseball team in the 1950s and is now owner of the Washington Redskins of the National Football League. Railey eventually left Cooke's band to front his own, the Roy Railey Orchestra. "They didn't have fancy names for bands in those days," Railey said. "Just Roy Railey and his Orchestra."

Fogg extended his hand in greeting. "Are these guys

causing you any trouble, Roy?" he asked, then he launched into a detailed description of his knee surgery, as if it was the funniest thing that had happened to him in years. "They gave me a local," he said. "I was awake the whole time. There was one guy working on my right knee, another guy working on my left knee. I told them, 'If you start coming up the middle, I'm getting out of here.'"

Railey himself went on the disabled list for the first time in 1993 for a week after blowing out his calf on his beloved Eaton Glider. "They put me in the hospital with all these sick guys," he said. "My doctor gave me all these blood tests, but I wasn't that bad. I thought I'd be out in time for the game that night."

Though Railey and Fogg and the rest of the grey heads at SkyDome are hired on a year-to-year basis, Wootton said he sees no reason to make any changes in the foreseeable future. "As far as Roy is concerned, he can work here until he can't do it anymore, whenever that will be. But I wish he'd be more careful on that bicycle. I came off the Gardiner Expressway one night and there was Roy, pedalling in the dark along the Lakeshore, by Greenwood Raceway, with those pant clips above his ankles."

After wintering in Florida after the 1993 World Series, Railey sent an application to Wootton for another season of honest work in the blue blazer.

Mario Coutinho sounds like a name for a slick, soft-handed shortstop, but the only time he steps on the field is before and after a game when he is studying the crowd and the innards of the SkyDome for problems and possible catastrophes. Coutinho's official title is Manager, Game Operations. Unofficially, once the gates open, Coutinho becomes the SkyDome's maître d'.

He is in his late twenties, with a handsome Italian face, black hair, always in a crisp shirt and well-tailored suit. He is "Unit 5," top walkie-talkie, supervising the runners, ushers, medical stations, peanut vendors and just about anything else that needs supervising. During the game he patrols all levels, starting at the doors when the gates open, then patrolling from 000 Level to 500 Level. He watches for troublemakers, drunks and overzealous "Baseball Annies," the women of all ages who prey on professional baseball players. He orders patrons out of the SkyDome for a variety of misdemeanours, often for interfering with fair balls, for which SkyDome has a policy of "zero tolerance." Touch a twisting spinner that is in play and curls by the field-level seats at either side of the field and you are gone.

Coutinho is a prime example of the running-off-to-the-circus school. The workers at the SkyDome are fiercely loyal to the place. They are also paid better than their counterparts at other major-league parks. The Blue Jays reward them with all-expenses-paid trips to another major-league city during the season. They are awarded rings for five, ten and fifteen years of service. And the top bosses never demand sub-servience. Paul Beeston is always "Paul," Pat Gillick is always "Pat."

In the late 1970s Cutinho was at the University of Toronto studying geomorphology, something to do with the origin and development of soils and land forms other than artificial turf. To get by, he worked at Exhibition Stadium, first as a runner, the lowliest job in the park, then as an usher, earning $18 a game. It was Fred Wootton who hired him.

After several summers, Coutinho worked himself to supervisor of ushers, making $50 a game. When he graduated, he got a job with IBM, working the midnight shift. This was it, all that book-cracking, essay-writing and cramming, the culmination of years of study. After three midnight shifts at IBM, Coutinho chucked it and reported to work full time with the Blue Jays—ran off to the circus.

Walking the SkyDome with Coutinho is like walking with an experienced bird-watcher in the woods. He sees things others don't, something out of kilter here, something new there. He knows every inch of the place, anticipates what can go wrong. Way across the field, behind the visitors' bullpen, a man and a small boy were watching the game from above the fence. Uh-oh. Could get cranked by a homer. SkyDome woul be liable because they are not supposed to be there. And if one of them did get cranked, he would not be easy to reach by the paramedics and the Ambu-Carts.

Speaking of bird-watching, the SkyDome is not Point Pelee, but interesting sightings are occasionally made. The SkyDome is built on landfill, over what years ago used to be a marshy shore where red-winged blackbirds nested. On a bright day in autumn, with high cumulus clouds, what look like specks of blown, drifting pepper up around the pods of the CN Tower are flocks of broad-winged hawks migrating to their winter home. At games on hot summer nights, black-crowned night herons often dip into the lights radiating from the open SkyDome as they fly from Mugg's Island for an evening meal of crayfish and minnows in shallow streams inland. Often a red-winged blackbird flaps back and forth along the screen behind home plate, looking halfway hysterical, though sometimes one will settle down and take in the proceedings. Gulls were a problem at Exhibition Stadium—it was like an airport for gulls—and when SkyDome was being built serious consideration was given to paying a falconer $150,000 a season to bring his falcon in after every game to chase away gulls descending to feast on the detritus of hotdogs and Big Macs. As it turned out, the gulls have avoided SkyDome. A few pigeons flap in now and then, but that's it. Oddly, the SkyDome does not seem to interest actual blue jays, who prefer distant suburbs and golf courses.

And speaking of bird-watching, there was the incident at Exhibition Stadium when Dave Winfield, then with the New York Yankees, was lobbing balls in the outfield between innings and one of his tosses hit and killed a seagull.

The incident had interesting ramifications for the Blue Jays. Some animal protectionists at the game complained and police arrived with a warrant for Winfield's arrest. Pat Gillick had to go to the Yankee clubhouse and tell manager Billy Martin that Winfield would not be able to go with the team to the airport because of what had happened. It was Gillick who drove Winfield to the police station, during which time he was impressed with the player's calm, mature way of coping with what was a difficult and embarrassing situation. Gillick told John Feinstein, who wrote the book *Play Ball*, "I was really impressed with Dave through the whole ordeal. A lot of people would have gone off, but he just dealt with it and got it over with. I actually enjoyed talking to him—we were together for several hours—so that winter, I invited him to come here for a banquet. He came and we sort of fell into a friendship." They remained friends, and when Winfield became a free agent after the 1991 season, Gillick remembered that evening back in 1983. He recommended that the Blue Jays sign him. They did, for $2.3 million, and in the deciding game of the 1992 World Series in Atlanta Winfield hit a key double that made the Blue Jays champions.

Coutinho raised his walkie-talkie to his mouth. "Unit 5..." In less than a minute the man and the boy were gone from behind the bullpen fence. Coutinho walked along the corridor by the concessions at 100 Level, when his walkie-talkie crackled again. "Unit 5, foul ball injury...." A wicked foul ball had hooked into the crowd by the left-field line, smashing a woman on the bridge of the nose. Right-handed batters always hit hooks to left, slices to right, and the reverse is true for left-handed batters. Balls hit directly to centre field have an honest over-the-top spin, which makes them easier to catch, but the centre fielder has much more ground to cover so he must be fast. Male fans always try to catch foul balls; women fans know better and do their best to get out of the way. When a woman gets hit it invariably is because she got caught between the flailing males trying to catch the ball.

The medics reached the woman quickly, administered first aid, an ice pack to the nose to control the bleeding, then helped her to her feet and up the aisle to the AmbuCart, where she was taken to one of the medical stations. Her son trailed along after her in the aisle, carrying a baseball glove. In the medical station Dr Noah Forman, an emergency physician at North York General who works all Blue Jay home games, examined the woman, whose nose was broken. She was in considerable distress. She kept asking, "Why didn't he *catch* the ball?" She meant her son with the baseball glove.

Forman's station is the busiest at SkyDome. Most ball injuries happen before the game, during batting practice, when fans gather by the low walls at field level, hoping for autographs. They are not watching the batting cage, where baseballs zip out like missiles. When the roof is closed, the sound of bat on ball is different, more vicious, than when the roof is open. There is a quick echo, like a rifle retort, which sounds like "Crack-*lasssh*." Some fans get badly cranked by liners and one-hoppers. Coutinho remembers one fan who reached to catch a liner with his bare hands and the ball tore through the web of skin between his thumb and index finger.

Dr Joe Madigan, another doctor who works the Blue Jay games—he started back in Exhibition Stadium in 1977, working out of St. Joseph's Hospital—is such a home-team loyalist that he wears a Blue Jay tie when he is at this medical station. Soon after SkyDome opened, when the glitches were being worked out, Madigan testified at an inquest into the death of a fan at the SkyDome who died of a heart attack at a game. There had been complaints that the SkyDome had opened too soon, before adequate medical facilities were ready, but the complaints were shown to be groundless.

Madigan was more concerned with the ramps to the different sections, especially the gaps between the ramps, where several fans have fallen. One man, attempting to jump from one ramp to another, fell from 500 Level all the way down to 000 Level and was killed. Steel girders were installed across the gaps to prevent this, but Madigan worries that someone might sit a child on the concrete ledge and, left unattended even briefly, the child could fall backwards through the space between the ramps. He also worries that someone reaching for a foul ball in the front row at 500 Level might topple over the short protective rail and land on someone in the 200 Level seats. He worries about it as if it is inevitable.

GAME PLAN

The highest and cheapest seats at the SkyDome are at 500 Level, which Coutinho prefers to many more expensive seats lower down. If you get a 500-Level seat behind home plate, you are only ten inches above the SkyBoxes, which lease for $225,000 a year. The 500 Level has the steepest seats of any sporting facility in North America, rising upward at an angle of thirty-six degrees. During a summer afternoon game, a woman who had never been to the SkyDome walked out of the tunnel to the open aisle, showed her tickets to the usher, then, looking down at the field, panicked when she became aware of the steeply raked seats. She grabbed hold of one of the metal railings. She would not let go. Coutinho called in two security guards, who pried her fingers, one by one, from the railing.

In the room on 000 Level behind the left-field foul pole next to the indoor batting cage, Kevin Shanahan was drawing a diagram of a ballpark.

"In the first and second innings I start here," he said, drawing an arrow to the top of the Blue Jays' dugout. "During the third inning I rest. During the fourth and fifth innings I'm here," he continued, this time drawing more arrows to indicate the circular television platforms above the outfield fence on the 200 and 500 levels. "During the sixth inning I take another break. Before I got the cooling unit I used to take a shower then. For the seventh-inning stretch I'm here." He made a large X on the field. "In the eighth I stand on the bench behind the left-field wall, beside the bench where the relievers sit to watch the game. That's where I was when I got ejected."

The ejection Shanahan is referring to took place on Saturday, May 22, 1993, during the eighth inning of a Blue Jay 7–0 rout of Minnesota. Twins outfielder Dave McCarty had made a spectacular catch on a drive to the wall by Roberto Alomar, but video replays showed McCarty had trapped the ball against the wall (meaning the ball hit the wall an instant before it hit his glove). Cito Gaston was arguing the

call with Ken Kaiser. It was Canadian-born umpire Jim
McKean who tossed out Shanahan, more commonly known
by his alter ego, B. J. Birdie.

"I thought I was doing a great job—moving around,
working the crowd," he recalled a few months later. "The
umpire thought I was arguing with the call. I never saw the
play. I was just doing my mock-rage routine because of the
out. Then Cito comes out so I keep it up. The umpire is
yelling and waving his hands, so I start dancing around some
more. How was I supposed to know he was waving his hands
because he had just kicked me out? That was the same day I
got my World Series watch."

Such is life as a major-league mascot, or, in the words of
now-retired Phillie Phanatic Dave Raymond, a "professional
idiot." The baseball mascots have been the most popular of
any sport, something Shanahan attributes to the nature and
pace of the game.

"Baseball works the best of any sport for this. It's so seg-
mented and there's always something strange happening. It's
like pulling on a slot machine."

Shanahan has been doing his thing since 1979, when he
was hired for a one-day tryout by Blue Jay president Peter
Bavasi. Bavasi gave him a shot after *The Toronto Sun* had interviewed Shanahan's father, a stand-up comic, and heard that
Kevin had been unsuccessfully trying to sell his services to the
Blue Jays. He was working as a moose at Ontario Place at the
time but was dreaming of bigger things. The *Sun*, knowing a
noble political cause when they saw one, put Shanahan on its
front page and implored the Jays to give him a try.

"They had tried one other guy, a CHUM [radio] chick-
en, but he burned out," said Shanahan, adjusting his head as
we walked through the 000-Level curved concourse toward
the Blue Jay dugout. "His second time out he ran out onto
the field during a break in play. No one told him he was supposed to do his tricks *between* innings. Most mascots burn out.
I'm an anomaly."

Compared to celebrities like the Phanatic and the San

Diego Chicken, who is reported to pull in a quarter million a year in game and other appearance fees, B. J. Birdie works in relative squalor, making maybe one-tenth of that in an average year. He used to work every home game. Then when Bavasi left he was reduced to sixty games. Now he only does day games on the weekend—about thirty a year. "The writing is on the wall," said Shanahan, who lives in imminent fear of going the way of the dodo. "All I ever hear from the Blue Jays is 'He must be doing something right, or we wouldn't have hired him.' With support like that, how can you go wrong?" he said dryly.

Just then a couple of boys, around ten years old, walked by and waved. "Hi-ya, kids! Okay Blue Jays!" shouted Shanahan in a high-pitched staccato that he describes as a cross between Bugs Bunny and Woody Woodpecker. "There is a certain Jekyll-and-Hyde quality to this," he said, then continued to bemoan his lack of job security after the boys had safely passed. For years now, Shanahan has done his shtick thinking every season will be his last. As far back as 1985, when he was the subject of a front page story in *The Globe and Mail*, Shanahan has felt unappreciated by the Jays, though much of his troubles have been of his own making. Seems he was not handling the heckling from season ticket holders behind the visiting dugout well back in 1985. He told the *Globe* that some fans were impugning the dignity of his profession and suggesting his children were embarrassed to have a mascot for a father. There were allegations that he was replying to their taunts in language not conducive to a family atmosphere.

Shanahan's troubles with the fans might not have become as public as they did were it not for the daily comic strip he was writing at the time for *The Toronto Star*. From time to time he would use the comic strip as a platform to air beefs with management.

"We don't expect someone we're paying to sit back and take shots at us," public relations director Howard Starkman told the *Globe* at the time.

"If it appears that Kevin Shanahan is using the comic strip as a forum to vent his own frustrations and anger—and I can't imagine he'd have any because he's just a clown—then he should stop doing it," added director of marketing Paul Markle.

"That one hurt," said Shanahan in the runway behind the dugout during the top of the first inning.

Shanahan's image on and off the field is an ongoing concern. Like judges, politicians and members of the royal family, Shanahan has to be careful not to involve himself in activities unbecoming a mascot. "I have to be careful of public impropriety because of my image with the kids. The Blue Jays wouldn't want me going down to Filmores [a strip club] and doing a Molson event. I have to be careful with the girls in the stands here, too. Teenage girls come up to me and give me a hug and I just stretch my arms out sideways and leave them in the air like a scarecrow and say, 'Go ahead.'"

After his first-inning routine, Shanahan went back up the runway and around to the visitors' dugout and waited for the bottom of the second. The 100-Level fans are the hardest to rouse, he said. The 500-Level bleacher bums are the easiest, and the most fun. "A lot of what I do depends on my mood or the mood of the fans. Normally I don't generate a movement, I react to one. That can be tricky at times because the visibility inside the head is so bad. I don't know what's going on. One day I gave a big cheer during a Yankee game after a Yankee hit because there was a section of New York fans cheering behind me."

It was a beautiful late-September day, temperature around twenty Celsius with a negligible breeze in an open SkyDome. The temperature inside B. J. Birdie's head was a great deal warmer and Shanahan was already sweating. The Phillie Phanatic told USA Today's Baseball Weekly when he announced his retirement what his costume felt like on a warm Saturday afternoon. "When it's ninety-five degrees this summer, put on your heaviest winter coat, boots and gloves, and stick a bag on your head. Then jog a mile and you'll get the idea of what I feel like."

Shanahan concurs. "When this place is closed it's hot and uncomfortable. And they only open it when it's hot and uncomfortable. Remember those freezing Aprils and cold Septembers at Exhibition Stadium? I miss those days. I'm like a lizard—sluggish in the heat, active in the cold."

After goofing around in front of fifty thousand fans throughout the afternoon, Shanahan was exhausted and retreated to the showers behind the groundskeeper's office. When he came out in street clothes a few minutes later he picked up the receiver from the wall phone.

"It's Bird, could you get me a cart?" Before a worker came by to escort him to one of the exits, Shanahan packed away his beak, two bird suits, ten sets of fluffy white three-fingered paws and the book he was reading at the time, *The Absence of the Sacred: The Failure of Technology and the Survival of Indian Nations*.

"The great part about this job is, I can walk out of here and no one knows who I am."

Blue Jays fans must have wondered over the years if a higher force was conspiring against them, so incredible have some past defeats seemed. There were those freak injuries to Tony Fernandez and Ernie Whitt in the last week of the 1987 season, when the Blue Jays lost the last seven games of the season and allowed the Detroit Tigers to clinch the American League East. There was the once-in-a-career game by George Brett of Kansas City Royals in Game Three of the 1985 American League Championship Series when the Blue Jays seemed poised to take a three-games-to-nothing lead. Even on the verge of their great triumph in the bottom of the 11th of Game Six of the 1992 World Series, General Manager Pat Gillick watched a perfect double-play ball bounce wildly past Alfredo Griffin at the last instant and wondered if it was just not meant to be.

It is a common thread throughout sports—the hope that God will be on our side for the big game. The ancient

Mayans of Central America, perhaps believing the gods showed their favour through sport, murdered the losing team after a championship game, which might explain why their soccer players get so weepy after a goal. The Olympics began as a religious event. Moving ahead to the late twentieth century, the Denver Broncos, losers of four Super Bowls, used to leave a space for Jesus in the huddle. And there was the devout Christian who played on the defensive line for the Los Angeles Rams who liked to say to his opponents, "I'm going to hit you with all the love within me" before trying to ram his opponent's nose into this cerebral cortex.

If God has not always been on the Blue Jays' side, it has not been because of a shortage of believers. Religious fervour was one of the defining characteristics of the talented under-achievers of the mid-to-late 1980s. Sunday chapel service after morning batting practice and the Wednesday-afternoon Bible study sessions had the zeal of a Memphis Rock church revival hour.

For the black players there was reliever Roy Lee Jackson, who pitched like he was in God's doghouse but preached the Word to anyone who would listen, and he found sympathetic listeners in Lloyd Moseby, Jesse Barfield, Tony Fernandez and quite a few others.

Joe Johnson, meanwhile, counted only ten wins during his two seasons with the Blue Jays, but registered two saved souls (Dave Stieb and Kelly Gruber). Even radio broadcaster Jerry Howarth was swept up in the missionary zeal of those days. He credits pitcher Don Gordon, with an assist from reliever Gary Lavelle, for his decision in 1987 to dedicate his life to Christ.

David Fisher, who has been giving spiritual guidance to Blue Jay and Montreal Expo players since 1976, still offers his services on Sunday mornings and Wednesday afternoons at SkyDome in the "green room," a nondescript, windowless refuge from secular concerns hidden between the 000 and 100 levels, accessible only via a stairwell tucked beside a storage bay, across from the Blue Jay bullpen. Fisher, forty-eight, has no formal religious training. He grew up in Peterborough, Ontario, attending a small Baptist-style gospel hall, and eventually bought a Christian bookstore in 1971, when he was twenty-six. He remembers the early days at Exhibition Stadium, when he conducted services in the weight room.

"Some of the fringe players were blown away by what went on in there," he told Sean one afternoon over coffee at a café on Danforth Avenue.

Religious services at SkyDome are more temperate affairs than they were in the luckless days of the mid-to-late 1980s. "Our present team has the best atmosphere I've every seen," Fisher said, meaning the 1993 edition of the Blue Jays. "Paul Molitor is more responsible than any other player for that. He is one of the finest examples I know of a man who has his life and priorities in order. He's a strong Christian, but he doesn't ram it down his teammates' throats."

That was in strong contrast to Dave Winfield, much beloved by the fans as the heart of the 1992 Jays but a perpetual no-show in the green room.

"In all the years I've done chapel—I've spoken with the Padres, Expos, Blue Jays and Twins—he has never been in a chapel service. And yet, when interviewed, he will talk abut his God-given talent. It's always been a puzzle to me."

About a dozen Blue Jays attended the Sunday services in 1993, with a core of seven—Tony Fernandez, Joe Carter, Paul Molitor, Darnell Coles, Mike Timlin, John Olerud, Mark Eichhorn—taking part in the more intensive Wednesday sessions. Fisher's wife, Carol, conducts parallel services for the players' wives. As with husband David's sessions, Carol Fisher keeps her meetings confidential. They do not even talk to each other about what they hear in the green room.

In-house chapel service is available at every ballpark in the major leagues, due to the diligence of a former Detroit Tigers beat writer named Watson Spoelstra. Like most self-respecting baseball writers, Spoelstra was a boozing wretch before asking for God's forgiveness when his daughter's health failed. He then realized that baseball players, who are seldom allowed to rest on Sunday, had no opportunity to attend church during the long season.

Aside from his volunteer work for the Blue Jays, Expos and Minnestoa Twins (he is the regional co-ordinator for the Baseball Chapel Network, which publishes regular newsletters on its activities), Fisher has worked informally with the Toronto Maple Leafs and writes thousands of letters of encouragement a year to athletes of all disciplines. He finds there are not as many born-agains in hockey as there are in the three other major team sports, though his first letter went to Mickey Redmond back in 1974, when Redmond played for the Detroit Red Wings and was slumping badly after a back injury. Redmond's back did not get any better, and neither did Redmond, but that did not dissuade Fisher, who often whips off twenty or thirty letters each day before his wife wakes up. For every thousand letters he sends, he gets maybe two dozen replies. "It's a small investment," Fisher said. "Just one stamp and a letter can change someone's life. I just felt it was something God would want me to do."

His first baseball letter was to former Montreal Expo star catcher Gary Carter, who got Fisher his in with the Expos in 1976, arranging for Fisher to distribute Bibles on a Sunday in May of that year. His first Blue Jay letter was to pitcher Dennis DeBarr, whose career line in *The Baseball Encyclopedia* reads as follows:

Year	Team	W	L	PCT.	ERA	G	IP	H	BB	SO
1977	TOR	0	1	.000	6.00	14	21	29	8	10

"He's one of the very few over the years who wrote back," said Fisher, smiling. "I still have his letter."

Slagging born-again athletes has always been a popular pastime in the world of sports. Players such as former Minnesota slugger Gary Gaetti, who lost the respect of drinking buddy Kent Hrbek when he became born-again and the respect of the Minnesota fans when he lost his batting stroke shortly thereafter, are cited as evidence that a heightened faith in the everlasting turns a ballplayer's instincts to goo.

"The majority of players do not lose their competitive edge," Fisher said. "Some do. But it happens in a non-Christian's life, too, and no one makes generalizations about them. I get a little bit frustrated when people say Christian athletes are wimps."

Because of the association in past years between religious zeal and bad baseball, Fisher believes Blue Jay management is wary of his activities, though outwardly tolerant. "Management does not put much stock in what I do," he said. "Cito does, but higher up, they might even see me as a threat, because of the bad rap the Christians got in the past. Like Tony Fernandez—maybe they thought I was making him the way he was."

Though there are some Jays who Fisher believes tell him things they have never told anyone before, he finds players on the visiting teams more forthcoming when they attend chapel on Sundays, like the fellow who confesses all to a stranger on a train because he knows he will never see him again. "Maybe the Blue Jays don't want to become transparent or vulnerable enough to share with me," he said. "Whereas a visiting player might feel there is safety with the distance between them and me, so they can unburden themselves."

Carol Fisher's sessions with the Blue Jay wives, or "Lady Jays" as they like to call themselves when doing charity work, are a more recent phenomenon, with no history before SkyDome. They also take place in the green room on Wednesdays, sometimes lasting well into the game. Attendance is sparse until the end of June, when the school year ends and those with children fly to Toronto for the summer.

Carol Fisher looks every bit the Baptist preacher's wife, with sensible clothes and lots of make-up. Her meetings are a combination of informal Bible study and support group counselling. It is a hard sell generating sympathy for the wives of multimillionaire celebrity athletes, but Fisher does her best.

She said they find it difficult to trust people, because offers of friendship in a strange city are often transparent attempts at ingratiation into the lives of their husbands. The women tend to stick together, she said, with the wives socializing with other wives and the girlfriends keeping to themselves.

There is even mistrust from the in-laws, Fisher said, with parents of Blue Jay players worried that their boy is being taken by a gold-digging harlot. They also have a vague sense of the potential darkness that lies beyond the cusp of their husbands' short careers, when they will no longer bask in the glow of idolatry, and are home every Sunday.

"The divorce rate is very high in baseball," she said.

Then there are the groupies, and unsolicited offers of service from across the continent. "I tell them not to even look at the mail," she said.

Diana Carter and Mariann Eichhorn are the veterans of the Wednesday meetings and the unspoken leaders in group discussions, though they like to maintain a wall of privacy beyond the walls of the green room, and will never discuss publicly what is said there.

"It is important that as women what is said in here stays in here," Fisher said. "They don't even talk to their husbands about it. Sometimes the wives can expose the vulnerabilities of their husbands and they do not want that getting around. It makes them feel good to share with other women who have common burdens—to see someone else who looks like they have it all but has troubles of their own."

= 7 =

Pulling the Trigger

Bottom of the first; 7:58 P.M.

Rickey Henderson saunters from the batting circle to the batter's box and digs in. Not too many people saunter. The essayist E. B. White once singled it out as one of the most overused verbs by thesaurus-dependent writers. After he had been writing for many years he realized most people just walk.

Not Rickey. He saunters. He saunters to the plate at the beginning of an inning. He saunters away from the plate between pitches. He saunters to left field when the inning is over. During the inning, he often saunters over to the left-field stands, chatting up the fans until the last instant before the pitch. Aside from his unfortunate habit of occasionally sauntering toward fly balls, Henderson's approach does not hurt him. It usually works to his advantage.

Henderson achieves the same effect as Mike Hargrove when he played for the Cleveland Indians and was known as "the human rain delay" for his intricate pantomime of ticks, tugs, taps, hitches and twitches after every pitch until he felt settled again in the box...just...so. It upsets the pitcher's timing. The pitcher starts thinking maybe he's not paying enough attention to his wife, maybe that letter from the tax people is serious, maybe he should have the canker on his tongue looked at. Then he looks down the sixty feet, six inches to the plate and the hitter still isn't settled and he gets pissed off and overthrows and there's no wrinkle on his fastball.

Another thing about Henderson: because of his size and his compact crouch, he has one of the smallest strike zones in the major leagues. At five feet ten inches, he is a short man by the standards of any other team sport except soccer, cricket and anything else the British do well. When batting, his head is nearly waist-height, his ass pokes back at the dugout and he looks like he is about to slam a line of books out from the bottom shelf of a library. Pitches thrown just above the belt down the middle of the plate often are called balls, and for anything slightly inside he jerks out of the way.

This is why Henderson has always been among the leaders in walks and on-base percentage. Hitters like Wade Boggs of the New York Yankees and John Olerud of the Toronto Blue Jays rely on keen eyes and ability to foul off borderline pitches to draw walks. Henderson creates the optical illusion that pitchers can't throw strikes whenever he steps to the plate. His stance is so deceptive it was the subject of an American League investigation in 1986 (when Henderson played for the Yankees) to decide whether his strike zone should be judged by his crouch or where he stands when he is fully upright.

In 1993 Henderson was again doing what he is paid to do, which is getting on base and scoring more runs than anyone else in the game. When Henderson surpassed Lou Brock's record for most stolen bases in 1991, he declared that his next goal was to break Ty Cobb's record for most runs. In 3,034 games over a twenty-four-year career, Cobb scored 2,245 runs, which averages 93 runs a year. So far, in fifteen years, Henderson has scored 1,586 runs, an average of 106 runs a year.

Henderson believes in runs. He thinks they are an important statistic. "That's how they keep score, isn't it?" he once asked. He also believes that the best player on the team is the one who scores the most runs. Which raises the suggestion: maybe that's why runs are the most underrated statistic in baseball, because runs are too simple and baseball prefers complexity (runs batted in, batting average, on-base percentage, total average). Scoring a run demands a peak effort in every offensive skill in baseball. The batter must first get on base (hit, walk, hit by pitch, error). He must move from base to base (speed, savvy). It helps if he has some power so he doesn't always have to rely on someone else to knock him in. Above all, he must have that instinct to score, or, as every sandlot coach insists, "to not die on third."

Henderson turned thirty-five on Christmas Day, 1993, so to break Cobb's runs-scored record he will have to continue averaging a hundred runs a season for seven years, when he will be forty-one, the same age as Cobb when he played his last game in 1928. It is possible, but it will demand every ounce of skill and effort he can muster.

In 1993 Henderson was hitting for average and power, putting up numbers comparable to his Most Valuable Player season in 1990. For the first time in Blue Jay history, Toronto had a classic leadoff hitter. It's odd, but, in an organization that has done nearly everything right from top to bottom from the beginning, the matter of who should bat leadoff has caused a collective brain cramp for seventeen years.

When the Blue Jays became a contender in the mid-1980s, manager Bobby Cox maintained a quaint loyalty to moody second baseman Damaso Garcia, a Dominican who regarded walks as an affront to his manhood. In 1984 Garcia hit a respectable .284, but walked only 16 times in 152 games, despite leading off the entire season. He swung at everything that did not bounce in the dirt or sail over his head. Cox regarded walks as statistical marginalia instead of one of the most vital components of the game.

After Garcia came Mookie Wilson, another leadoff man who could make Mitch ("Wild Thing") Williams of the Houston Astros (formerly of the Philadelphia Phillies) look like a control pitcher. When Roberto Alomar arrived in 1991, the Jays had finally acquired a legitimate leadoff hitter. As the *Elias Baseball Analyst* said in its annual preseason book (on Alomar as a prospective leadoff hitter): "Alomar brings to the plate exactly what the doctor ordered." Alomar seemed such a natural leadoff hitter that manager Tom Kelly selected him to lead off the American League side for the 1992 All-Star Game. Gaston himself selected Alomar as the leadoff hitter in the 1993 All-Star Game.

Problem was, Gaston used Devon White for the real games, despite the fact that White drew fewer walks, stole fewer bases, struck out more, hit for a lower average and hit more home runs. Why this is so, only Cito can say. One could make a stronger argument to use White at cleanup instead of leadoff. All that changed, however, on July 31, 1993, when the Blue Jays acquired Henderson, the best lead-off hitter in the history of baseball. The earlier trade for Tony Fernandez, giving up only Darrin Jackson to the Mets, proved to be the best deal the Blue Jays made in 1993, but the trade for Henderson was the most interesting deal of the season. At the time of the trade, Henderson was having a career year, but a series of debilitating and incongruous injuries—getting hit by a pitch on the bony part of his left wrist during his first week with the Jays, burning his foot with a freezing solution a few weeks later—diminished his numbers for the rest of the season. He did manage to keep scoring runs, though. And his acquisition by the Blue Jays had a dual purpose and effect: to demoralize opponents, and to remind the Blue Jays that their front-office guys were dead serious about winning another World Series. The argument that Henderson decided to dog it after joining the Blue Jays doesn't make sense. He has always enjoyed postseason play, he revels in World Series contests and, most significant, he knew he was playing for a new contract in 1994.

The deal was Henderson for blue-chip pitching prospect Steve Karsay and outfielder Jose Herrera. It was regarded as an unusual move, considering Toronto was scoring tons of runs and their most obvious need was starting pitching. Dave Perkins of the *Star*, the unofficial dean of the press box, said it didn't "feel right," not like the acquisition of David Cone from the New York Mets in August, 1992. Ultimately, even Pat Gillick, who made the deal, admitted publicly he might have goofed. This was during the American League Championship Series, when Henderson was in a slump, and Gillick said if he had a second chance he would not have made the deal.

Late in July, hours before the trade for Henderson, Martin and Gillick were chatting in the press box, along with Dave Perkins of the *Star* and Steve Milton of the *Spectator*. It was a comfy, freewheeling discussion, with names of prospects being tossed about left and right. This was when the Blue Jays and Yankees were tied for first, with Boston only a game and a half behind. Henderson had been playing well for the Oakland Athletics, hitting .327, with 17 home runs, 77 runs scored, and 31 stolen bases. No question he was an igniter, a pest. Martin's contribution to the discussion was this, to Gillick: "How would you feel if the *Yankees* nabbed Henderson?"

When Martin mentioned this to Sean, Sean asked, "What did Gillick say?"

"Nothing at all," Martin said. "He looked at me kind of funny. Then he smiled and walked away."

Whatever, the Henderson trade symbolizes the Blue Jay way of doing business in the 1990s. It symbolizes everything about professional baseball in the 1990s.

The Henderson trade was finalized at ten minutes before midnight on July 31, 1993, in Oakland, California, but the chain of events that led to it began four months earlier on a warm, sunny afternoon early in April at Grant Field in Dunedin, Florida.

Derek Bell, the talented but dippy outfielder, was standing on second base in a game against the Detroit Tigers. So far, so good. After a phenomenal season with the Blue Jays'

Triple A club in Syracuse in 1991, and a disappointing, injury-plagued season in 1992, Bell came to spring training in 1993 as the Blue Jays' starting left fielder. There was some token competition from career bench-warmer Turner Ward, but essentially left field was Bell's to lose. Bell's talent was never in question, though everything else about him was. The year before, when the Blue Jays clinched the American League East, Bell trashed Dave Stieb's locker in the uproarious Blue Jay clubhouse celebrations. He angered veteran teammates when, in a supreme violation of baseball's code of rookie humility, he loaded squashed and empty beer cans, all wet and sticky, into Stieb's locker after whooping it up like a howler monkey on the field after the clinch. Next day, in a meaningless contest, Detroit pitcher Scott Aldred drilled Bell twice, hard, in retaliation for his antics the day before.

After the 1992 World Series, the front office scratched its collective head when Bell went AWOL for the victory parade in Toronto and the receptions with Prime Minister Brian Mulroney in Ottawa, and President George Bush at the White House.

"If there's one guy you'd think would love a parade, it'd be Derek Bell," Paul Beeston said, still puzzled months later. "But he just didn't show up—not in Ottawa, not in Washington."

Beeston, Gillick and Gaston made Bell one of their off-season projects, taking turns phoning him at his home in Tampa. They all swooned over his talent, but they were trying to figure him out, get a handle on him. He was still a kid, only twenty-four, but a twenty-four-year-old going on fourteen. "Derek's an entertainer," Beeston said. "You're never going to win if you only keep putting regular people on the team. Sometimes you need people who are a little different. Well, Derek Bell is different, but he's got an immense amount of talent. If he ever has a Hall of Fame year, watch out!"

Still, Bell "styled" a bit too much during spring training for Gaston's liking. Henderson's styling did not bother Gaston because Henderson had proved he could play the game. Bell hadn't proved a damn thing, not in the major leagues. When Bell was doubled off second after a lazy infield pop-up, something went tilt in Gaston's head and he lashed out at Bell in a rare display of public anger at a player.

Next day, Bell was on a plane to San Diego, traded straight up for outfielder Darrin Jackson.

Jackson, it was said, had a better attitude than Bell. He was thirty years old, but he was a crackerjack centre fielder, with a strong, accurate arm that led all major-league outfielders in 1992 with eighteen assists. He had decent power, with seventeen home runs, and enough speed for the Padres to have considered using him at leadoff. Jackson's shortcomings were food selection—he came down with a powerful dose of food poisoning the day he was traded to Toronto—and hitting American League pitching. Jackson spent a lacklustre two months in right field for the Blue Jays—Joe Carter had obligingly moved over to left to make use of Jackson's arm in right—then Gillick traded him to the New York Mets for prodigal son Fernandez.

The Fernandez reacquisition bore the Gillick trademark signature of making several passes at a player before grabbing him. Once Gillick's interest is piqued, it tickles him for years. He made attempts before 1993 to obtain both Rickey Henderson and Seattle pitcher Randy Johnson. He was also obsessively interested in getting Jim Abbott, the one-handed pitcher who was traded to the Yankees from the California Angels before the 1993 season. Gillick's interest in Abbott went back to Abbott's high school days when scout Don Welke told Gillick this big kid with a stump for a right hand had big-league stuff.

Fernandez, of course, had a long, sometimes brilliant, but often troubled relationship with the Blue Jays in the 1980s before being traded to San Diego. He was moody, a slacker. One time he was so self-absorbed he forgot to take his turn at bat. Fernandez often seemed more interested in converting teammates to religion than converting ground balls into double plays. Gillick still liked him as a slick shortstop and effective hitter, but he was suspicious that Fernandez was about to ditch baseball for a career as an evangelical preacher, so after the 1990 season he sent him off to the San Diego Padres as part of a blockbuster trade: Fernandez and Fred McGriff for Roberto Alomar and Joe Carter.

Fernandez stayed in baseball, however, remaining an all-star shortstop, so Gillick kept an eye on him. During the 1992 World Series Gillick made serious overtures to bring Fernandez back to Toronto, but a deal had already been made to move him to New York. Gillick mentioned this to Martin one evening in his office at the SkyDome early in April. When Martin asked about Fernandez's so-called bad attitude, Gillick quickly replied, "I *wanted* him back. If his attitude was that bad I'd never have tried to get him back."

Gillick was more interested in obtaining a pitcher, a quest that would continue all season, but the Fernandex deal just popped up and Gillick pulled the trigger. Besides, shortstop Dick Schofield had broken his left arm and replacements Alfredo Griffin (another reprise player) and Domingo Cedeno were not up to the job on a full-time basis. One morning Gillick was chatting with the Mets, asking how things were going, and in less than an hour the deal for Fernandez was done—paperwork and all. It was like a couple of kids with bubble-gum cards saying, "Got'm, got'm, need'm."

Tony was back.

In one of the most astonishing welcome-back stories ever printed in a Toronto newspaper, on Saturday, June 12, 1993, Dave Perkins of the *Star* wrote:

> Tony Fernandez is exactly the kind of chicken-hearted, self-centred clown the Blue Jays needed to get rid of before they could win the World Series.
>
> It is almost inconceivable that they would bring him back again.
>
> It wasn't until they thoroughly cleaned out the club-house of brittle brains like Fernandez that they took the big steps in October....

Then, Perkins got nasty.

With Jackson gone, Carter moved back to right field. The trade was a huge break for Rob Butler, the young man we met in Plant City back in spring training, the day he got those hits off Jose Rijo of the Cincinnati Reds. Butler was brought up from Syracuse the day of the Fernandez trade. He got his first major-league hit that Saturday afternoon against the Tigers in Detroit, though the Jays were thrashed 12–1. Butler showed promise in the outfield, at the plate, on the bases, and he looked nifty in his high socks. With the gap in left field filled, it was time again to look for someone who could pitch.

There were some out there, notably Tim Belcher, a workhorse starter for the Cincinnati Reds. There were rumours Belcher was available, one based on the suggestion that having grown up in Sparta, Ohio, a couple of hours from Cincinnati, he felt too much pressure playing for the home-town Reds. No matter, Belcher was making $3.75 million a year, and as much as Gillick wanted pitching he also wanted to hold the reins on the Blue Jays' payroll, keep it in the $46-million range.

Then, on June 22, in a game against the Yankees at the SkyDome, Butler slid head first into second base and ripped the ulnar collateral ligament in his left thumb. No one in the press box had ever heard of such an injury until the familiar voice of Howard Starkman intoned the diagnosis over the intercom. After examining Butler, Dr. Ron Taylor said it is an injury skiers sometimes get after tumbling and catching a thumb in the straps.

Butler would be out six to eight weeks, which meant back to the drawing board.

For Gillick, that is a lovely place to be. He has been at the drawing board since the Blue Jays began, monitoring every draft choice, trade and sale since 1976 when he was lured away from the Yankees. After pitching in the minor leagues for five years, then scouting and doing front-office work for the Houston Astros and Yankees over the next thirteen years, during which time he briefly considered a career in the FBI, Gillick cranked up the Blue Jays from scratch. After some predictable start-up coughing, he soon made them a perennial winner, if not a dynasty.

He has shown a remarkable ability to adapt to the changing nature of his team, and the game itself. Gillick used to be called "Stand Pat" for his reluctance to make a deal. He once went 608 days without making a single trade, from the 1987 season to the 1989 season. Now he is the most feared and respected general manager in the major leagues. In five of the last six years up to 1993, Gillick made late-season deals to bolster the team. In 1987 he acquired pitcher Mike Flanagan. In 1989, Mookie Wilson. In 1990, John Candelaria and Bud Black. In 1991, Tom Candiotti. In 1992, David Cone, the most spectacular late-season acquisition in Blue Jay history. No matter how Cone performed—and he performed very well—his mere presence in the Blue Jays' rotation in that hotly competitive race of 1992 took the wind out of the enemy sails.

In earlier years, when Toronto did not have the money or the talent it does now, Gillick had to be a different kind of general manager. These days he can afford to spend his time finding the right kind of imported chocolate for the dessert tray because the gourmet meal has already been prepared. But until recently he had to make his own bread using the cheapest ingredients he could find. He hired master scout Epy Guerrero and sent him to the barrios of the Dominican Republic to find unpolished gems like Damaso Garcia, Tony Fernandez, Alfredo Griffin and George Bell. If he didn't get them signed himself, he kept them in his prodigious mental files and either traded for them later (as he did with Griffin) or bought them for a song in the Rule 5 draft, during which players not protected on other teams' forty-man rosters could be purchased for $25,000. The only proviso was that the drafted player had to remain on the major-league roster for at least one season—a small price to pay when you are dealing with players like Bell, Willie Upshaw, Kelly Gruber, Manny

Lee, Jim Acker and Jim Gott. He had so much success with the once-obscure procedure that in 1985 they doubled the price to $50,000.

Gillick's desk on 300 Level of the SkyDome faces a window overlooking Lake Ontario. It is crowded with files, notes, telephone directories, a telephone with many buttons, a model of a two-masted sailing ship and stacks of media guides from all teams in both leagues. In April Martin had a session with Gillick to discuss the psychological testing of major-league prospects, and the new emphasis on "attitude" and "character." Nothing new in that, the Blue Jays have been doing it for years, Gillick said. How many years, he wasn't sure, so he got up, walked to the door and yelled a question down the corridor to Gord Ash, his assistant. Ash said they've been doing it since 1984.

His phone rang and Gillick took a call from an old friend in California, a woman he has known for forty years, a friend of the family. Years ago, in his teens, Gillick used to go out with her sister. It was a long call. Gillick mainly listened, commiserating now and then with "Mmms" and "Ahhs." The woman had just lost her husband to AIDS. They have three children, aged fifteen to twenty, but she and her husband had been separated for four years. The woman and her children had been tested for the AIDS virus. The results were negative, but she worried.

When Gillick hung up he talked of retiring at the end of the 1994 season, most likely to be replaced by Ash, the local boy who started with the Blue Jays selling tickets. Gillick had a curious reaction to success, with his moods seeming to have an inverse relationship to the fate of the team. When they are on a roll, he often seems restless and ill at ease. When they are slumping, Gillick seems chirpier, like the fireman who hears the alarm bell after too many games of gin rummy at the station.

"Guys who have been around for a while, they usually get pushed out," Gillick said. "They outlive their welcome. I've seen it happen a lot. I don't want to get in that situation, where you get pushed, terminated, fired—whatever you call it. I don't want to go that way. I'd also be making room at the top, just like the ball club does with the players. Same thing happens in this end of the business."

He might stay with the Blue Jays in an advisory capacity, but he does not want to be involved with the team on a daily basis, commuting from his home in Mississauga. He expects to stay in Toronto after he retires. Unlike the players, the Blue Jay executives live in the city. It is one of the conditions of employment, which never bothered Gillick because he likes living in Toronto, and is particularly fond of the vibrant live-theatre scene. Brian Williams, the CBC announcer, once encountered Gillick and his family at the skating rink at City Hall on New Year's Eve, enjoying the cold, snowy night.

"Why don't any of the players live year-round in Toronto?" Martin wanted to know.

"Taxes, pure and simple," Gillick said. "It's a big whack. You stay more than half the year in Canada and you're considered a resident, which means 15 percent more in taxes—$150,000 a million. Someone like Joe Carter, making $6 million a year, that's a $900,000 differential. That's a whack."

The Texas Rangers were in town for a two-game series. Jack Morris would be starting that night, his fifth start of the 1993 season. So far, he had not won a game, had lost three and had given up 25 earned runs in 17 innings for an embarrassing earned run average of 13.24.

"Is this a crucial outing for Morris?" Martin asked Gillick.

"Naw," he said. "I think he's throwing the ball okay. He'll be all right."

There had been talk that Morris had been tipping off his pitches, that hitters knew what was coming by the way he took the ball out of his glove.

"We've been talking about that," Gillick said. "It came up at a meeting today. We have books on guys that tip off their pitches."

Gillick, the former pitcher, got up from his chair and,

standing in the middle of the office, dressed in a shirt and tie, demonstrated Morris's windup. The tie flapped over his right shoulder as he stretched, raising his cupped hands over his head.

"See, the open glove? It can tip off a fastball, a curve. Even guys like Morris can get careless. But I think he's throwing the ball okay."

There are two important midseason trading deadlines in baseball: July 31 and August 31. After July 31, any player traded has to clear waivers, a procedure that allows every other team in the major leagues to block a deal by making a claim for the player. In some years, 1992 was one, the July 31 deadline is not a problem. General managers routinely put their whole roster on waivers in early August and it is considered a breach of protocol for another team to put in a claim for a player because once the claim is made the original team can still pull the player off waivers.

Nobody wins—it just creates bad blood.

That is why David Cone was available in late August, 1992. He had cleared waivers without incident. The real deadline is August 31, the last day a player can be acquired and still be eligible for postseason play. It wasn't always so. The rule used to be that the last significant period of unrestricted inter-league trading was at the general managers' winter meeting in December. There was always a flurry of pressure-cooker wheeling and dealing at these meetings, the action Gillick enjoys and at which he excels.

In 1993 it was different. At midsummer, every team except the Milwaukee Brewers and Cleveland Indians had a shot at winning the American League East. At the end of April, the Detroit Tigers led the division by two games. At the end of May, the surprising Tigers were still on top, by two and a half games. At the end of June, Toronto led by two games. By the end of July, the Blue Jays and Yankees were tied for first, and the fifth-place Tigers were only seven games back. Sandwiched in between were the Red Sox and Orioles.

Gillick knew that his rivals would do whatever they could to block a deal.

Protocol, schmotocol.

In the week leading up to July 31, the Blue Jays' biggest needs were a left fielder and a starting pitcher. But Toronto already has WAMCO—White, Alomar, Molitor, Carter, Olerud—the most potent lineup one through five in baseball. The sixth hitter, Fernandez, was no slouch either, slashing doubles and triples and maintaining a plus-.300 average. (An advance scout in the SkyDome press box one summer night suggested that an effective way to handle the Blue Jays might be to walk the first six guys and pitch to Ed Sprague.)

Starting pitching had been a disaster all season. Dave Stewart had injury problems, Juan Guzman had strike-zone problems, Jack Morris had Jack Morris problems. The best pitching prospects available were Tim Belcher of the Cincinnati Reds, Dennis Martinez of the Montreal Expos and Randy Johnson of the Seattle Mariners. Belcher and Martinez would be free agents at the end of the 1993 season, while Johnson was despised by Seattle manager Lou Piniella and considered too expensive by Seattle general manager Woody Woodward.

All eyes turned to Pat Gillick as the man most likely to swing a deal for one of the three pitchers. He had a reputation now. He was known, and respected, as someone who could "pull the trigger." Paul Molitor said there was a sense of dread in Milwaukee in 1992 as the August 31 deadline approached and the Brewers were scratching and nipping at the Blue Jays' heels. He knew Milwaukee couldn't afford to make a deal, but the Blue Jays could. When the Blue Jays got David Cone, Molitor said there were shock waves of despair in the Brewer clubhouse.

This year would be different. For one thing, George Steinbrenner was back running the New York Yankees. He might not be as smart as Gillick, but he could match the Blue Jays dollar for dollar, and the Yankees had a splendid batch of tradeable prospects in their minor-league system. Also, the

Boston Red Sox, Baltimore Orioles and Detroit Tigers all felt they were a player away from making it to the top.

Gillick started working the phones. It has been said of Gillick that he never met an airport telephone that he didn't like. On an average day he makes between twenty and twenty-five calls, most of them what he calls "maintenance calls" to other GMs. ("Hi, Pat here. What's doin'?") Once in a while he gets lucky and reaches someone in the middle of a divorce, nervous breakdown or bad-hair day, someone who might in a reckless moment trade a Devon White for, oh—a Junior Felix.

At the beginning of the week leading up to the July 31 deadline in 1993, the Blue Jays clung to first place, barely, half a game ahead of the Yankees. Monday the Blue Jays had a day off, the Baltimore Orioles arrived Tuesday for a two-game series, then the Detroit Tigers came to SkyDome for four games. By week's end the Blue Jays and Yankees would be tied for first. The deadline would be the stroke of midnight Saturday, after Juan Guzman and the Blue Jays dealt with the Tigers.

Most of Pat Gillick's energy focused on the Cincinnati Reds and Montreal Expos. He was concerned about Belcher's midseason slump, so negotiations proceeded slowly. The Martinez trail was warmer, but there seems to be an unspoken code that limits dealings between the two Canadian teams. The Blue Jays and Expos have never made a deal. When the Blue Jays had pitcher Denis Boucher, a marginal prospect, on their roster, the Expos might have given up a Dennis Martinez to get him. Boucher is French Canadian and the Expos knew he would be a valuable marketing tool with Québécois fans. Alas, and *au revoir*, the Jays made him a throw-in in a trade with Cleveland.

There is a similar dynamic in U.S. cities with two teams: in Chicago between the National League Cubs and American League White Sox, in the Bay Area between the National League San Francisco Giants and American League Oakland

Athletics, in New York between the National League Mets and American League Yankees. It worked in Gillick's favour in 1992 when he managed to pry David Cone away from the Mets. Cone in a Yankees uniform would have hurt the Jays (and Cone in a Brewers uniform might have derailed the Jays).

At SkyDome that week, Gillick took Dave Stewart aside one afternoon to talk about Rickey Henderson. Gillick knew Henderson had a no-trade clause in his contract, so he asked Stewart to call Henderson and do a soft sell on the merits of playing in Toronto. Stewart and Henderson had grown up together in Oakland and had played against each other in high school, with Henderson in the outfield and Stewart a misplaced catcher. Gillick had talked to Stewart earlier in the year about Henderson, when he thought he had a chance to get him in the spring.

On Wednesday, Bob Elliott of *The Toronto Sun* wrote a column, quoting his always impeccable anonymous sources, saying the Blue Jays were after Henderson. It was the first public stirring of the deal.

So far, however, no serious negotiations had taken place. Gillick knew from experience that nothing important really happens until the last forty-eight hours before the deadline. This would be especially so in 1993, because the teams out of the race with talent to deal would, in Gillick's words, "try to bleed things right down to the wire" because there were so many contending teams lining up at their doors. By Friday, Gillick had given up on Martinez, who would ultimately stay in Montreal. He was actually traded to the Atlanta Braves, but he exercised the no-trade clause in his contract when he learned that Atlanta would not guarantee him a spot in the starting rotation.

On Saturday morning the *Sun* printed a picture of Henderson's head superimposed on a Blue Jay body (which turned out to be former Blue Jay shortstop Manny Lee). The talk at breakfast all over Toronto was about Henderson and the prospect of the Blue Jays assembling one of the most feared lineups in years.

As for Gillick and Ash, a pitcher remained their number-one priority and the possibilities had been reduced to two: Belcher and Randy Johnson in Seattle. Gillick had always admired the long-haired, giant southpaw, and in the summer of 1993 it looked like Johnson finally was coming into his own. He was not as wild as he had been earlier in his career, and was fanning hitters at a Nolan Ryan pace (a pace that would result in 301 strikeouts, tops in the league by a wide margin). Larry Hisle, the Blue Jays' hitting coach, said, "It's not just that he has great stuff. He's so tall he seems to be halfway to home plate when he finishes his delivery."

Earlier in the week, Seattle had asked the Blue Jays about catcher Carlos Delgado and pitcher Steven Karsay, both with the Blue Jays' Knoxville affiliate. Oakland had been asking about them, too. Gillick said they were "untouchables." Delgado was one of the best minor-league prospects in all of baseball. Karsay, too, was considered blue chip. Only twenty-one years old, Karsay was a first-round draft choice in 1990. He had an excellent curve, his fastball rang in at upwards of ninety-two miles an hour and he had a wicked change to go with it. When Karsay took his regular turn in the Knoxville rotation on Wednesday night, Oakland had a scout in the stands to watch him, just in case. Roger Jongewaard, Seattle's assistant general manager, scouted Karsay personally early in 1993 and predicted he was two years away from being a fifteen-game winner in the majors.

Pitcher Ron Darling of Oakland rated Karsay as "the best pitching prospect I've seen since Dwight Gooden."

What had the scouts drooling was that Karsay had what they call "a good make-up." Some scouts mean the same thing when they say a prospect has "good face." It is something intangible, but understood by all. One definition is that it is a combination of inner fire and outer calm, but it is more than that. Scouts who have been in the game their whole lives still can't explain what they mean by it; they just know it when they see it, and everybody saw it in Karsay. (In mid-

September, when the Oakland Athletics came to SkyDome, Karsay asked manager Tony La Russa to re-jig the rotation so he could face Rickey Henderson and the team that drafted him. "That," said Blue Jays vice-president and fifty-year baseball man Bobby Mattick, "is what I mean by good make-up.")

Gillick countered by offering Seattle a variety of players, with the fulcrum of the deal being veteran pitcher Tod Stottlemyre. Stottlemyre had been a curious, maddening, confusing presence on the Blue Jays since he joined the team in 1988. His career wins and losses before the 1993 season stood at 51–51, which sums up Stottlemyre perfectly. He has good velocity, four major-league pitches, a competitive temperament and excellent genes. His father, Mel, starred as a pitcher with the Yankees for eleven years in the 1960s and 1970s, compiling a won-loss record of 164–139, with a career earned run average of 2.97.

Young Todd never seemed to be able to put everything together. He wasn't mediocre, or injury prone; he simply kept failing to rise to expectation. He could be good, then ordinary, then brilliant—threatening a no-hitter—then awful. He was erratic as hell.

Young pitchers with potential are always dealt away reluctantly, more reluctantly than young hitters. Stottlemyre, however, was not getting any better, and Gillick was getting older, and Gillick felt he deserved better than to have to suffer this way in the penultimate year of his career. It was time for the dump. Problem was, Seattle didn't want Stottlemyre. "Even if we liked Stottlemyre we didn't want him in a deal because of his salary," Jongewaard said.

Stottlemyre was making $2.3 million with the Blue Jays and the only reason Seattle was considering dealing Johnson was to trim the payroll and get some good prospects in return.

As the morning turned to afternoon that last Saturday of July, Gillick and Ash decided on a major shift in strategy: they would abandon Plan 1 and go for what they would later describe as Plan 1a—Rickey Henderson. They had given up on Belcher by noon. Belcher ended up with the Chicago White Sox later that day. They were still talking to Seattle about Johnson in the afternoon, but they weren't getting anywhere with Seattle, and they thought they might get a better deal with Oakland. But that wasn't the whole story. The whole story sheds a lot of light on why Toronto has won five division titles and two World Series in their seventeen-year history, while Seattle, their expansion twins, has managed only one season in which they won more games than they lost.

Despite many attempts over the years, Toronto had made only one minor deal with Seattle. They came close to a multi-player deal a few years ago when Seattle agreed to send outfielder Henry Cotto to Toronto for a truckload of prospects. It was all set to go to the commissioner's office, the paperwork was done, then Seattle owner George Argyros abruptly cancelled the deal.

Argyros was the worst kind of baseball owner—loud, meddlesome, unpredictable. He was a West Coast version of George Steinbrenner. In fact, he often expounded to Mariners front-office staff what admiration he had for the way Steinbrenner operated. Talk like that is not good for company morale. General managers are busy people and do not like having delicate negotiations voided by a brute hand just when all the pins are in place. It makes everyone look bad and hurts the credibility of GMs in future trade talks. It is not that rival GMs think their counterparts are lying; it is that they know the person they are talking to is not in charge, and might not deliver on his promises.

By contrast, the Blue Jays' ownership is the textbook ideal: stable, silent, reliable, with deep pockets. As *USA Today*'s *Baseball Weekly* said in a survey of all twenty-eight owners that ranked the Jays number one by a wide margin: "Every owner, general manager and manager should be required to spend a three-day seminar in Toronto to see how baseball should be run."

When the team was founded in 1976, the split was

45–45–10 between Labatt Breweries, Imperial Trust Limited and the Canadian Imperial Bank of Commerce. Imperial Trust was a holding company of the late R. Howard Webster, who was instrumental in the granting of the franchise in 1976. The Webster family maintained their share of the ownership until they sold their 45 percent to Labatt in November, 1991. The Blue Jays' ownership currently consists of John Labatt Limited, which owns 90 percent, and Canadian Imperial Bank of Commerce, which owns 10 percent.

Whatever the split and the percentages, the company philosophy has never changed—hire the best people, and let them do their job.

In 1993 the working hierarchy was elegantly simple. Gillick reported to Paul Beeston, president and chief executive officer. Beeston reported to George Taylor, Labatt's chief executive officer. That was it. Unless a trade meant going over budget, Labatt would be informed more as a courtesy than anything else. As Beeston explained, "The last thing you want is for the owner to go to a cocktail party and have someone tell him, 'We just got Rickey Henderson.' And the owner says, '*What?*' That's known as CLM—a Career Limiting Manoeuvre."

Labatt has never interfered, has never vetoed a deal. Even at the end of July, 1993, when the Blue Jays were $2 million over their $45-million ceiling, Beeston had a brief chat with Taylor just before the trading deadline, explaining why they needed money for either Johnson or Henderson. Taylor said okay and that was that; both deals were pre-approved.

Beeston rarely pulls rank on either Gillick or Ash. "It's not even a matter of rank," Beeston said. "That's not the way we do business here. Their offices are three doors away from mine. I always know what they are doing. It's a team effort. I'm like a fan. I tell them what I think they should do and they go the other way. It's great. If I take away the decision-making process from them, I take away their ability to enjoy their jobs. Besides, they are as good as anyone I know at exceeding their budgets, so they always have to come back to me, anyway. That's the beauty."

Argyros sold the Mariners after the Cotto debacle, but the situation in Seattle in 1993 was still not as ideal as it was in Toronto. In Seattle, the general manager had to report to a consortium of nearly a dozen part-owners. There were too many engineers in the caboose, increasing the risk of the train going off the rails at a moment of indecision at a critical juncture.

The Mariners are not the only team that operates this way. The San Diego Padres, which went to ruin in 1993, have twelve owners. And having fewer owners, or even a single owner, does not always mean a better system. In many ways, baseball ownership resembles government, involving a delicate balance of compromise, leadership and decision. One-person rule can be efficient, but there is always the risk of rule by an unenlightened despot. The Cincinnati Reds are saddled with Marge Schott, who can do more damage all by herself than any consortium.

An oligarchy dilutes the damage any one owner can inflict, but it is not as steamlined. The Blue Jays operate like a monarchy: according to the constitution, the owners have unlimited theoretical power, but they know the country would be thrown into chaos if they interfered in the workings of Parliament.

The structure in Oakland is similar to Toronto's. Wally Haas has the money and the final say, but he gives general manager Sandy Alderson as much autonomy as Labatt gives Beeston and Beeston gives Gillick. In his book *Play Ball*, author John Feinstein says Alderson went so far as to ask Haas to leave the room while he, Tony La Russa and the coaches and scouts debated whether to trade Jose Canseco to the Texas Rangers in 1992. Plus, Gillick and Ash had dealt with Oakland before. "We know these people and what their normal course of behaviour is," said Ash.

The Oakland Athletics were playing at home on Saturday, July 31. The negotiations between Gillick and Alderson were heating up in midafternoon, Toronto time, when it was still morning in Oakland. Gillick was not getting anywhere with Seattle and, worse, he felt he was not making headway with Oakland. Things were tight in the American League East: the Blue Jays and Yankees were tied for first, and the Yankees looked to be coming on strong—with ol' horse trader Steinbrenner back on the scene. Boston, Baltimore and Detroit were also in contention in this exciting race. Gillick, sensing that the 1993 Blue Jays' chances of repeating as World Series champions were in serious jeopardy, made a startling move that turned out to be the crucial breakthrough: he agreed to include Karsay in the deal.

Not only did he want to acquire Henderson, he also wanted to prevent anyone else, such as Steinbrenner, from getting Henderson. Baltimore had also been sniffing around earlier in the week, and if they added Henderson to their already strong lineup they would be a troublesome opponent in the AL East.

Gillick, however, hated to trade away any blue-chip prospect, especially a starting pitcher. A few players, Cecil Fielder comes to mind, have returned on other teams to haunt the Blue Jays. The only pitcher of note to wreak havoc in an enemy uniform was Doyle Alexander with Detroit during the calamitous 1987 stretch run, which was perhaps fitting retribution, as the Blue Jays had stolen him from the Yankees.

Gillick called in the generals for a group meeting. Many of them were at SkyDome, and they gathered in Gillick's office. The others joined the discussion by speakerphone on a conference call. All told, Gillick heard from Ash, Beeston, vice-presidents Al LaMacchia and Bobby Mattick, director of player development Mel Queen, special assistant and former pitching coach Al Widmar and several scouts. Notable among the scouts *not* consulted was Neil Summers, who had courted Karsay when he was playing high school baseball in Queens, New York.

As a former scout himself, Gillick knew how disappointed scouts are when one of their "discoveries" is traded. Before the 1990 draft, Summers often had visited Karsay at his house, got to know his parents and had taken the young pitcher to dinner. Gillick sensed that Summers's contribution would be clouded by emotion, so he did not include him in the brainstorming session that Saturday afternoon.

As Ash explains, "The scouts have a different relationship with the players than player development staff or people in the front office. They have signed them and guided them in the early course of their careers, so trading them away is like dealing their own son. Summers put a lot of heart and soul into this guy. But the job of the person in the big chair [he points to Gillick] is to see the big picture. The scout's job is securing talent that allows us to do our job. We have confidence in them that they can replace a Steve Karsay. They don't see that. All they see is a subtraction and it's painful for them."

Gillick always likes to consult as widely as possible before making a decision. He wants to hear what everyone has to say, and, just as important, when the smoke clears he wants everyone to feel they've had their say. After that, says Ash, the organization rallies behind the front office, no matter how acrimonious discussions have been before the deal. "It is like the cabinet of a political party. Once the decision is made, everybody is supportive of it."

After a couple of hours of negotiations with Oakland, the brain trust in Gillick's office occasionally glancing out at the yachts on the lake, the deal with Oakland narrowed down to Henderson for one of three pitching prospects, plus a player to be named later who was lower on the depth chart. The pitchers were Karsay, Jose Silva and Paul Spoljaric. Silva was a right-hander in Hagerstown, playing A ball, striking out more than a batter an inning and holding opposition hitters to a miserly .188 batting average—lowest in the minor leagues. Spoljaric was a fireballing, twenty-two-year-old lefty playing in Syracuse who was struggling in 1993 after an all-star season in A ball the year before. Spoljaric also happened to be Canadian, born and raised in Kelowna, British Columbia. That always counts for something, helps maintain fan loyalty.

Sandy Alderson of Oakland gave Gillick the right to withdraw one name from the list of three pitchers, after which Alderson would take one of the remaining two for Henderson. Neither Gillick nor Alderson would say after the fact which two players were left for Alderson to choose from. General managers are uncomfortable discussing deals once they are done. They do not want players in their organization to know that the people who drafted them were willing (in Stottlemyre's case *hoping*) to ditch them.

But one can guess. Obviously, Karsay was one of the players left unprotected. And because Spoljaric was tentatively pencilled for a spot in the starting rotation as early as 1994, Silva was almost definitely the other. Regardless, the significance is that Karsay, the player Gillick would later say was the best prospect he ever traded, was not even considered Toronto's best pitching prospect. The fact is, Gillick traded away a player who was, at best, Toronto's second-best pitching prospect for a future Hall of Famer having one of his best years, which is all one needs to know about the depth of the Blue Jays' farm system.

"That is why I can make these deals every year," Gillick said. "It's not just the money. The scouts are disappointed when we trade prospects they scouted, but it is because they are so good that we can trade for players like Henderson and Cone. They keep on replenishing the stock."

Now that Karsay was on the table, it was time for Gillick to poll his advisors on the merits of the deal. Opinion was divided. Some did not want to lose a pitcher with possibly years of good service ahead of him for a two-month lease of Henderson. Others did not mind the leasing business as much, but felt that bait should be used to catch a pitcher.

In the end, it was Gillick's decision. Unlike the Cone deal a year earlier, he was not getting a clear consensus that this was a deal that should be made. Gillick, after a big gulp, phoned Alderson, took aim and pulled the trigger. It was, he said later, one of the hardest decisions he ever made. "It's the one deal I think could come back to haunt me," he said.

"This is the biggest chance we've ever taken. The other guys [Whiten, Kent, etc.]—everyone was pretty much in agreement that they should be moved. We hated to lose them but it wasn't the end of the world. Karsay could be the end of the world."

Little did he know that the fun was just beginning.

The Athletics were playing baseball when the tentative deal was made about 7:30 P.M. Toronto time.

The Blue Jays had enjoyed a fine day at the SkyDome, defeating Detroit 3–1 to remain tied with the Yankees in first place. The roof was open, the temperature was in the high seventies and there was a gentle breeze blowing in from left field. Juan Guzman was the starting pitcher, and despite giving up ten hits in $6^1/3$ innings, he managed, somehow, to keep the Tigers off the scoreboard. The Tigers left fifteen runners on base, ruining an otherwise creditable performance by their starting pitcher, none other than David Wells. Boomer had started the season well with Detroit, but this loss brought his record to ten wins and seven losses, and he was never the same again.

The Blue Jays won, but they were lucky, and the game again demonstrated that they needed some pitching help—another starter, maybe a good middle reliever. Nobody expected Guzman to keep pulling rabbits out of a hat all season long.

The deal for Henderson had to be tentative because of the no-trade clause in Henderson's contract. Alderson had to sort that one out before the deal became official. About half an hour later—eight o'clock Toronto time, five o'clock Oakland time—Alderson tracked down Henderson when the A's game was over and told him about the trade to Toronto.

Henderson immediately called Stewart, his old friend in Toronto, and peppered him with questions about the city and the team. Henderson and Stewart had been through a lot together in Oakland, including three consecutive World Series, one of them marred by the disastrous earthquake of

1989. With established stars like Mark McGwire, Jose Canseco, Dennis Eckersley, as well as Henderson and Stewart themselves, the Athletics had been considered a dynasty, with more to come. But Stewart was now with the Blue Jays, Canseco with the Texas Rangers, Eckersley wasn't the same old Eck, and the Athletics were in last place in the American League West.

"The ship is sinking," Stewart told Henderson on the phone. "I think you should jump while you can."

Stewart had another thing in common with Henderson: a chequered relationship with Alderson. He felt that Alderson had used Stewart's home-town loyalty and intense involvement with charitable concerns in Oakland as a way to low-ball him into agreeing to terms below his market value. Leaving Oakland was more a matter of principle than money, he said. Stewart had received other offers, including one from Boston that was competitive with Toronto's $8 million over two years. When Toronto made its offer, Stewart instructed his agent to tell Boston he wasn't interested.

On the phone to Henderson, Stewart explained his reasons for choosing Toronto. "Gillick, Beeston and Ash have all proved to be people who put the athlete first and the game second," he told Henderson. "They want you to be a healthy athlete and a happy athlete. They want to know about your family life, about you personally. It's not just a baseball relationship."

Henderson's problems with Alderson had begun almost from the time the ink was dry on his four-year, $12-million contract, signed in 1990. At the time, that made him the league's second $3-millon-a-year player, right after Kirby Puckett of the Minnesota Twins. Henderson won the Most Valuable Player award in 1990, with a .325 average, 28 home runs, 65 stolen bases and 119 runs scored. He also distinguished himself in the 1990 league championship series and World Series. And he had been selected to the All-Star team, the ninth time in eleven years.

No matter, the next year Canseco signed a deal for $2

million a year more than Henderson, which infuriated Henderson. He accused Alderson of reneging on a pledge La Russa had made to "take care of him" if salaries in the rest of the league spun out of control while his stood still. Henderson became an unhappy camper, sulking through the remainder of his days with Oakland. By the spring of 1993, Alderson was saying for the record that he was willing to deal Henderson for less than his market value, and had been "willing to do so for some time."

It is one of the occupational hazards of professional baseball in the 1990s. No sooner does a general manager assemble a championship team than it becomes fractured by ego-driven salary squabbles among the top players. If teams are not bled dry because of their inability to afford the greatness assembled, as happened most recently to the Pittsburgh Pirates, they are prey to a poisonous atmosphere at the clubhouse.

Henderson is more vocal than other players about the financial pecking order, but most other top players feel the same, especially with regards to what they consider discrepancies on their own teams. Henderson already was ticked off that inferior players on other teams were making more money, but it was Canseco's contract, and Canseco's clubhouse gloating, that really got under his skin. That the Blue Jays have been able to field teams loaded with all-stars with a minimum of in-house complaints is a tribute to the type of players they recruit, and the way Gillick, Beeston and especially Cito Gaston treat them.

Gaston has played the game, he's a big man—physically and temperamentally—and he knows how to treat players so their egos don't get knotted up in their jocks. In many important ways, Gaston represents the ideal manager of the 1990s. Back in the spring, Gillick told baseball analyst Peter Gammons that managing a baseball team is more complex today because society is more complex. "Time was when a manager had natural authority that went unquestioned," Gillick said. "Now that's simply not so. The concept of *team* is far less important than it was twenty years ago. The 1960s changed that. Certainly contracts and money did."

Gene Tenace, the Blue Jays' bench coach, can't understand why Gaston doesn't even make the short list in any of the manager-of-the-year awards. "All successful managers know how to handle ten people, the pitching staff," Tenace said. "Cito's good at that, too, but his real strength is handling all twenty-five players on the team. He instils confidence. A lot of managers break down players mentally, and they can destroy a player. Cito knows how to handle individuals, personalities. He has feelings for people. The players know it, and they respect him for that."

Managing a team of all-stars, many of them millionaires in their twenties, is one of the hardest things to do in baseball, and one of the least appreciated skills. Gaston is well paid as a manager—he makes about $300,000 a year—but he is a peon compared with players who make penthouse salaries, $4 million and $6 million a year. It does not make managing any easier to be outearned twenty to one by the workers you are supposed to be managing. And these workers are acutely aware of the status and power that comes with big money.

One afternoon in the press box at SkyDome, Dave Perkins of the *Star* told Martin a story about an incident that happened at Exhibition Stadium in the late 1980s. Perkins was sitting in the Blue Jay dugout with Lloyd Moseby, talking about the exploits of baseball great Lou Gehrig. Perkins mentioned that one season Gehrig knocked in more than a hundred runs *on the road*. Jesse Barfield, the strong-armed outfielder for the Blue Jays, walked by and overheard this. "That's impossible," Barfield told Perkins. Perkins showed the figures to Barfield to prove that not only was it possible, but it had been done. Barfield then asked, "How much did Gehrig make that year?" Perkins guessed about $40,000. Barfield turned to Moseby and said, "See, he couldn't have been that good. He didn't make no cake."

Fans who begged Gillick to be more aggressive in the free-agent market in the 1980s did not appreciate that contracts are not signed in isolation. Sign a Dwight Gooden or Jose Canseco to a huge-money deal and it has ripple effects up and down the lineup, especially if the free agent turns out to be a dud.

That is probably why Gillick went after Joe Carter much harder than he did David Cone after the 1992 season. He could depend on Carter to drive in a hundred runs and hit thirty home runs every year. If anyone complained about Carter's $6-million salary, Gillick could tell the griper that if he did what Carter did year after year he would be paid accordingly. End of conversation. If Gillick signed Cone and he had a mediocre year, as he did in 1993—pitchers are a much more perishable commodity than position players—he would soon have Juan Guzman or Pat Hentgen or Duane Ward on his back. (Baseball salaries are always mentioned as yearly sums. It is easier to relate to them in weekly sums, which in Carter's case means he pulls in a weekly $115,384.61, which provides a lot of quarters for the laundromat.)

In Oakland, Alderson knew he was in for a battle with Henderson over the no-trade clause. According to the deal with Gillick, it was Alderson's responsibility to resolve it. This would turn out to be the last ripple from the Canseco deal, and the first from Stewart's telephone conversations with Henderson.

Alderson had already talked to Miles McAfee, Henderson's agent, who left for the stadium in Oakland in the seventh inning. At five-fifteen Oakland time, eight-fifteen Toronto time, Henderson and McAfee talked one-on-one in Alderson's office to discuss Henderson's options. The trading deadline was just under four hours away, nine o'clock Oakland time, midnight in Toronto. If the deal collapsed, Oakland had the right to keep Henderson for another year if they offered him arbitration. McAfee reminded Henderson that Alderson had once offered him $1 million to remove the no-trade clause.

Alderson and owner Wally Haas then joined Henderson

and McAfee. Alderson told Henderson he would grant him unrestricted free agency at the end of 1993 as a condition of the deal, but he did not offer him any money to buy out the no-trade clause. After a few minutes, Henderson left to meet his daughter for dinner. McAfee thought that was a good idea, as Henderson was becoming increasingly agitated. "What's in it for me?" he kept asking. And then he told McAfee, "I don't have to do anything. I can keep my butt right here and go to arbitration next year."

Though the two sides had not even begun to discuss dollars, Alderson stepped outside to talk to a scrum of reporters at around five-thirty and announce the tentative deal, subject to resolving the no-trade clause. When he returned, McAfee kept pushing his point that Oakland was unloading a third of Henderson's $3-million contract for 1993, and getting two prospects in return. If you don't make it worthwhile for Rickey financially, McAfee told Alderson, there's no deal.

The meeting broke up at around seven, two hours to deadline, without any specifics on the table. McAfee drove to his downtown Oakland office. Alderson remained at his office at the stadium where he telephoned Henderson, who was now at his mother's house. Alderson offered him $125,000 to scrap the no-trade clause. Henderson called McAfee. "No way," Henderson said. "Not even close."

Alderson, growing frustrated, was patched through to Beeston at Splendido's, a restaurant in Toronto as swank as its name, where Beeston was having a late dinner with his family. Alderson wanted to know if the Blue Jays would split the cost of buying out the nettlesome no-trade clause. "No way," Beeston said, either Oakland pays the shot, or the deal's dead.

At about this time, Gord Ash received a call from Jongewaard in Seattle, whom he had been talking to sporadically throughout the evening. Jongewaard had gotten wind that the previously untouchable Karsay was now part of the Henderson talks. Jongewaard suggested to Ash a counter offer—Randy Johnson for Karsay and Mike Timlin, the Blue Jays' gritty middle reliever.

GAME PLAN

Ash didn't know what to do. He wished all this was happening at the winter meetings, where he could meet Jongewaard in person. Ash considered himself good at reading faces, looking for telling signs—a twitch, a frown, a brow raised. For Ash, it is like playing poker; it is not just what card you play, but *how* you play it. Now he was playing poker over the telephone. Gillick trusted Ash's instincts, and whenever possible liked to have him in the room with him when he was talking turkey. "He might get a different reading on a tone in a guy's voice from one conversation to another that I did not," Gillick said. "There might be a nervousness, a dryness in the voice, any change in attitude from a previous call." Ash sensed a renewed urgency on the phone line from Seattle. He called Gillick immediately.

Gillick and Ash were in a quandary. The deal with Henderson had been announced, but negotiations in Oakland over the no-trade clause were going nowhere. Seattle had always been unpredictable in trade talks; now they were willing to deal Johnson. Johnson had been Gillick's number-one priority all along, right up until lunch that Saturday. The Blue Jays needed pitching. They already were stacked offensively without Henderson—WAMCO made sure of that—and nobody with the Blue Jays entertained the quaint notion they were seeking Henderson for defensive purposes (though inserting Henderson in the leadoff spot would spell HAMCO—a more felicitous acronym for a Henderson-studded lineup one cannot imagine).

After hearing from Ash, who relayed the news from Seattle, Gillick realized he was being offered Johnson for terms comparable to the Henderson deal, and without the hassle of the no-trade clause. Gillick was in his element. He loves it when it comes right down to the wire, and there is no baseball executive in the majors more experienced or adroit at these eleventh-hour, high-stakes negotiations. Nothing gets by him. Earlier in the week, when one general manager had tried to squeeze more out of Gillick than he was prepared to give and said he had a better offer elsewhere, Gillick sensed a bluff and called him on it. "Okay, then," he said. "I'll watch for it on CNN."

End of discussion.

Gillick called Alderson and issued an eleven-thirty deadline (Toronto time) to come to terms with Henderson because he had another deal in the works that he was prepared to pull the trigger on if the Henderson deal fell through. And no, sorry, Toronto would not give Oakland a dime for the no-trade buy-out.

Looking back at the flurry of negotiations, Gillick later admitted that if Seattle had talked earlier in the day the way they were talking as the deadline approached, he would have made the deal for Johnson. But Gillick had never put Karsay on the table when he talked to Seattle. Karsay only became part of any deal after negotiations with Seattle had closed earlier in the day. Jongewaard of Seattle never could figure out why Gillick offered Karsay to Oakland first.

"I was surprised Oakland could get Karsay for a guy who wasn't signed past 1993," Jongewaard told Sean. He considered Johnson more attractive than Henderson, not only because he was a front-rank pitcher, but he had a contract that would include the 1994 season. "I thought they needed a pitcher more than they needed another hitter," Jongewaard continued. "But I'm not the one to tell Gillick how to do his job. We were hoping that either the Henderson deal would fall through, or the Blue Jays would change their mind."

Gillick may have been hoping the same thing. Changing his mind, however, was out of the question. He had a verbal agreement with Alderson to give Oakland until eleven-thirty to iron out the Henderson deal. Gillick knew if he went back on his word, however tempting it might have been, his reputation would be tarnished, which could skewer future trade talks.

Meanwhile, in Seattle, Jongewaard ensconced himself in the owners' box under the field-level stands behind home plate at the Kingdome and kept sending and receiving calls from Ash at the SkyDome in Toronto. The Mariners were in the middle of a game and Jongewaard tried to follow the action between telephone rings. Between innings, manager Lou Piniella walked over to the owners' box from the Seattle dugout to get any updates.

If Jongewaard and Ash were going to revive the Johnson deal, they would have only half an hour to do so, between eleven-thirty and midnight Toronto time. Jongewaard felt the cold sweat of pressure, as he had already failed to come to terms with the Yankees and Philadelphia Phillies in earlier entreaties for Johnson.

As eleven-thirty approached, Alderson and Henderson were getting closer, but still had a lot of middle ground to make up. Alderson called Gillick and asked for a ten-minute extension. "Okay," Gillick agreed, "but not a minute longer."

At eleven-thirty Henderson called Stewart again. He said, "Hey, Stew, I don't know what's going on. Sandy's being pretty hard. It doesn't look good."

At eleven-forty Gillick and Ash prepared to call Jongewaard and hope against hope that something could be salvaged from the day. McAfee gave Henderson Alderson's final offer to buy out the no-trade clause: $500,000.

It was up to Rickey. Oakland was his home town, where he grew up and played high school baseball, where his mom still lived. His best years in baseball had been in an Oakland Athletics uniform. He remembered Stewart's last words of advice: "You're a great player, Rickey. Great players belong on great teams."

Henderson liked the sound of that, but he was still confused. In a sudden inspiration, he decided to ask his mother, Bobbie, what she thought he should do. "They've been doggin' you here long enough," his mother told him. "Go for it." That was all Rickey needed to hear.

The deal was on.

Henderson called McAfee. McAfee called Alderson. Alderson called Gillick. Gillick called Ash. Ash called Jongewaard. Gillick called Beeston. Alderson called Haas. But there was one more hurdle to be cleared: signing the papers.

Henderson's mother lived about twenty minutes away in Oakland Heights. There was not enough time for Henderson to drive to the stadium. He agreed to meet halfway, at a softball park off the freeway. Henderson got in his car and drove from his mother's to the softball park. McAfee headed to the softball park with the papers to be signed. Mickey Morabito, travelling secretary for the Athletics, and Eric Kubota, the A's assistant scouting director, also drove to the softball park. It was in a seedy part of town, and it was getting dark. It was only minutes before nine o'clock, midnight in Toronto. The four men met in a nearly empty parking lot, then gathered around McAfee's black Mercedes, which was not an everyday occurrence in the neighbourhood, unless it was another drug deal going down.

"We got some strange looks," Morabito said.

On the Danforth in Toronto, Rob Butler, the Blue Jay rookie, was watching television at his father's house, resting his injured and taped thumb, when he learned on the late news that Rickey Henderson was now a Blue Jay. For Butler, the year had begun with such promise, with those hits off Jose Rijo on the second-last day of spring training on a sweet afternoon in the Florida sunshine. Now that Rickey Henderson was on the team, left field would be his until further notice. Rob turned to his father and said, "Well, Dad, there's always next year."

=== 8 ===

The Clubhouses

Psychiatrists, lawyers, FBI agents, Coca-Cola executives—they all have the ability, buttressed by oaths of confidentiality, to keep their mouths shut about certain things. For others—bartenders, night porters, mafiosi, lovers, priests, journalists—the codes are unwritten but as rigidly enforced. Nobody likes a snitch.

So it is for Ian Duff, thirty-three-year-old visiting clubhouse manager at the SkyDome. Early on a game day afternoon in May, as the Detroit Tigers gradually filed in, Duff spoke of the code. "All clubhouse managers know it," he said. "It goes 'What you see here, what you hear here, let it stay here when you leave here.'"

The visiting clubhouse is not as splendid and palatial as the home team clubhouse, certainly not at the SkyDome where the Blue Jays dress and undress and shower in rooms Nero would have envied. The visiting clubhouse suffers by comparison, but as visiting clubhouses go in the major leagues it is better than okay. The meals are good, the service excellent, and though the room is rather narrow and reminiscent of a well-appointed railway car, it is tidy and comfortable.

Happy, too. The Tigers, always a loosey-goosey club under manager Sparky Anderson, whose surface amiability camouflages no-nonsense authority, had clobbered the Blue Jays the night before. In the visiting clubhouse, one could feel the power of the Tigers, who always seem to find a solid core of big muscular white guys—Mickey Tettleton, Rob Deer, Kirk Gibson—with big black Cecil Fielder thrown in for good measure.

Duff's position as manager of the visiting clubhouse makes him a big tease for gossipy journalists. One can only imagine what Duff has seen and heard during sixteen years in the company of millionaire baseball players. He has seen rookie sluggers when they first begin to realize that stardom may not be a dream. Veteran pitchers in moments of solitude after being sent to the showers early, when they begin to realize for the first time that their dream is ending, and real life awaits.

One can only imagine, because Duff isn't saying anything.

"If there are things I see when only the players are around—say, a fight between two guys—and I told a reporter, the team would be very unhappy with me, as would the Blue Jays' front office. I just wouldn't do it."

Duff is interrupted by Sparky Anderson, walking by in skivvies, looking every inch the paterfamilias with his white hair and wise, grizzled, twinkling face—a Santa Claus without the beard—that has watched two lifetimes of baseball and may be going for a third. In the summer of 1993 Sparky was fifty-nine, but he has looked fifty-nine all his life, and probably will look fifty-nine when he is seventy-nine. Of all the managers in the major leagues, Sparky Anderson is the one most people like to take home to dinner to talk about baseball and life. Sparky approached Duff for the first request of the day, which Duff already knew: ham sandwich, white bread, lettuce, mustard.

Duff is one of the longest-serving visiting clubhouse managers in the major leagues. He knows most of the players and team routines. He knows which teams ban alcohol in the dressing rooms (Detroit and the California Angels), which teams want the locker-room layout on the road to be the same as at home (Kansas City Royals), which players want a McDonald's cheesburger waiting for them when they come in from batting practice (Frank Tanana). That is about as juicy as Duff gets with his story-telling. "I'm an employee of the Blue Jays," he explained in his laconic manner. "But I would never tell them any of the things I see. I'm the first contact with the Blue Jays for most of the players and it's important to make a good impression so that if they become a free agent, maybe they will want to come back here." Those twin yet separate loyalties are essential components of Duff's job. Player loyalty ensures lucrative tips, which constitute a greater share of his income than his official salary with the Blue Jays. Duff will not reveal just how generous the players are.

As for his employer, after finishing high school in 1976, at age seventeen, Duff joined the Jays for their inaugural season as a part-time home clubhouse attendant. While Torontonians were celebrating the Blue Jays' snowy Opening Day 9–5 win over the Chicago White Sox earlier in the day, Duff kept vigil overnight at Exhibition Stadium because the locks had not yet been installed on the clubhouse doors.

Duff seems to have been destined to be a professional fly-on-the-wall in one form or another. He looks the part of a background man. His height is average, hair of average length and thickness, with a nondescript pair of glasses resting on a modest nose on top of a not-too-trim, not-too-straggly beard. He would be the guy used for scale in a police lineup between the fat guy with the scorpion tattoo and the midget with the three-inch facial scar. The only other career that interested him was a behind-the-scenes job in television or film. It did not matter what exactly, as long as it was anonymous, essential and inside.

"I felt like I was in dreamland," he said of his first days on the job. "I thought it was the greatest job in the world. I wasn't in awe, though. A lot of the guys we had in those days were just kids trying to make it."

Since the lateral move to the visiting clubhouse, Duff has

struck up lasting friendships over the years with players like former Boston Red Sox slugger Jim Rice, Kansas City Royals Cy Young winner Bret Saberhagen and future Hall-of-Famer George Brett, plus other established stars like Robin Yount, Don Mattingly and Jeff Reardon.

Some of Duff's most difficult moments on the job have come during the Blue Jays' greatest moments of triumph. Four divisional titles and the 1992 ALCS championship were clinched at home, which meant that in some of those years Duff had to keep counsel with a locker room of broken-hearted ballplayers cursing, crying, or simply numb. He slipped over to the winning clubhouse for a while when the team was celebrating its first division title in 1985, but in future years he stayed with the losers, as a show of respect.

"I have a lot of respect for Tony La Russa and the whole Oakland Athletics team, so I stayed there last year when we won the ALCS. It's a dog assignment to work in the loser's dressing room, and with this team, more often than not this has been the losing room. I'm happy when the Blue Jays win, but I also feel bad for these guys. That's why, in a selfish sense, I was glad they won in Atlanta last year. I got to run out on the field and celebrate with the guys."

The visitors' clubhouse wasn't the losing clubhouse this night, to the chagrin of the Blue Jays and the 50,488 fans, who watched the home side lose a dispiriting contest to Detroit, this time 13–8. In two games the Tigers scored twenty-five times and tonight they banged out five home runs, two by Cecil Fielder, two more by Kirk Gibson, another by Tony Phillips. All the Detroit home runs came off young Pat Hentgen, who lasted three innings and emerged looking like he had been in a car accident. It was the first time in the 1993 season, apart from their opening-day loss in Seattle, that the Blue Jays had had a losing record. The cleats clicking down the steps to the visitors' clubhouse sounded like castanets at a party that was just getting going. Duff would not have to fake a hangdog expression this night.

Aside from his general housekeeping duties and player

requests, a good chunk of Duff's time is spent in the laundry room. After the game it takes an hour just to spray clean the dirt marks on the uniforms. Before throwing them in the wash, he checks the pockets for batting gloves or any $50 bills Baton television broadcaster Fergie Olver may have given the players for on-camera interviews.

Duff rarely leaves SkyDome before one o'clock in the morning on a game day and never works less than twelve hours a shift. During the transition between one team leaving and another arriving, he has been known to work forty-eight hours straight. When the Blue Jays are on the road, and during the off-season, Duff's time is his own. He remains single. "You don't meet a lot of women in my line of work."

Dearth of dating prospects notwithstanding, Duff likes being right where he is: on the inside. "I don't know if I could ever sit in the stands and watch nine innings anymore. I'm too used to being in the clubhouse, or sitting on the bench. This is the best job in baseball, other than being a player. I'd miss the bullshit if I left. It's different on the visiting side, but there is still a camaraderie here."

Over on the other side of the field, under the third-base stands, is where Duff hopes to be some day. It is usually the happier place, according to Jeff Ross, manager of the Blue Jay clubhouse. "I can understand what Ian goes through," he said five hours before a September night game against the Oakland Athletics. "It's not as much fun there. Here, when the Jays are winning, you feel a part of it—you ride the ups and downs with them."

At the moment, Ross was riding a down. The night before, the Blue Jays had lost a horrible game to Oakland, 11–7, but the score does not nearly indicate the true depravity of the game. It was played indoors, went eleven innings, lasted nearly four hours and it was the Blue Jays' fourth consecutive loss. The fans either knew what was going to happen, or, coming off a World Series championship season, they have become astonishingly blasé, because they began streaming out at the end of the tenth inning and by the time the eleventh began the SkyDome ws barely half full. Consider this: the score after ten innings was 6–6, the pennant race was white-hot, with the Yankees only half a game back and winning by a run down in Texas. No matter, gotta go, so thousands rose from their seats at the end of the tenth and headed to the exits to get a jump on the postgame rush.

In the top of the eleventh, Brent Gates of Oakland drew a leadoff walk. When he took off on a steal of second, Pat Borders sailed the ball high over Roberto Alomar's head—it looked like Borders had thrown a Frisbee—allowing Gates to move on to third. That turned out to be the hole in the dike, after which Oakland scored five runs. After the game, reporters crowded into Cito Gaston's office, down the corridor from the players' dressing room, and someone asked Gaston if it was the ugliest loss of the season.

"It's up there," Gaston said.

As Dave Perkins explained in the *Star* next morning, "Last night's loss is either the beginning of the end for the 1993 team or it is the absolute ebb and everything goes in one direction—up—for the remaining 23 games."

Across the way, in Duff's clubhouse, loud rap music boomed as the Athletics enjoyed what merriment they could in what for them had been a dismal season. They had lost six straight games, lost fifteen of their last sixteen games, and were on the verge of mathematical elimination with nearly a month to go in the season. Beating the defending champions in the heat of the pennant race is something to be savoured, however, so they savoured it: *Thump! Thump! Thump!* All that stuff.

In the hours remaining before the second game of the series, Ross was on a down, quietly going about his business, trying to remain unobtrusive. The Blue Jays were playing their worst baseball of the season at precisely the wrong time. Ross knew from experience that he would shoulder some of the blame.

"Whenever we are struggling, the bats are no good and I have to order some better ones. I'll be happy when we start to win again. They like the equipment a lot better when we're winning."

As if on cue, Darnell Coles walked into Ross's cramped office down the hall from the palatial dressing room and asked if his shipment of Cooper bats had arrived. "Tomorrow," Ross told him, spitting a stream of tobacco juice into a paper cup by the phone on his desk. Unlike his counterpart on the visitors' side, Ross does not have a great deal of experience dealing with the surly moods of a losing team. After growing up in Montreal and working part-time for the Expos on the grounds crew and in the clubhouse, Ross was hired as visiting clubhouse manager for the Jays in 1977. "They offered me the head groundskeeper job, but I looked around the CNE and didn't see any ground. I didn't think it would be enough of a challenge."

Ross worked in the visiting clubhouse for four years, following his favourites, the late 1970s Boston Red Sox teams of Rice, Fisk and Yastrzemski, before handing over the reins of the visiting clubhouse to Duff in 1981 and moving to the home side. Duff can be forgiven for thinking he has been given the short end of the stick over the years. During the first few seasons, when the Jays were routinely losing more than a hundred games a season, Ross was surrounded by visiting players who were quite enjoying themselves as they beat up on the expansion Blue Jays. The visiting teams would be in a good mood as soon as they arrived from the airport, so assured were they of picking up two or three easy wins on the road. The customers were happy, tips were good. Then when Toronto showed the beginnings of respectability, only two years away from the start of their eleven years and counting streak of winning seasons, Ross switched to the Jays' dressing room. The customers were happy, tips were phenomenal. After both the 1992 and 1993 seasons, the players voted Ross a full share of playoff bonus money, which in 1993 came to $127,920.77. He was the only non–player, other than coaches or trainers, given a share. Duff got a Christmas card.

The Blue Jay clubhouse is conceded to be the most

splendiferous in the major leagues. Television monitors hang from the rafters so players can watch other baseball games—or basketball, football or hockey games. Or "The Dating Game," if it's on. ("The redhead—take the redhead, dummy!") The centre of the large room has curved granite stanchions, forming a staggered oval. On the granite stanchions are cartons of baseballs to be autographed, trays of bubble gum and the usual assortment of freebies distributed to the players by corporate and commercial hangers-on. The players' lockers are spread around the room, against the walls. They really are not "lockers," but open stalls, where the players' uniforms and civilian clothes are carefully hung. Stacks of mail from fans spill down from an overhead shelf. Each stall has a stool where the player sits to pull on his sanitary hose and cleats or to sit and answer how-does-it-feel-to-be-you questions.

At the south end, a short, white-tile corridor leads to an open shower room, where there are fourteen stalls. Off the north end of the clubhouse is the workout room, where players can heft weights, work on specific muscle groups on Nautilus machines and immerse themselves in a hot whirlpool or stretch out on a narrow padded table for a soothing massage. Farther north is the private lounge, where players have their pregame snacks—apples, oranges, watermelon—and choose from an assortment of juices, bottled water and Gatorade. There is a bright red Naugahyde couch, the carpeting is Blue Jay blue, the walls providing a pleasant blend of teal. The training room and lounge are strictly off limits to the media, a place of refuge, a safe escape for players who want to brood or bitch, make a phone call, sometimes settle on-field disagreements, but mostly save themselves from the inanities of the querulous scrum that buzzes in from the press box after every game. (In the early 1980s, on a West Coast trip, the Blue Jays brought in a stripper for a little postgame, *Bull Durham* frivolity, but that is one of the luxuries of being in the visitors' clubhouse, where the local media is not much interested in what the visitors say or do after the game.)

There is a corridor from the clubhouse that runs under the third-base stands directly to the dugout. This is the alley the players, coaches, trainer, batboys and manager use before, after and during games. They walk by the huge railway wheels used for rotating the stands for baseball, football and other events at the SkyDome. A short walk along the roadway from the clubhouse, at 000 Level, is the indoor batting cage, used all year round. (For postseason games, the indoor batting cage is made over for a media interview room.)

Along the east wall of the clubhouse, starting at the corner stall, is Joe Carter's place, which is a double locker. Then there's Mark Eichhorn's stall, then Todd Stottlemyre, Pat Borders and Duane Ward. Ward is one of the few players who smokes cigarettes in his undies, encouraging any of the reporters who smoke to light up with him. After Ward comes Tony Castillo, then Danny Cox (the only player born in England), then Dave Stewart, Alfredo Griffin and Roberto Alomar, who also has a double locker, with photographs of family. The SkyDome dressing room, however palatial, does not have as many lockers as the dressing room at Exhibition Stadium had, and Ross likes to assign what few double lockers there are to the players most likely to be surrounded by scrums of reporters after the game. The last thing a fringe player like Willie Cañate wants after yet another unnecessary postgame shower is to sit on his stool at eye level with the behinds of a crowd of journalists listening to Alomar talk about what a glorious game he just had.

There is the entrance to the showers, then the stalls belong to Al Leiter, Mike Timlin, Randy Knorr, Juan Guzman, Darnell Coles, Turner Ward, Tony Fernandez and Ed Sprague. Along the west wall: John Olerud (perhaps due for a double locker in 1994?), Paul Molitor, Dick Schofield, Pat Hentgen, Jack Morris, Devon White, Cañate, Rob Butler. Then the aisle of coaches: Bob Bailor, Galen Cisco, Gene Tenace, Rich Hacker, John Sullivan and Larry Hisle. The door beside Hisle leads to Gaston's office.

David Garrick, SkyDome president of corporate affairs,

has been in the Blue Jay clubhouse a few times when a new player arrives from the minors. These are the young men who have been riding the buses, stretching their daily meal money, washing their faces in gas station washrooms. When they enter the clubhouse they reverentially sit on the stool at their stalls, looking around the room at the names above the stalls around them: CARTER...OLERUD...MOLITOR... ALOMAR. "It really blows them away," Garrick said. After a while, an adventurous one walks over to one of the granite stanchions, picks up a chunk of bubble gum, unwraps it, pops it into his mouth, then goes back to his stool and lets the major-league feeling wash over him.

If there is a power side to the clubhouse it is along the west wall, where Olerud, Morris and Molitor have stalls side by side. Last year, Winfield's stall was along the west wall and many postgame sessions were held here as the caramel-voiced Winfield elaborated on baseball and life and the universe. Winfield also was the judge of the kangaroo court that dispenses justice for flagrant and unflagrant, on-field and off-field violations. In 1993 the court judge was none other than Alfredo Griffin, a bench jockey throughout most of the season, but one of the most respected and liked players on the team. The players along the west wall hardly constitute a clique, though; young Hentgen, Butler and Cañate have stalls interspersed among Olerud, Morris and Molitor.

Tony Fernandez was the next player to visit Ross. He told Ross he wants to order a pitching machine and have it sent home to the Dominican Republic. Ross wrote down the request, then pointed toward Sean, who was seated across from Ross with a notepad.

"See what happens when you don't play well," Ross told Fernandez. "They come to interview me."

In other years, that kind of ribbing would have sent Fernandez into a week-long sulk. But after a few years in San Diego and a few months with the lowly Mets, Tony was thanking his Lord for small mercies. "He is much happier now," Ross said when Fernandez was gone. "When he left the Blue Jays he didn't realize that all organizations do not treat their players as well as Toronto does."

A few minutes later Pat Hentgen walked in. He asked Ross if he could arrange a tour of the local Polo shirt factory for September call-up Doug Linton. "No problem," said Ross. "Ask for Simon when you get there. He runs the place. He'll get you a good deal."

Third-base coach Nick Leyva, recently promoted from Syracuse after Rich Hacker's automobile accident, poked his head in and asked. "Can you get me some Phantom tickets?" Ross said, "No problem." Hacker, a close friend of Leyva, was badly injured in an automobile accident when he took advantage of the three-day midsummer break to visit his home in Belleville, Illinois. As he was driving in from the airport around midnight, suddenly a pair of headlights appeared in the darkness, coming straight at him. Youngsters had been drag-racing on the highway and one of the cars rammed head-on into Hacker's van. He was in a coma for a week, clinging to life, but he recovered enough to throw out the first pitch in one of the ALCS games at the SkyDome in October.

When Leyva left, Duane Ward walked in, his ever-present cigarette in his pitching hand. He asked Ross if "the shirt" was ready for the evening game. Ward meant the blue T-shirt he has worn under this uniform all year, every year, since he started with the Jays in 1988. It is part of his superstitious routine that includes throwing his warm-up jacket into the air, rather than handing it over, when one of the ballboys greets him as he jogs in from the bullpen in the ninth. Sean knew about the jacket routine, but he did not know about the shirt. He felt a great appreciation for Ross's work upon hearing this, and just a little queasy. Ward's ragtag good-luck T-shirt looked like it could have walked to any of the washing machines, jumped in and given itself a good back scrub. Ward has pitched in 377 games since he joined the Blue Jays. And he sweats a lot.

"I had to send it out for repairs this time," Ross said.

Things did not turn out any better that night, and the Blue Jays lost a 2–1 squeaker to the Athletics. They were ahead 1–0 going into the ninth, but Oakland scored two in the top of the ninth. The next night the Blue Jays lost again, their sixth loss in a row, this time 7–4 when the Athletics scored three times in the top of the ninth. After the Oakland sweep, the Blue Jays and Yankees were tied for first, with twenty-one games left.

That turned out to be the season's ebb, for the Blue Jays then went on a tear, winning nine in a row. After shutting out the Boston Red Sox 5–0 at the SkyDome on September 21—Stottlemyre pitched a masterful nine-inning shutout against Roger Clemens—the Blue Jays were in first by five games. The race was over. All Duane Ward hoped for now was that his T-shirt would be ready for postseason play.

"No problem," Ross said.

═ 9 ═
Covering Baseball

Behind the third-base stands at Grant Field in Dunedin, Florida, there is a small square sign atop a chain-link fence: "Press and Handicapped Entrance." Choose your own punch line. At the SkyDome in Toronto the media have their own entrance, Gate 9, but in some ways that sign at Grant Field would be as appropriate here. A good number of big-league baseball players feel the former and the latter are synonyms and act accordingly.

Consider this exchange between pitcher Jack Morris and *Globe and Mail* beat writer Neil Campbell on Sunday, April 11, 1993, after the last game of Toronto's season-opening series against the Cleveland Indians. Morris pitched dreadfully. He gave up base hits to the first two Indians he faced, then served up a three-run homer to the third hitter, Carlos Baerga. He was gone before the third inning was over, leaving with zero wins and an earned run average of 16.71.

Morris was changing into civilian dress—blue jeans, cowboy boots, Western shirt—when a media scrum of about fifteen print reporters gathered at his locker and waited inches away in respectful silence for the television reporters to show up and get their clip for the six o'clock news. This was the understood thing. A postgame session with Morris was necessary—Morris knew that—but no one in the scrum was looking forward to it. And there was no way Morris would answer the same perfunctory questions twice for stragglers.

No one wanted to be the first person to start this unpleasant business, so Campbell, new to the baseball beat this year after writing mostly about horse racing, did the honour as a show of good faith to the veteran baseball writers.

CAMPBELL: So…Jack…what happened?
MORRIS: They hit my pitches, all four of them. It didn't matter what I threw. Baseball's not easy. It's humbling at times. Shit happens. I don't overanalyse things. One-sixteenth of an inch difference and Baerga's ball stays in the park. It would be different if I was a young kid and hadn't been through this before. I have. But it doesn't mean it doesn't hurt. I can't tell you I feel good right now. I don't. I feel like shit. I got my ass beat. I accept that. No one feels worse than I do.

The usual postgame musings from the losing pitcher. Morris had given the media what was expected of him, but when Campbell persisted by asking him about any previous slumps comparable to what he was going through at the moment, an entirely appropriate follow-up to Morris's talk of "having been through this before," Morris lit into Campbell with a venom that made the rest of the scrum cringe.

"I don't care what happened in the past," Morris snapped. "I'm not gonna go back into my stats for you. Do your own fucking homework. The fans in Detroit never knew me. You don't know anything about me, either, and you never will. All you do is make judgments on me."

Morris stared into Campbell's eyes the entire time. To his credit, Campbell persisted, asking Morris when he would be able to put this outing behind him.

"Dinner's coming up," Morris shot back, the suggestion

being that all would be forgotten as soon as he began his meal.

Finally, Dave Perkins of *The Toronto Star* put Campbell out of his misery and stepped in. He asked Morris, "Is that true? Can you do that?"

"No, that's not the truth," Morris said. "I can't put it out of mind until the next chance to prove myself. On days like this I think it's better to be a hitter. I have to live with this for five."

The exchange is instructive for several reasons. It is a typical example of how mean spirited baseball players can be toward the media when things are not going well. It shows how rookie baseball writers are treated relative to veterans— both by players and by the writers themselves (more on this later). It also reveals how self-censoring the baseball media corps can be. Here was Morris-the-man coming out—raw, angry, afraid. As the season wore on and Morris kept getting shelled, he would talk more and more about going back to his ranch in Montana and playing soft-toss with his kids and less and less about how flat his fastball was that day or if he was tipping off opposing hitters with his delivery. But on this day, Morris had not yet resigned himself to the real possibility that his seventeen-year career was ending. His pain was palpable to everyone in the room, yet none of this was reported in the *Sun,* the *Star* or *The Globe and Mail* the next day.

Having never written exclusively about baseball before the 1993 season, we felt like outsiders much of the time, not part of the tribe. At various times we felt it from the players, front office staff and the daily baseball writers. Exacerbating this feeling was the uniquely languid pace of the baseball season. From the time spring training begins in February until the World Series ends in late October, countless hours are spent in the middle of things—sitting in the dugout, hanging around the batting cage, walking through the dressing rooms—long before the games begin and long after the games end. From four in the afternoon until forty-five minutes before the first pitch at seven thirty-five, the media are allowed access to every nook of the SkyDome except for the showers, training room and players' lounge. On a typical game day, the media have so much time to kill that most of them spend more time kibitzing with each other than they do talking to players.

For those who are not accepted by the players or the media it is a paranoid's delight. It is like being invited to all the "A" list dinner parties, then being seated alone in the kitchen with a TV dinner. You are where everything is happening, but you never really feel part of things. You find yourself spending much of the time trying to pretend you are not listening in on someone else's conversation.

Like prison culture—where armed robbers look down on break-and-enter artists, and rapists look down on pedophiles—there is an unofficial but clearly defined hierarchy among the Blue Jay media in terms of access to the players. At the top of the hierarchy are the radio announcers Tom Cheek and Jerry Howarth and former players-turned-TV-personalities like Tommy Hutton and Buck Martinez. They pal around with the players on off days and fudge the rules about clubhouse access by wandering into the areas that are off limits to the rest of the media.

Cheek and Howarth are the most closely associated with the team—they even get World Series rings—but the others exert their authority in subtle ways. After one home game in June, Sean and Martinez chatted while waiting for the elevator to take them to the basement level where they could walk under the stands through the dugout to the field. There are two elevators, one for Blue Jay personnel, one for everybody else. The Blue Jay elevator opened first and Martinez hopped on. "See ya," he said, as Sean waited for the elevator for everybody else.

Next in line are the beat writers, who have to write game reports to deadline every day and who go on most of the road trips. They include Dave Perkins, Tom Slater, Al Ryan and Jim Byers of *The Toronto Star*, Mike Zeisberger, Bill Lankhof and Bob Elliott of *The Toronto Sun*, Larry Millson and Neil

Campbell of *The Globe and Mail* and Steve Milton of *The Hamilton Spectator*. As columnists, Perkins and Elliott are more inside than the rest because they can get candid comments from the players, coaches and office staff without having to name them in print. But they all have plenty of time to schmooze with the players and coaches on the golf courses, the buses and in hotel restaurants and bars on the road.

Next comes the mass of radio, television and print reporters who attend only the home games. They gain access by virtue of simply hanging around long enough, but they do not get the sense of the daily grind of the long season that the beat writers do. They also do not get the same access to the players and coaches, access which comes easier on the road when the players and coaches stay at the same hotels, are away from their families and have time to spare. The beat writers make a big deal of this access, but none of them ever gets all that close to the players. As a group, players tend to regard print reporters as "pond scum." They see print reporters as disrespectful of their talent and reputation—certainly not respectful enough—and thus people not to be trusted. Not like Cheek and Howarth, or Hutton and Martinez, who are essentially loyal shills. Although the players do not always express it as such, they also sense that print itself these days, with the exception of certain high-profile columnists, is on the fringe, and not a little *déclassé*.

Next down the hierarchical ladder are sports journalists who do not file stories every game. They are general columnists who might write once or twice a week about baseball; general assignment sports reporters chasing down an angle; magazine writers who focus on a particular player for a particular story; and book writers. We were in this category, which is a shade above the last and most loathsome character, the "press box tourist" who hangs around watching baseball for nothing, gorging on the bountiful lunches, dinners, snacks and drinks while everyone else wonders exactly what they do to earn and living. "I call them 'foofs,'" said Perkins a few hours before a night game last summer. "This press box is full of foofs. They get credentials for one game, they're floaters. They show up, have dinner and do nothing—just get in the way. Toronto has a lot, but it's not as bad as New York or Boston. They have foofs there who sit in the press box and stand up and cheer. In Fenway Park, the press box is full of little old men wearing Red Sox caps. They'll be standing behind you, looking over your shoulder, reading what you write, saying, 'Look at what this guy's writing about the Sox!' You have to turn around and say, 'Hey! Fuck off! Get outta here!'"

When we began a weekly baseball column for *The Globe and Mail* in April, the newspaper provided us with season passes, but other factors early on made access difficult. Perhaps because of the increased profile that winning the World Series gave the Blue Jays, a new style of kiss-and-tell journalism evolved and the players became increasingly suspicious of the motives of journalists they did not know. *Frank* magazine, an Ottawa-based gossip sheet devoted primarily to the peccadilloes of politicians and national journalists (So-and-so has been involved in a "horizontal jogging" relationship with So-and-so), began printing salacious rumours about the alleged sexual habits of some Blue Jays. At the same time, *Toronto Life* carried a cover story on Roberto Alomar by writer Michael Posner. It delved into rumours that had been circulating for weeks in the press box but had never been written about.

The story mentioned that during a game, while he was playing second base, Alomar scoured the stands looking for postgame action. According to Posner, Alomar noticed an attractive blond sitting behind the Blue Jays dugout, then asked a newspaper photographer to pass her a note asking her to join him for drinks at a bar on Queen's Quay on the Toronto waterfront. She accepted. They had dinner, shot some pool and she visited Alomar at his SkyDome Hotel suite, but the relationship soon ended, leaving the woman with what she called "a sour taste." In his *Toronto Life* story, Posner quoted the woman as saying of young Alomar, "He's not the angel everyone thinks he is. I keep hearing from other women, maybe ten of them, all of whom had met Roberto Alomar in much the same way. He was only interested in one thing and when he didn't get it, that was it."

The story infuriated Alomar. He began a media boycott. Suddenly the motives of everyone in the press corps were questioned. An atmosphere of mistrust prevailed. When the Blue Jays arrived home from a road trip, with the Alomar boycott presumably still in effect, Sean noticed Alomar chatting amicably with Perkins of the *Star*. Curious, Sean asked Perkins if the boycott had been lifted.

"There's no boycott," Perkins told him. "Alomar just isn't sure who the real baseball people are this year. It's only fair. We have to get some reward for all the time we spend on the road with these guys."

Martin had it easier than Sean. He has written a weekly baseball column while on staff at *The Globe and Mail* during the early days of the Blue Jays, then the newspaper invited him back to write about baseball when he was a freelance writer in the early 1980s. He had also played fastball with some of the current beat writers in a press league he helped to found in the late 1960s. At spring training in Florida, he stayed at the *Globe and Mail* condominium, where he became the designated driver for the *Globe* writers, going out to dinner and playing video games late into the night. He was friends with current and former baseball writers such as Kevin Boland of *The Financial Post*, Ken Becker of Canadian Press and Alison Gordon, who wrote baseball mystery novels and used to cover the baseball beat for the *Star*.

Sean generally was treated as a tag-along whose chief talent was obliviousness to accusations of nepotism. No one explained the rules to him, certainly not Martin, who wanted him to discover them on his own (and secretly worried that too much exposure to the innards of baseball might erode Sean's love of the game). In the postgame sessions in Cito Gaston's office, Sean usually stood at the back of the room so the beat writers could get what they needed quickly for their deadlines. This was fair, he thought.

Then Sean started to feel uneasy about his silence after hearing of the almost universal disdain the writers and players had for *Globe and Mail* columnist Marty York when he used to write about baseball. The writers considered York gutless for writing nasty bits about the Blue Jays, but always stationing himself anonymously at the rear of the scrum, or avoiding the clubhouse altogether. No reporter likes to keep asking the good questions for the benefit of his competitors without ever having the favour returned, especially when the competitor keeps writing critical stories that make the team grumpy. The writers most respected were fellows like Perkins who, the day after writing in his column that Tony Fernandez was a chicken-hearted, self-centred clown, walked into the Blue Jay clubhouse, stationed himself at Fernandez's locker and asked if he had anything to say for himself. And there was former *Star* and *Sun* columnist John Robertson who, after attacking second baseman Damaso Garcia mercilessly for weeks, actually apologized in the clubhouse in front of the entire team when Garcia went on a hot streak.

With this in mind, Sean felt obligated to contribute more to the scrum discussions. He saw an opening late in July, when Gaston announced the roster for the All-Star Game in Camden Yards in Baltimore. (As manager of the 1992 World Series winner, Gaston became manager of the American League All-Star team.) Gaston had selected no fewer than seven Blue Jays to the team and there were groans of objection throughout the league that more deserving candidates—Mickey Tettleton of Detroit, Rickey Henderson of Oakland, Kenny Lofton of Cleveland—should have been selected instead of Devon White and Paul Molitor. Sean had talked with Pat Gillick that afternoon and learned that Gillick had already received a complaint from the brass in Cleveland about the Lofton omission.

So, during a silence in the postgame session in Gaston's office—a session that was going nowhere in terms of news value—Sean piped up what he had heard from Gillick and asked Gaston for a reaction. Gaston's reply was typically succinct: "Tough." Sean would have preferred to keep the Gillick tidbit to himself, but he felt pleased that he had done a small part for what he thought was the greater good of all.

Uh-uh.

Next day, Larry Millson of *The Globe and Mail* took Sean aside in the Blue Jay dugout. He said he wanted to speak to him privately. "You shouldn't have done what you did last night," Millson said.

"Done what?" Sean asked. He did not have a clue what Millson was talking about.

"The question in Cito's office. You shouldn't have done that. Those guys have about ten minutes before deadline, let them get what they need first."

"Sorry, Larry, I had no idea. No one was saying anything."

"Sometimes they take their time, trying to steer Cito in a certain direction," Millson said. "Then you come along and change the topic and give him a chance to slip away."

"Sorry, Larry, no one told me. I thought I was supposed to ask questions once in a while so you guys don't think I'm a tourist."

"Not then," Millson said. "I just thought I should let you know. Some of the guys were pretty upset about it."

Sean wished he had said that Gaston had not said anything worth quoting in four years as manager. He was still bewildered that his question had triggered such a heated response. Martin had always maintained that the art of asking questions is a neglected art in journalism, that blunt questions get blunt replies, woolly questions get woolly replies. He also thought journalists were too deferential to the people they covered. When he was in his twenties, *The Globe and Mail* sent him to the airport to intercept Prime Minister John Diefenbaker, even though it was a Sunday and the national press had an understanding that Sunday was Dief's day off. No matter, and still on a three-month apprenticeship, Martin found Diefenbaker and a large entourage on one of the top levels at the airport. He sidled up to him, then rode down an escalator with him, all the time pestering him with questions as the frowns of the national media burned in on him. The interview resulted in a front-page story on a no–news day. Better, a senior *Globe and Mail* reporter who had been part of the entourage told Martin's city editor that he had done an admirable job smashing the barriers of protocol.

Millson's intentions were good. He is one of the most hard-working and amiable of the upper rank baseball writers, always generous with advice or a candid talk about his own life and work. Millson is an excellent reporter, one of those muckers unafraid to go into the corners, and with no pretensions to poetic journalistic style. He is also one of that strangely common breed of journalist who talks better than he writes, delivering intelligent insights into the game that are too philosophical ever to find their way into his game reports.

One Saturday afternoon in May, Millson and Sean were talking abut the surprising Toronto Maple Leafs, who were engaged in a thrilling playoff run that would take them within a game of the Stanley Cup finals. There was a lot of discussion in the sports pages about whether Toronto was a hockey town or a baseball town. The accepted group-think wisdom among sports writers was that Toronto is and always will be first and foremost a hockey town. Sean considered the debate rather silly, and said so in his weekly *Globe and Mail* column, reminding readers how irrelevant the Maple Leafs were when Toronto went into paroxysms of joy over the Blue Jays in the autumn of 1992. He could not understand why Toronto could not be a baseball *and* a hockey town.

Millson talked at length about the multicultural mosaic of Toronto. He described conversations he had had with cab drivers from Asia and Africa who had never seen snow, let alone a hockey game, but were avid baseball fans. Millson pointed out, quite rightly, that an entire generation of post-1967 immigrants had grown up in Toronto believing that the Blue Jays were the only game in town. Only white Toronto could even begin to claim that Toronto was a hockey town. Millson's comments were sensitive and well presented, but he never once chose to use them in a story.

That same day, Millson the mucker spoke trenchantly about the over-romanticization of baseball, and the tendency among some of the best writers to turn tobacco-spitting, semi-literate jocks into gods. "This game is a grind, that's all it is," Millson said. "I don't know why people romanticize it so much. The beat writers certainly don't because they know what a grind it really is, from February until October. A few weeks ago we had Reggie Jackson here for an old-timers game and he was talking to one of the Blue Jays on the field. If Roger Angell had been here and seen them, he probably would have imagined them talking about the cut-fastball or Vida Blue or something like that. He's not putting it on— that's the way Angell sees the world—but we know how these guys really are. They were probably talking about getting laid last night."

Millson has been covering the Blue Jays full time longer than any other baseball writer and remains one of the best liked of the press corps, covering the team since its inception except for 1991. That was the year *The Globe and Mail* was in the midst of seriously downgrading its sports department. Millson was forty-eight years old, and he thought he might be out of a job. Instead, the newspaper shifted him to news. During spring training that year he was covering a rooming-house inquest, and when Opening Day rolled around he couldn't attend because the inquest jury was deliberating that day. It was the first opening day he had missed since the Blue Jays started in 1977.

He was reassigned to cover baseball in 1992 and remained the *Globe and Mail's* top baseball reporter in 1993. During the season, when the Blue Jays are in Toronto, his day begins at six o'clock, when he gets up to have coffee with his wife, who leaves at eight o'clock to teach English as a second language. When she is out the door, Millson goes back to bed, sleeps until ten o'clock, then gets up and starts working.

He keeps box scores from both leagues on computer disks, which he often studies in the morning. He videotapes most Blue Jay games, so some mornings replays parts of a game to see what happened—a pickoff, a catcher not blocking the plate, a hit-and-run. He might watch one play twenty times, until he's sure he's got it right. He leaves his apartment at two o'clock, briefly visits *The Globe and Mail*, checks his mail and memos, then walks across the street to the SkyDome.

"I used to get there earlier, but now they don't open the clubhouse until four o'clock. I don't know why baseball writers didn't protest that more. Maybe a lot of them didn't want to get there earlier. Lots of times I used to be in the clubhouse at noon, but the four o'clock thing started last year."

In the early years, Millson was close to outfielder Lloyd Moseby and pitcher Jim Clancy. Moseby was a kid of nineteen, not yet a real Blue Jay, when Millson first met him in Florida. He needed a ride to the minor-league complex in Dunedin, so Millson and his photographer gave him a ride and Moseby spent most of the time talking about his idol Muhammad Ali. When Moseby made it to the Blue Jays, he remained friends with Millson. "He didn't have much of an education, but he was very bright, with a quick sense of humour," Millson remembered. When Millson was pulled off sports, he went to the batting cage before a game to say goodbye to Moseby. When he said he was going on news, Moseby's response was, "That's great!" Other players and other writers had felt sorry for him, leaving baseball, going back to the civilian world, but Moseby's mind didn't work that way. He considered Millson's reassignment to news a promotion. "You've been doing this way too long," he told Millson.

Millson's last deadline for an evening-game story is eleven-thirty, after which he goes for a few beers with the writers. Most nights he pals around with Al Ryan, known as "Bear," who writes game stories for *The Star*. "The other night Bear and I sat around at his place drinking beer and listening to Steely Dan. I didn't get home until six in the morning. My wife is good about it. When I got home at six, she said, 'Okay, you can stay out an hour beyond normal for every night you get home on time.' So if I get home five nights in a row on time, she allows me a night out."

The road games are the hardest on family life, and on Millson's health. He sympathizes with players who endure midseason slumps, always packing and unpacking, staying in hotel rooms, eating in coffee shops. It is especially hard on the writers because their work begins when everyone else's ends—after the games and the clubhouse scrums. The players at least get their exercise, which provides a physical release.

"On the road you do a lot of drinking and staying up late because you're wound up, pumped up with coffee," Millson said. "You can't sleep. On the West Coast you check into hotels at four in the morning and get calls at seven because of the time difference. I once spent seventy-two consecutive days on the road, starting with spring training. The lifestyle of covering baseball is selfish. I've not had to face a lot of problems at home when my daughter was in her teens. My wife was there alone. I should have been there. Everybody has crises, and she was always handling these crises by herself. It's a very selfish way to make a living.

"This is the most tiring beat on the newspaper. And at the office, you're always being second-guessed because everybody thinks they are a baseball expert. They wouldn't dare second-guess the medical reporter, or the labour reporter."

Before a game in June, Sean and Neil Campbell sat in the Blue Jay dugout, watching the pregame goings-on on the field and around the batting cage. Suddenly, changing the topic, Campbell asked Sean, "Do you want a job?"

"Doing what?" Sean asked.

"Covering baseball."

"For who?"

"*The Globe and Mail.*"

"Come again?" Sean asked.

"I can't stand this anymore," Campbell said. "I'm sick of dealing with these assholes."

With that, Campbell walked away, looking like the television anchorman in the movie *Network*, after his on-air nervous breakdown when he began muttering, "I'm mad as hell and I'm not going to take it anymore." He never told Sean exactly what had set him off, but he made it through the season somehow. One of his happier days was toward the end of the season when ESPN, the American all-sports network, had chosen a Sunday Blue Jay game for its national broadcast. That meant the game was shifted from the afternoon to 8:30 P.M., which meant the game would end after the *Globe's* early Sunday night deadline and he would not have to go down to the locker room for postgame interviews.

Campbell is certainly not the only Toronto baseball journalist to develop a temporary or permanent disdain for the players. It is a common occupational hazard, a process of disillusionment that is exacerbated by the love for the game that propelled many of the journalists to cover baseball in the first place. Martin's friend Ken Becker covered the Blue Jays for a season for the *Sun* back in the early years and emerged totally disillusioned. He was, and is, a keen and knowledgeable baseball fan, having grown up in the Bronx. That is the home of the Yankees, but through his father Becker inherited a devotion to the Brooklyn Dodgers. He was heartbroken when Walter O'Malley moved them to Los Angeles in 1958, a day he still considers one of the blackest in baseball. He hoped that covering the Blue Jays would bring him close to the game again, perhaps allow him to get to know some of the players. The only player he got to know and respect was John Mayberry, the large, big-hearted first baseman. The rest he considered self-centred louts. When his season as a beat writer ended, Becker wrote a personal, embittered account of his experience in *Toronto Life*, including the sense of disgust he felt seeing players on the team bus laughing at the people in the slums as they were going through the Bronx on their way to a game against the Yankees. Becker still writes elegantly about baseball from time to time for Canadian Presss, but he will never again cover baseball full time. He loves the game too much.

GAME PLAN

When Martin repeated this story to Perkins, he said, "Guys like us who are not part of the scene, but are close to the scene, we're in an interesting position. The public, the fan, has to think that these guys [the players] care. About Toronto, the fans, the team—about *something*. That's the basis of being a fan. If a fan ever got to ride a bus with these guys for three days they'd be appalled. They'd realize the players care absolutely nothing about them. There are exceptions, but most players loathe the fans. From the safety of the bus they make all kinds of remarks about fans. The saddest sight is one o'clock in the morning, leaving the stadium on the road, and there'd be clusters of Blue Jays fans, pathetic creatures holding scraps of paper, wanting autographs. They're there essentially to wave at the bus, and the players are making jokes about them, saying, 'Get a life!' They have disdain for anybody who isn't a ballplayer. And that applies to anyone in the media.

"Money has a lot to do with that. It's taken by these guys as a mark of something. The closest I ever came to being 'one of the guys' was back in '88 during an exhibition series in Puerto Rico and it pissed rain for three days. We never got out of the hotel. But there was this big casino in the hotel lobby. I got on this two-minute run at the dice table, made thousands of dollars, and ended up clearing more than $3,000. Suddenly, I was being looked on with respect. I was making money. The players talked about this. It was a big deal."

Martin knew Perkins from their days together at *The Globe and Mail* and later at the *Star*, when they both played on the same office fastball team. Perkins is a big man, with a full brown beard, which gives him the formidable countenance of a northwoods lumberjack. He could crush the ball, launching it to adjacent roofs and tennis courts, but he was not blessed with what baseball calls "soft hands." If office fastball had enjoyed the luxury of the designated hitter, Perkins could have become a local legend.

He has a wicked sense of humour. Days before the All-Star break in July, Perkins was part of a scrum around John Olerud by the batting cage. Olerud had been selected by the fans as the All-Star first baseman, and, low-key as Olerud is, his placid face betrayed a hint of anticipation at starting in the big game, which would be played at Camden Yards in Baltimore. Asked what he thought of being in the game, Olerud launched into what for him would be considered a frenetic ramble. "I think I'll be very excited," quiet John said.

"How will we *know*?" Perkins asked.

In 1993 Perkins had been covering the Blue Jays for eight years and had earned himself a column with his gruff, no-nonsense style. His column measured 720 words, which he could write in a span of twelve minutes, as he did in Atlanta after the concluding game of the 1992 World Series.

His "Welcome Back Tony Fernadez" column last June has become something of a classic in the Toronto baseball writing fraternity because of the amount of vitriol in it—a rare thing indeed in the chummy world of sports journalism—but Perkins said Fernandez actually took the criticism quite well. "We had a long talk and that was that. I told him that's how I felt at the time and that's what I'm paid to do. The public took it far worse than he did. I got hundreds of calls on my voice mail. I even got a death threat. I've had players say they'll take a poke at me. I've always said, 'Pu-leeze do. Pay my mortgage.' That straightens them out. David Wells once told me he was going to hit me. I said, 'Boomer, you go ahead, take your best shot, because I'll hit you back.' He didn't know what to say. He just kind of laughed. Then we both started laughing and that was the end of it."

Overall, Perkins said, the 1993 edition of the Blue Jays was the most pleasant to be around since he started covering baseball full time, relatively speaking. "There are fewer assholes on this team than any other team," he said. "Last year's team was pretty good, too. But that's strictly a 'Who cares?' It doesn't have a bearing on my job. The only reason I do this is because I like the game. The rest of it is just awful tedium."

The writers, said Perkins, can get as drained by the long season as the players, and there are times when he does not even want to think about baseball. When the Blue Jays were in California on a road trip last summer, Perkins, Tom Cheek and Cito Gaston got together one morning for a round of golf on an off day. "We don't talk baseball all the time," Perkins said. "You'd make yourself crazy. Cito loves to talk about things that aren't baseball, which we all do. After the golf game, which was a lot of fun, Cito said, 'What do I owe for my share of the rental cart?' Just like a normal guy. Then the next day I go to him and ask, 'How come your pitching staff's so horseshit?' I didn't want to ask him that on the ninth green. It was my day off, too."

Most beat writers gravitate to one or two players, whom they get to know better than the others over a season. Martin's friend Kevin Boland got along well with infielder Rance Mulliniks during the 1992 season. Boland writes a column for *The Financial Post*, as well as books on Dave Stieb and Kelly Gruber. (Few people know that Alison Gordon, who covered the Blue Jays for the *Star* for five years, also wrote a book about Stieb—one of the least liked players in Blue Jay history. It was her first baseball mystery novel, *The Dead Pull Hitter*. As she told Martin once night over several glasses of red wine, "I guess enough time has gone by for me to say that he was the player who gets murdered when someone smashes his head in with a baseball bat," she said. "That's what makes writing fiction so satisfying.") Mulliniks, though he was not playing regularly in 1992, was always thoughtful and articulate. Ask him three good questions, Boland said, and you could depend on Mulliniks to deliver three cogent, unclichéd answers.

"Yeah, Rance was like that," Perkins said. "You have certain guys you like to take care of, because they will take care of you. They will tell you when you're right or wrong. They'll put you on the right track if you're on the wrong one. They learn in a hurry who the important writers are, and who are not."

Dave Winfield was easily the most popular Blue Jay with the fans in 1992, and he astonished many baseball journalists that year by using the word *symbiotic* in a front-page interview with the *Star* when he asked the fans to be more boisterous at games. We never understood what the fuss was about. After all, Winfield was a grown man of forty-one at the time, and *symbiotic* is in the vocabulary of the average high school honours student. Perkins, too, thought that Winfield's influence was overrated.

"With Winfield," Perkins said, "there's the perception and there's reality. The public cares more about perception; I care more about reality. The reality to me is that Dave Winfield— great, great player on the field, hustles hard on the field—was the greatest self-promoter I've ever seen. He was as phoney as a three-dollar bill—*in my opinion.* Maybe what he is is a 'genuine phoney.' He was out for Dave Winfield. The only time I ever saw him lead anything was into the trainer's room after a tough loss. [The trainer's room is out of bounds to media.] I'm not knocking Dave Winfield the great ballplayer. To watch him hustle last year was a real treat, because this has not been a hustling team for a long, long time. Winfield talks in sound bites. He'll ask, 'How long do you need?' If someone needs a twenty-second sound bite, he'll give it to them.

"Some players, like Devon White, you ask the right question and you can trigger him. He's not a talkative guy, and getting things out of him can be difficult, but if you ask the right question and phrase it well, you'll get him talking. And he talks very well. I think the world of Devon White. Last year when he made that catch in the World Series [against the wall in deep centre field] I was the first guy to compare it to Willie Mays in 1954. Now everybody does."

John Olerud?

"Forget ballplayers, he might be the most even-tempered *human* I've ever seen. I've never seen anybody this side of a respirator who's as low-key.... I'd love to see his pulse line on a graph—it would look like the horizon...."

In *Sports Illustrated*, a writer said Olerud's resting pulse rate was forty-four beats a minute, about as low as a hibernating bear.

"I believe it. Like a Trappist monk. I don't think I've ever been able to get John to spew, really unload. He's very polite. He answers all questions the best he can, but I've never been able to make him a chatterbox."

Joe Carter?

"Joe's a cliché machine. There have been times when I'd say, 'Hey Joe, wait a minute here. I'm not some guy from a radio station looking for a cliché.' But he's okay. I don't have any problems with Joe."

Rickey Henderson?

"To me, Rickey Henderson is the biggest hot dog I've ever seen. He turns it on, turns it off. A lot of people in the clubhouse suspect that's true, but when it comes time to be on the record—coaches, manager, players—they say, 'Aw, gee, poor Rickey, he's had some injuries. He's trying....' Blah, blah, blah. When Rickey wants to play he's tremendous. When he doesn't want to play, which to me seems like most of the time, he's an empty suit."

Paul Molitor?

"Molitor understands that we are here, we're going to stay here, and we have a job to do whether he likes it or not. The day in Boston when Tommy Craig freeze-burned Rickey Henderson, I thought I died and went to heaven. I'm having a picnic with this, because it's so bizarre. The next day, Molitor says, 'You columnists have any fun with that stuff?' I said, 'Matter of fact, yes, I did.' Then Molitor says, 'I heard of players giving a guy a hotfoot—never a *trainer*.' I said, 'Why didn't you tell me that yesterday? I could have used that line.' Molitor has a great sense of humour. He does everything but take your notes for you. I love him."

The consumate players' manager, Cito Gaston, on and off the job.

Audio programmer Nick Poulakis, "the DJ of the Dome," with his daughters Sarah (left) and Stefanie.

Home Sweet Dome — the SkyDome celebrates its fourth birthday with a world-class cake.

Affable, low-key and in charge: Blue Jays president and CEO Paul Beeston.

CBC's Brian Williams: the curiosity of a cat and the energy of a cub reporter.

The architect of victory, Blue Jay executive vice-president Pat Gillick.

The incredible Canadian, Dr. Ron Taylor, has earned four World Series rings, two as a player and two as the Jays' team physician.

Assistant General Manager Gord Ash began with the Blue Jays as a part-time ticket seller.

George Holm, director of stadium and ticket operations: 3.4 million tickets sold before the first pitch of '93.

Going out on top.
Bullpen coach
John Sullivan
retired after the
1993 season.

Walk softly and carry a big stick. Batting coach Larry Hisle and
1993 batting champion John Olerud.

Jay clubhouse manager Jeff Ross (left) and trainer Tommy Craig —
keeping the equipment and players in shape.

Covering the bases: first-base coach Bob Bailor (left) and former
third-base coach, now special assignment coach, Rich Hacker.

=== 10 ===
The Wizard of SkyDome

At four o'clock on a sunny afternoon at the SkyDome, Nick Poulakis was selecting the song tracks for an evening game against the New York Yankees.

It was the Yankees' first visit to SkyDome in 1993, which meant the last of the Blue Jay reunions this season. Dave Winfield, Kelly Gruber, Tom Henke, Manny Lee, David Wells, Bob MacDonald and David Cone had all come and gone, looking strange and out of sorts in the uniforms of opposing teams. Now Jimmy Key was in town. He would be starting for the Yankees next evening, the second game of a three-game series.

After the Blue Jays won the 1992 World Series—Key won two of those games, winning the climactic Game Six in relief—Key waited on a cruise ship during the winter baseball meetings for a faxed offer from the Blue Jays. When no offer was tendered, Key signed a four-year deal with George Steinbrenner's Yankees. Of all the champion Blue Jays, once fans had recovered from the shock of Winfield's departure (he was replaced by Paul Molitor, after all) the loss of Jimmy Key proved to be the saddest of all. He was such a nifty southpaw, and he had been a Blue Jay nine years. He always looked so young, like the fresh-faced kid down the street who knocks on the door and asks if he can mow your lawn. Early in the 1993 schedule it became apparent the Blue Jays needed Key's pitching more than they realized when they so blithely let him fall into Steinbrenner's hands.

When the game starts, Poulakis sits at a keyboard at an open window high over home plate, just west of the press box on the third level of SkyDome. The room where he sits is small and crowded with electronic geegaws, microphones, two-way radios, autographed baseballs, posters and hundreds of compact discs. To his right, at the same high window, is Murray Eldon, the public address announcer. Behind them is Matt Carnovale, who operates a cockpit of audio controls, looking every inch the hard-core rocker he is. They are the only people who belong in the room, but during every Blue Jay home game the place fills up with SkyDome people and an assortment of hangers-on who drift in to pick up on the vibes. People also drop by for a smoke, as the audio booth is one of the few unofficially designated smoking areas in the SkyDome (another being Paul Beeston's office, always redolent of his Monte Cristos).

"I've got to find the Alabama CD," Poulakis said as he riffled through his collection of thirteen hundred compact discs. While he searched, his face was hidden by a mane of thick black hair that fell to the shoulders of an old baseball jersey. "Here it is," he said, pulling the CD out from a tall shelf at the rear of his audio room. "It's not mine, it's Jimmy Key's. He lent it to me last year."

If SkyDome is Oz to traditional baseball's Kansas, then Nick Poulakis is the little wizard who rings the bells, blows the whistles and sends puffs of smoke shooting into the sky. He represents the modern generation of baseball fans—the MuchMusic rock and rollers who get hives when they hear "Take Me Out to the Ball Game" and other odes to schmaltz.

Martin kept dropping by the audio booth throughout the season, usually to escape the no-cheering-in-the-press-box crowd. There he could smack a high five, or cheer an Alomar fielding gem, or commiserate with the folks in the

JumboTron room next door, or simply enjoy the nuttiness of the moment. He always came away with another joke.

"Did you know Tony Fernandez thinks God's name is Andy?"

Pause.

"After he heard that song, 'Andy walks with me, Andy talks with me...'"

Groan.

The audio booth is not green grass and blue skies or "Casey at the Bat" territory. It is funk, rock and upbeat C&W territory. It is a cultural, generational phenomenon that slides by the Fogies of baseball, but explains much of the remarkable success of SkyDome. "This is a spaceship in here," Poulakis likes to say. His official position is Audio Programmer/ Operator, which is what it says on his business card, the top half of which is the shape of the SkyDome horizon. His other business card says Rocking Bird Entertainment Service, which is more like it.

Martin took to calling Poulakis "the DJ of the Dome," and the audio booth "the soul of the Dome." He knew it would get a predictable reaction from his Fogie friends, most of whom regarded Poulakis and his high jinks as the arch-enemy of everything pure and traditional about baseball. Poulakis is the one who triggers the glass-smashing sound effects for foul balls, the hokey "noise metre," the screams, the trumpeted cavalry *Charrrge!* and the one who gives the order that detonates the fireworks for Blue Jay home runs. The serious folk in the press box regard these activities with considerable disdain.

Throughout most games, Poulakis is connected by head-set to Myles Patterson, who works from a perch high over centre field—*high* over centre field, just beneath the roof when the roof is open. Patterson is known as "Bam Bam" for reasons that become obvious when he is at work at the SkyDome. Most people can't see him when he is at work, or they see him perhaps as a speck way up there above Devon White, above the massive and gaudy television screen that is

JumboTron. If Bam Bam were anywhere else equivalent in Toronto he would be standing on the roof of a thirty-one-storey building.

To see Bam Bam at work you need binoculars, but even then it is unlikely you would make out his moustache or his bulk: six feet four inches, 235 pounds, sheathed in faded jeans and a bulky sports shirt, with a satchel of equipment dangling from his right hip. In the satchel are small, round cardboard boxes containing Bam Bam's "airbursts." They are wrapped in clear plastic bags and look like miniature fruit cakes, each containing pellets the size of corn niblets that explode in red, yellow, green, orange, blue and what Bam Bam calls "strobe white." When the white pellets explode, they create a glittering, sparkling effect.

Earlier in the season, the big deal was blue. It is difficult to achieve blue in pyrotechnics, the art of fireworks. Even Bam Bam does not know how it works. "You'd have to ask a chemist why," he said. Bam Bam sets off his airbursts only for Blue Jays' home runs, and at the end of the game if the Blue Jays win, which meant there were many games in 1993 when he spent half an hour carefully assembling his explosives before the game, stood there through nine innings with a headset on looking down at Poulakis in the audio booth, his finger over the buttons of his "firing board," waiting for Poulakis's "Thar she goes!" or "Yes!" or some other Poulakism indicating a homer (he can be very inventive, as we shall see). In 1992, if the Blue Jays lost and also failed to hit a home run, Bam Bam could always count on the seventh-inning stretch and the rhythmical explosions that went: "Okay [Bam! Bam!]...Blue Jays [Bam! Bam!]...let's [Bam]...play [Bam!]...ball." (Bam! Bam!) Then the front office told him to knock it off. That meant that sometimes in 1993, Bam Bam went entire games without setting off a single airburst. Then he had to spend another half hour tearing it all down again, feeling like the frustrated general in *Dr. Strangelove* who never gets to show what his machines of war can do.

As for the music Poulakis plays, it actually is shut off in the press box, which means it can only be heard by the fifty thousand–plus fans.

And the players. Definitely the players. They take their music very seriously.

Before one game, Sean went down to the field for batting practice when Joe Carter was taking his pregame cuts. The music Poulakis was playing that afternoon had the bouncy calpyso "feeling hot-hot-hot" chorus made popular by Club Med commercials. "What is *this*?" Carter grunted, stepping out of the batting cage. He looked up at Poulakis in the audio booth high over home plate, then shouted, "This isn't Disneyland!"

Poulakis knows what the players want. They tell him. On the field window side of his cramped control booth is a metal rack with single-song cassettes in a vertical row, each with the name of a player in that night's starting lineup. The way manager Cito Gaston operates, Poulakis rarely has to shuffle his tapes around.

Some players are pickier than others. For the leadoff position, Devon White's exclusive property early in the 1993 season, Poulakis played anything with a heavy funk bass line. For number-two hitter Roberto Alomar, Poulakis picks one song at Alomar's request each season and plays it at the beginning of every at-bat from April through October. First it was "Guns in the Sky" by INXS. During the 1992 championship season it was "Too Legit To Quit," and in 1993 it was "Hip Hip Hooray" by the group Naughty by Nature.

Getting to the meat of the order, Paul Molitor likes anything by Bruce Springsteen, which for much of the first half of the season was "Better Days." Carter likes a mix of funk and hip-hop, and he is very picky, preparing his own selections for Poulakis. Two days earlier, Carter had hit his fifteenth home run, then singled in the winning run in the bottom of the twelfth to beat Boston 3–2 to complete a four-game sweep of the Red Sox.

"I knew he was going to do it," Poulakis said. During

morning batting practice, Poulakis played Carter's take right through, and Joe was appreciative. "When he hit that one out, Murray Eldon and I looked at each other and said 'See, see.'"

Poulakis chooses all John Olerud's music. Sometimes it's "Tall, Cool One," by Robert Plant, sometimes "I Can't Dance," by Genesis. He has also used the "feeling hot-hot-hot" song because of the punny "Olé, Olé" chorus. For the 1993 season Poulakis was using Joe Cocker's "Leave Your Hat On." Olerud wears his batting helmet when he is playing first base, even when he is being interviewed off the field. There was that life-threatening aneurism, to be sure, but Olerud also happens to be rather accident prone. Once he was standing too close to the batting-cage netting and got cranked by a foul tip, resulting in a great deal of unnecessary pain and blood. Another time the pitcher whirled, fired a pick-off throw to first, then watched in horror as the ball whistled by Olerud's head as the usually laconic first baseman succumbed to a fit of loquaciousness and was enjoying a conversation with gabby outfielder Kirby Puckett of the Minnesota Twins. Poulakis kept playing "Leave Your Hat On" all season, but Olerud and his wife, Kelly, did not pick up on the subtlety until late in the season when they heard the song at the annual Blue Jay picnic.

Next in the lineup, Tony Fernandez, who had been a challenge for Poulakis since he'd returned to the Blue Jays from the Mets. At first Fernandez did not request his own music, so Poulakis chose Bobby McFerrin's "Don't Worry, Be Happy." It elicited a broad grin from the often sour-faced shortstop, and for a time Fernandez was hitting at a wicked .350 clip. Then one day a mysterious request reached Poulakis, probably relayed from Fernandez himself: Stop playing "Don't Worry, Be Happy." Apparently Fernandez was getting seriously razzed by his teammates, so Poulakis switched to a song called "Freedom." Fernandez immediately fell into a slump and his average dropped below .300.

Getting into the act, Fernandez decided to take charge of

his own music. He sent Poulakis a tape of a bouncy Latin American number. It had a few seconds of instrumental music, then lyrics with a religious theme. Fernandez went on a tear, slapping doubles and triples and lifting his average back over .300. As the season wore on, Fernandez became as picky as Carter. There is time for only a few bars of music as the hitter walks to the plate, which meant that Fernandez could hear only the instrumental beginning. Before one game he relayed another message to Poulakis: Get to the lyrics. He had become convinced that the more words he heard, the better chance he had for extra-base hits. Poulakis, of course, obliged, and Fernandez went off on another doubles, triples tear.

"Don't mess with the karma of the music," Poulakis said.

He remembers a time when changing a song had disastrous results. That was when Dave Stieb complained before a game that he was sick of hearing his song, called "Cat Scratch Fever." A pitcher's music—starter or reliever—is played only once, when he first toes the rubber. Stieb wanted something new, so Poulakis picked a new song. Stieb injured himself soon after, young Juan Guzman emerged as the new ace of the staff and Stieb was never the same again. In the 1993 season, Stieb, long gone from the Blue Jays, was trying to work himself back to the majors. He didn't make it, and midway through the season he finally was flushed right out of professional baseball.

As the Yankees prepared for batting practice, Poulakis flipped through his CDs to find suitable music for the opposition. Nothing too upbeat. Let's see...oh, here, yes—"Autumn in New York," Frank Sinatra. Good. And, hmmm—how about "If You Could Read My Mind," Gordon Lightfoot? Uh-huh. That'll do 'er. *Just like a paperback novel....* Oh, yeah, try to crank one over the infield to that.

Poulakis gained a measure of international notoriety during the 1992 American League Championship Series when the Athletics came to SkyDome and he played classical music, interspersed with tinkling dollops of Hagood Hardy, to put the Oakland hitters to sleep during their batting practice. An Associated Press writer caught on to what was happening and wrote a story that was picked up by newspapers across the United States. It brought phone calls from across the continent, from the local paper in Butte, Montana, from *The Village Voice* in New York.

For a series between the Minnesota Twins and the Blue Jays in May, Poulakis played selections from a CD called "Bugs Bunny on Broadway" during the Twins' BP. Puzzled Twins batters listened to the maddening cacophony of Bugs Bunny singing "Figaro" from a track called "The Rabbit of Seville." And there were sounds of applause and kettledrums, and noises that sounded like plastic plates falling on a hard floor, like a tape rewinding at high speed. The Blue Jays outscored Minnesota by a total of 20–3, sweeping the three-game series.

It was Poulakis who first came up with the idea of playing rock music during player introductions. In his twenties he had worked at a series of jobs, including shipping/receiving clerk at Etobicoke General Hospital (where he made videos of surgical procedures), the assembly line at Chrysler and cameraman for YTV. Poulakis fell in love with the SkyDome after paying $125 to sit in 500 Level for the lid-lifter in 1989. He came to love the place so much that in 1991 he married his second wife outside Gate 11 before an Argo game.

Between the first and second Blue Jay games at SkyDome, Poulakis got a call from an acquaintance who had the job he has now in the control booth. He was offered a job in which his single task was to carry a microphone out to the field for the singing of the national anthems.

"It was great," he recalled. "I got paid for a six-hour shift for doing fifteen minutes of work. Then I got restless and suggested they start playing music for the players. Before that I felt the introductions just weren't personal enough."

Occasionally Poulakis gets complaints from the players over his selections. In 1992, when now-departed infielder Jeff Kent was slumping, he found the Superman theme song played before each strikeout increasingly grating. When Kent told him to knock it off, Poulakis changed it to a song called "Don't Bother Me When I'm Working."

At every home game the fans are different, as the audiences at any play, musical or concert are different. There is no explaining it. Some nights the crowd wants to cheer and needs little assistance from Poulakis or anyone else. Other nights they are as sombre as shareholders at an annual meeting. Some nights they arrive quiet and leave exuberant; other nights they arrive exuberant and leave quiet.

"I just want to add some colour to the game, some zip," Poulakis said. "Baseball's a square game. And we don't have the folklore they have at Yankee Stadium. If the worst they can say when they leave is that the music was too loud, that's good, as long as they've been entertained. That's my job, to entertain them. And myself."

As much fun as Poulakis was having in the new season, from a strictly aesthetic standpoint he did not like the 1993 edition of the Blue Jays as much as previous teams. "It's all rap and country music now. They traded away all the rockers. Metal maniacs like Gruber and Stieb and MacDonald and Wells are all history." As with the boys in the gounds crew, Wells's name brought a smile to Poulakis's face. "He used to ask for 'Born to Be Wild' all the time. One day we were standing by the dugout talking about music and he said, 'Nick, if you can come up with a better theme song, let me know.' Then a light went off in Wells's head. 'I got it!' he said. He wanted Alice Cooper's 'No More Mr. Nice Guy.'"

The keyboard Poulakis uses during the game has a template indicating what keys produce the desired effects. For the Yankee games in June, some of the tried and true effects were written in pen by the keys:

Car skid
Alarm
Ha Ha Ha
Bugle
Nowhere to Run

Glass

Rock You

There are many others, of course. The template is always being updated as new effects are created and old ones are discarded. Poulakis was considering a chicken squawk as a new gimmick for foul balls, one that would be co-ordinated with the JumboTron, which would show a parade of chickens marking in single file across the JumboTron screen with the printout: Fowl...Fowl...Fowl.... Poulakis thought it was hilarious. Most everyone else thought it was, well, sort of okay.

The JumboTron room is next door to the audio booth, separated by a glass partition with sliding windows. The JumboTron room is much more serious, with more workers doing more things on more machines. There is a sense of self-importance about the JumboTron crowd. There is an intercom connection, so the two rooms can communicate with each other, but the JumboTron room is not as much fun as the audio room. It is perhaps significant that JumboTron uses two capitalized letters in the same word, like SkyDome itself, while the audio booth is just that—a booth. It is small and funky and light on its feet. It is hard to be light on your feet with all the equipment in the JumboTron room.

Everyone in the JumboTron room knows their job and performs their interrelated tasks with a minimum of instruction. Dan McPhee, JumboTron's technical producer, is a bright, imaginative fellow, can have as much fun as the next guy, but he often seems burdened with a terrible responsibility overseeing the mammoth JumboTron screen so conspicuously dominant above centre field. "Coverage of baseball is very routine," McPhee said. "It's not that the producers have no imagination. The nature of the game lends itself to routine."

This was borne out during a football game at the SkyDome—Winnipeg Blue Bombers versus Toronto Argonauts—when Martin attended with the roof opened to a bright, crisp, September afternoon. It was a journey to the past for Martin, a chance to see his once-beloved blue-and-gold Blue Bombers, and the quaint excitement of the Canadian Football League. In the second half he wandered from the football press box to the audio booth to say hello to Poulakis who was working the football game. It was a different Poulakis at work this time, not nearly the laid-back, inventive trickster he had known at baseball games. Maybe he was having a bad day, but more likely it was the frenetic pace of football that frazzled Poulakis. There were no convenient breaks between innings, no predictable processions to the plate by the hitters, no opportunities to do his favourite set pieces (apart from a looooow foghorn noise to elicit the "Argoooooos" chant from the crowd). Whatever it was, Poulakis did not seem to be having as much fun as he usually does.

The closest McPhee gets to crisis management is when one of the 67,200 "Trini-Lites," each containing two "Pixels" with the primary colours of blue, green and red, goes out. Each Pixel is about the size of a deck of cards and when they burn out a white spot appears on the 110-by-33-foot screen—a twelfth of an acre, big enough for an average-sized house with a backyard swimming pool—and McPhee has to walk halfway around the stadium to the back of JumboTron above centre field. Behind the screen are powerful fans blowing toward the field to keep the JumboTron cool. The worry is, if JumboTron overheats, JumboTron may explode. To get behind the JumboTron, McPhee has to navigate five levels of catwalks and enough wires and cramped corridors to make it look like a scene from *Alien*. He cannot see the white spot from behind the screen. He has to guess where it is, and test the screen one Pixel at a time, while getting instructions on his headset from the people back at the control centre. "No, Dan, not quite, a few inches to the left, please."

Each Trini-Lite costs about $100, meaning that replacing all the bulbs would cost nearly $7 million. But JumboTron is a big moneymaker for SkyDome. A full-package corporate sponsorship, which includes a forty-five-second spot for each game or event and a rotation among the still ads shown in the corner during at-bats, goes for $250,000 year.

When JumboTron was built by Sony of Japan, at a cost of $17 million, it was the biggest video screen in the world. It has since been nudged into second place by an even bigger Sony screen in Japan, but SkyDome's JumboTron still dwarfs any similar screen in the major leagues. The screen in Miami's Joe Robbie Stadium measures 36 feet by 27 feet, one in Anaheim Stadium measures 35 feet by 26 feet and the screen in San Francisco's Candlestick Park is a mere 32 feet by 24 feet.

It has taken on a life of its own. SkyDome attracted a near-capacity crowd for the sixth and final game of the 1992 World Series, beamed in from Atlanta. It was eerie—a packed stadium, nobody on the field, but all heads turned toward the mammoth screen beyond and above the outfield fence. David Garrick, SkyDome's vice-president of corporate affairs, expected a crowd of about 15,000 and was staggered when the final tally showed 45,501.

Early in the 1993 baseball season, JumboTron carried the NHL playoff game between Toronto Maple Leafs and Los Angeles Kings, which attracted 17,000 hockey fans. When the series went to a seventh game, another 30,000 fans trekked into SkyDome to watch it on JumboTron, nearly twice as many as watched the game at Maple Leaf Gardens.

JumboTron also carried the final episode of the popular television program "Cheers," which attracted 33,000 viewers to SkyDome. This prompted Garrick to try for a JumboTron première of the movie *A League of Their Own*, but he was not able to close the deal. Unfazed, in early 1993 Garrick was planning to use JumboTron for Hollywood premières and monster bingo games.

There are five on-field cameras: third base, first base, above home plate, behind centre field, under the roof high above centre field. Needless to say, most baseball purists object to the JumboTron, regard even its name as vaguely menacing. But since the first full-scale video screen was unveiled at Dodger Stadium more than a decade ago, only the Chicago

Cubs, Detroit Tigers and Cleveland Indians had not joined the video age in 1993.

Judging by the hysterical response from just about everyone within seconds of being spotted on JumboTron, it is a great hit with Toronto fans. No doubt a substantial portion of the fifty thousand–plus baseball fans go to SkyDome to see themselves on television, bathing for a few seconds in their Andy Warhol fame. Why otherwise civilized people choose the one moment when they are being seen by more people than at any other time in their lives to behave like jackasses is a mystery of the television age. When one of the cameras isolates a patch of crowd, they jump up and holler and wave, as if trying to flag a search-and-rescue plane.

Being in the control room with McPhee, watching the five cameras in constant motion picking out fans at random during breaks in play, feels Orwellian. The ability to shoot extreme close-ups of any one of fifty thousand people conveys immense technological power. The slightest mistake, the most innocent deviation is magnified a thousand times on JumboTron. You must be very careful. There are men in the crowd with their mistresses, women in the crowd with their lovers, executives at a Wednesday get-away afternoon game who are supposed to be attending a sales conference. Any shot of otherwise harmless cleavage caught by one of the five JumboTron cameras looks Brobdingnagian on the huge screen.

Any randy moments?

McPhee said no.

"But once we shot a guy talking into his cell phone and he ducked for cover the second he saw himself. We'll never know what he was up to."

And that's just stuff on the periphery; there are the umpires to consider, and the tall foreheads of Major League Baseball. Major League Baseball, that formless and powerful entity—like God and Mammon—has decreed that no moving images must appear on JumboTron while the batter is in the batter's box. Major League Baseball also prohibits close calls on replays. No balls and strikes, either, a right the umpires won during a labour dispute in the early 1980s. Fans are allowed to see the beginnings of a play on replay, but not the end, and McPhee does not want the fans to know the play is being censored.

"There is a very valid reason for not showing replays," he explained. "In other sports replays can be forgotten, but in baseball there is an awful lot of time between plays, a lot of time to question whether the umpire made the right call. It's not really a safety issue. What it does, it creates tension between the umpires, the players and between the two teams that may affect the outcome of the game."

McPhee runs a tight, efficient ship. His JumboTron cameras delicately avoid any of the windows of the SkyDome Hotel, for fear of capturing a lurid moment such as the one that happened in 1989 when a couple undressed and made out in full view of a packed house. Sometimes they'll show a snippet of a pillow fight in one of the hotel rooms, but only after much deliberation, and only very briefly. (Lord knows who might walk out of the bathroom from a shower.) He has avoided any horrendous goofs, which is an accomplishment in itself in the new age of Monster Video. "It's a pretty well oiled machine in here," he said. "A lot of the communication is non-verbal. Like a football team after the snap, everyone knows what they have to do."

One night Jack Morris was getting bombed, a regular occurrence in 1993, and after three consecutive hits one of the JumboTron cameras switched to the bullpen. As if on cue, Mark Eichhorn started to limber up. Two batters later Morris was gone, and another camera panned the dugout to catch a glimpse of Morris as he whipped his jacket off the bench and stomped off to the showers. While Eichhorn warmed up on the mound, a bored cameraman aimed into the sky above the open dome and found the underbelly of an airplane directly overhead. Adjusting the lens, he focused on the electronic advertisement for a local strip club: Filmores…Girls… Girls…Girls….

Uh-oh, switch to camera one.

In the audio booth, on a wall above the sound effects organ, there is a picture of Anne Murray with a diagonal red slash across the singer's smiling face. "We are in an Anne Murray–free zone," Poulakis explains.

The thing is, Murray Eldon likes Anne Murray, likes her a lot. He met her in the early 1970s when her song "Snowbird" appeared and rose to the top of the charts in North America. He met her again when she sang the national anthem in the snow at the Blue Jays' first home opener in 1977. He still gets the warm fuzzies when he meets her, and never knows what to say. "I always do the fan thing and say, 'You're so great.'"

Eldon has been doing broadcast work of one form or another, primarily radio, since graduating from high school in Midland, Ontario, in 1966. Married with two sons, Eldon has missed only two home games since he started announcing regularly in 1978. He estimates he has talked to forty million fans at Blue Jay games.

As one might expect, there is a cultural divide between Poulakis and Eldon. Eldon is forty-six years old, only thirteen years older than Poulakis, but they seem a generation apart. Poulakis is the long-haired rocker in jeans and sweatshirts. Eldon is the slacks, tie, buttoned-down, leisurewear man. Toward the end of a game, Eldon sometimes loosens his tie.

"I always ask for Anne Murray but he never plays her," Eldon says as Woody Williams relieves Al Leiter in the eighth with two outs and two runners on. Eldon can continue a conversation in the audio booth until the split second before announcing the next batter. Williams strikes out the next hitter, end of inning.

"Maybe he'll play something by Anne on my birthday in July," Eldon muses aloud as the teams exchange places on the field below.

"Against Kansas City?" Poulakis says without taking his eyes off the field. "On a Friday night? That would make for a real fun evening."

"He always knocks Anne Murray, but the only reason

she's not played anymore is because she was overplayed in the past because of the thirty percent Canadian content regulation," Eldon says.

"That's not why," Poulakis says. "I don't play her because she sucks. But I play her sometimes."

"Not enough," says Eldon, his voice capturing a perfect mock whine.

"There just aren't enough Sundays in the year."

From the rear of the audio booth someone refuses to let the Anne Murray discussion die. "I hear she bowls overhand," the voice says. Eldon nearly breaks up as he leans toward his microphone to introduce the first Yankee batter in the top of the ninth.

The one moment Eldon will always be remembered for is his announcement to the fans prior to Game Three of the 1992 World Series at SkyDome. That was after the infamous upside-down-flag incident before Game Two in Atlanta, when a member of the U.S. Marine Corps carried an inverted flag onto the field for the playing of the Canadian anthem. Major League Baseball issued an apology to Canada early in the game, but photos of the flag were displayed prominently in Toronto newspapers the next day. By the time Game Three was gearing up, hawkers outside SkyDome were selling miniature upside-down American flags and T-shirts wih an inverted flag and the slogan Sorry, Eh.

There had already been some embarrassing jingoism in Atlanta when a local paper there ran a front page headline before the opening game of the series that said This Is Our Game. Now, with the flag furore, the off-field shenanigans were threatening to focus attention away from the memorable baseball being played on the field.

Between the second and third games, the public relation wings of Major League Baseball and the U.S. Marine Corps got together to draft a pregame strategy. They agreed that the incident was too serious and potentially explosive to ignore. The prospect of Canadian fans booing the American anthem in front of 100 million American viewers gave the people at

CBS the shakes.

So, before the singing of the anthems, Eldon took over for a few minutes, told the crowd what they already knew about what had happened in Game Two, then quickly defused the situation by announcing, "To show their respect for the Canadian people, the Marine Corps has requested the privilege of again carrying the national flag of Canada and has requested that the Stars and Stripes by carried by the Royal Canadian Mounted Police. The Toronto Blue Jays ball club and its players request your courtesy, and ask everyone to join in honouring these two great nations, by standing together for the singing of both anthems."

It worked. The announcement had been carefully worded by Major League Baseball and the Marine Corps, so carefully that writer John Feinstein, in his book *Play Ball*, an overview of the 1992 season, singled out the word *privilege* for special praise in his analysis of Eldon's address. For a man whose job is to be familiar yet anonymous, it was a heady experience for Murray Eldon to be for a brief and shining moment the focus of the North American sporting community.

"It wasn't so much what was said, just that it was an apology, from baseball to the fans," he said. "The marines, the Braves, even George Bush had apologized, but that's not what the fans were looking for. We had no idea what the reaction from the fans would be but something had to be done. I would have hated for it to be known as the upside-down-flag World Series. Thankfully it worked, and we were able to get back to baseball."

Perhaps because of his higher profile in the World Series, on Hallowe'en a few days later, kids were knocking on his door, asking him if he could do a "Robertoooo Alomar" or Eldon's wonderful "Devoooon White" (the surname enunciated as a breathless gasp).

"Maybe I should do an album," Eldon says as Duane Ward starts mowing down the Yankees in the top of the ninth. He allows a few seconds to pass, then says to Poulakis, "Sorry, I meant to say *compact disc*. Album is passé. I would never be passé." Eldon winks at Poulakis. Poulakis rolls his eyes.

"I'll bet he won't mention his embarrassing correction," Poulakis says. Eldon looks across, wondering what's coming, expecting the worst. "You remember, that time you said [Poulakis does a fair imitation of the Eldon voice], 'Ladies and gentlemen, the Blue Jays would like to welcome you to Don's Boner Clinic.' Then you had to make that correction, you had to say 'blood donor clinic....'"

Ward retires the side, for his nineteenth save. The Blue Jays win 5–4, their seventh consecutive win, which puts them a game away from first place. Poulakis signals to Bam Bam high in the rafters of SkyDome to ignite the game-winning fireworks.

Eldon has switched off his mike. There is a newcomer in the audio booth and Eldon can't resist. "People don't appreciate just how important my job is up here," he says. He then pauses, lights a cigarette. "If it wasn't for me, it would be chaos down there. The batters would all come to the plate at the same time."

= 11 =
Chatter

Ride the bush-league buses with the Reading Phillies or the Spokane Brewers or the Chattanooga Lookouts, and suddenly it is easy to understand why a major league dugout is a place of such addictive conversational pleasures. In the world of the minor leaguer, which is split between short hours of athletic adventure and long hours of idleness, talk becomes a staple of sanity; the man who does not have a way with a yarn, a joke, a tale of pathos, or an epigram drawn from his own experience is condemned to be an outsider.

This rich verbal tradition...[t]his passion for language and the telling detail is what makes baseball the writer's game.

—Thomas Boswell, *How Life Imitates the World Series*

In the third inning of a game at the SkyDome, we slipped a note to Louis Cauz, the official scorer that evening. The note read, "Do you know of any major-league teams with six players who scored 100 or more runs in the same season?"

When he is scoring a Blue Jay game, Cauz sits in the front row of the press box in front of a microphone, with guides and scribblers and the official scoresheet in front of him. During the game he decides if a hit is a hit, an error an error, a passed ball a passed ball, then he tells the rest of the press box, then Cauz's decision is flashed on the JumboTron above centre field. The job carries enormous responsibility, and pays $75 U.S. a game. Cauz's scorecard goes to Major League Baseball in New York after the game and, after a twenty-four-hour period of grace during which the official scorer can change any of the rulings of the game just scored, it becomes part of baseball history, forever.

Cauz is an author and a former baseball writer for *The Globe and Mail*. He has been a student of baseball since he was in short pants, and during the 1993 season he became our court of last resort (along with the Elias Bureau in New York, if we needed a second opinion). His home in west-end Toronto has shelves crowded with baseball books. He uses different coloured scribblers for notes of all Blue Jay games, so by the end of each game his scorecard looks like it has been annotated by Jackson Pollock.

In the sixth inning, during a pitching change when he slipped back to the lounge for a hot dog, Cauz got back to us, as we knew he would. "That's impossible," he said, meaning six players on the same team scoring a hundred or more runs in the same season.

We knew that wouldn't be the end of it, either. Sure enough, next morning a remorseful Cauz called Martin to say that not only is it possible, that it has been done. Six players on the 1931 Yankees scored 100 runs or more: Lou Gehrig (163), Babe Ruth (149), Ben Chapman (120), Earle Coombs (120), Joe Sewell (102) and Lyn Lary (100). We wanted to know because at the time it seemed a possibility that the 1993 Blue Jays might duplicate the feat of 1931. Up to the game Cauz was scoring that evening, the Blue Jays had five players who had scored at least 100 runs: Paul Molitor (114), Devon White (112), Rickey Henderson (112), Roberto Alomar (105) and John Olerud (100). A sixth, Joe Carter, had 85 runs scored with only two weeks left.

During the 1993 season, some of us gathered at Cauz's home for morning "chatter sessions" over coffee and muffins. Besides Cauz and the O'Malleys, the other regulars were Trent Frayne, the writer, and Brian Williams, the announcer.

Part of Cauz's work was to prepare Williams for his CBC telecasts with Tommy Hutton.

There was no keener student of baseball this summer than Williams. He began training for his baseball telecasts in spring training in Florida. One evening early in the season we noticed him sitting off by himself at the end of the press box, watching the game on the field and on a monitor over his head. We had seen him doing this in spring training. This time, thinking he might like some company, Martin walked over and sat beside him, only to discover he was calling the game, his left hand cupped over one ear, rehearsing. "Alomar to his left...it's 4–3...the Indians go down one, two, three...."

Williams had the curiosity of a cat, the energy of a cub reporter, but he is ebulliently, shamelessly profligate with his information. One night he gave us some fascinating stuff on Rob Butler's father, who happens to be from a place called Butlerville, Newfoundland. He had even dragged us from the batting cage and introduced us to Butler's father, who was sitting in the stands behind the Blue Jay dugout. The only problem—Williams did the same for the *Star*, the *Sun*, 13 radio reporters, 15 out-of-town columnists and 27 small-town papers from Brampton to Owen Sound. He can't shut up. So much for the exclusive.

Over dinner in the lounge behind the press box that evening, we shared a table with Frayne, one of Canada's top sports writers. He is a neighbour of Cauz, married to writer June Callwood. They are a remarkable couple, with so much newspaper ink in their veins that when they both worked for *The Globe and Mail* they chose the newsroom for their wedding reception. Cauz was talking about a game at the SkyDome the year before that was interrupted by an invasion of mating gnats engaged in a breeding frenzy in the warm, humid night air. The game had to be interrupted to close the roof, to halt the invasion and perhaps dampen the ardour of the gnats. Cauz was the official scorer that night, so in his game report to Major League Baseball he would have to include a reason for the game being interrupted.

"Fucking gnats," Frayne suggested.

Cauz said, oh sure, but he would also have to explain to Major League Baseball how the game was able to resume.

"The gnats fucked off," Frayne said.

Such was the weighty tone of our "chatter sessions," which continued over two days in Cauz's dining room, with a tape recorder plunked down beside the blueberry muffins and coffee pot.

SEAN: The first time I clued in to baseball I was in the fifth grade, ten years old. Our teacher, Mrs. Webb, was retiring that year. She was a big Red Sox fan. That was '75, the Cincinnati/Boston World Series. We were all Cincinnati fans, if we were fans at all, I don't know why, and over the course of the seven-game series she converted the entire class to the Red Sox. I still remember the day after Game Six. We were too young to see the end of the game in the twelfth inning. We came into class in the morning and she had this clothesline drawn in chalk on the black-board with a little red sock hanging on it and the words We Won! in big letters.

TRENT: Was that the Fisk home run?

SEAN: That was the Fisk home run.

TRENT: Jeez, I *covered* that game! There you are, in grade five!

MARTIN: I used to like the Pittsburgh Pirates, when they were always in last place but they had Ralph Kiner going for sixty home runs. Then they won it all in 1960, the Mazeroski home run. That's when my interest peaked, dropped right off. It was the end of my love affair with the Pirates.

TRENT: Really?

MARTIN: Is that Canadian, or what?

Interruption here as Cauz leads everyone down to the basement to show his collection of beer bottles and cans. They are on tables, shelves, bookcases—a lifetime collection of beer bottles, from all over the world. Some are still capped, their contents aging. Then it was upstairs, where Cauz produced a wrinkled copy of the scoresheet of a game he scored late in the 1992 season, when the Milwaukee Brewers defeated the Blue Jays 22–2. The Blue Jays used six pitchers, none of whom went four innings. What was of consuming interest to Cauz, however, was that the game tied an astonishing, little-known record in the American League. The Brewers scored in all but one inning, the fifth. In all the hundreds of thousands of games played in the American League since the turn of the century, no team has ever scored in all nine innings. This does not mean both teams scoring in every inning. In the 22–2 pasting of the Blue Jays, the Brewers scored in every inning but the fifth, and in that inning they had runners at first and third, which means they came within ninety feet of achieving what no American League team has ever done. (Let's say eighty-five feet, for the runner on third surely must have been leading off from third base.)

Back to the dining-room table for more muffins, a fresh pot of coffee and more chatter.

MARTIN: I was just in Montana with Fergie Jenkins. He told me about the time when Cal McLish taught him the slider one winter. Fergie was playing in Puerto Rico at the time. He struck out Roberto Clemente with his Cal McLish slider, and he couldn't wait for spring training because he knew now he was a major-leaguer. He felt he had a secret weapon. Then we won twenty, and twenty and twenty...

LOUIS: Do you know Cal McLish's full name? It's Calvin Coolidge Julius Caesar Tuskahoma McLish. His nickname was Buster.

TRENT: I remember being baffled when Jenkins was

with the Red Sox, in the dressing room. I asked
him what was his secret with the Cubs, winning all those games in that little bandbox. And
he said, "I throw strikes." I hadn't the faintest
idea what the hell he was talking about. Throw
strikes? Hell, don't they all throw strikes? I went
for years wondering what the hell he meant.

LOUIS: He had the lowest ratio of walks to strikeouts of
anyone in baseball.

TRENT: He threw strikes!

BRIAN: What's he like today? Is he happy? (Jenkins's
live-in girlfriend had committed suicide the
previous winter, taking his three-year-old
daughter's life, as well. Before that, Jenkins's
wife died from injuries in a card accident.)

MARTIN: He's got another woman, an ex-Las Vegas
dancer. She brought along her mother to dinner on their first date. Now she's living at the
ranch. He's working as a roving pitching scout
for the Reds.

BRIAN: He's one of our great sports stories.

LOUIS: There aren't too many Canadians on the horizon to make the Hall of Fame.

BRIAN: Do you know what position has the fewest
members in the Hall of Fame? Third base.
Only five: Eddie Mathews, Brooks Robinson,
Pie Traynor...

LOUIS: Talking about third basemen, Kelly Gruber
lived just four doors down from me.

BRIAN: Here's something I used on the air last Friday
night. Whitey Herzog (manager of the
California Angels, the team Toronto traded
Gruber to after the 1992 season) came to the
broadcast booth and I asked him, "Where's
Gruber?" He said, "You tell me." And then he
said, "That boy is never going to play baseball
again."

200

SEAN: Did you see the press conference he gave when he came back to Toronto for the first time this year?

BRIAN: That's as close to a walking nervous breakdown as I've ever seen. He had his son sitting on his lap the whole time.

SEAN: I talked to Steve Karsay last night. (The Blue Jays' ace minor-league prospect who was traded for Rickey Henderson late in the season.)

BRIAN: What's he like?

SEAN: Your basic twenty-one-year-old kid out of Queens, New York. He doesn't have a real thick Queens accent. It seems the younger the player, the more prone they are to clichés. He's very polite, but he spoke in *Bull Durham* lingo.

BRIAN: Let's be honest. If a football player—I don't care how stupid he is, I don't care if he goes to Texas A&M and majors in basket-weaving—at least he's around people who can write and complete sentences. And if they go to Notre Dame or Michigan, they're going to have to study. These kids in baseball have been out of school since they were seventeen or eighteen, riding the buses in Alabama and Arkansas.

SEAN: We think of baseball as naturally the more intellectual, intelligent sport....

LOUIS: Dick Beddoes and I used to go up to this Chinese place at two o'clock in the morning when we were at *The Globe and Mail*, and we were talking about the same thing. He said the most intelligent group of athletes were the wrestlers. He loved chatting with wrestlers. Gene Kiniski would always be eating at this place and he'd have Kiniski over to the table chatting. Baseball players read far too many newspapers. They get all the clichés out of there. But of all the athletes I've been around,

201

baseball players have the greatest sense of humour. I'm talking abut the minor-league days when I used to hang around the old Toronto Maple Leafs, riding the buses with them. One time at the Maple Leaf ballpark, they had eight hundred, nine hundred people, and Jimmy Gosger, an outfielder who went on to play with Boston, was looking at the stands and said a fat lady got stuck in the turnstiles and the people couldn't get into the ballpark.

BRIAN: They spend more time together than any other athlete. A football player plays only on Sundays, only 16 games. He's in his home every week. They never stay on the road for a full week. In hockey, they don't go on extended road trips like baseball teams, and they only play 80 games. Same in basketball. In baseball it's 162 games. The game lends itself to sitting around telling stories.

SEAN: I read the most wonderful baseball story in Kevin Kerrane's book on scouting, *Dollar Sign on the Muscle*. He actually borrowed it from Roger Angell. This scout Ellis Clary is in Live Oak, Florida, to look at this high school hitter, and he can't find anybody to pitch batting practice to him. Then this tenth-grader walks by, a total stranger, and he asks him to pitch. The kid did not even play on his school team but Clary was more impressed with his pitching than he was with the hitter he went there to scout in the first place. A few years later he goes back to Live Oak to see the pitcher again, and he still wasn't playing organized ball. He hadn't thrown a pitch since he threw batting practice the last time. Clary asks him if he knows anyone who can catch him and he brings a friend from the high school team, but the kid throws so hard that his friend can't catch the ball. Then just for fun, Clary asks them to switch and the catcher throws so hard that the other kid can't catch *him*. Clary signed both of them as pitchers and they both make it to the majors. The guy who had just walked in off the street the first day was Ray Corbin. He pitched for the Minnesota Twins for five years. Then Clary tells Angell, "He's still be there but he hurt his arm. Good ballplayer. But if he'da been a guy like Sandy Koufax, that'd be a hell of a story, wouldn't it?"

LOUIS: Clary is still a scout, with the Blue Jays, in Valdosta, Georgia. Great sense of humour.

BRIAN: Do other hockey people sit around and do this? This is almost hot-stove-ish. Baseball lends itself to this sort of discussion.

LOUIS: Look at that shelf there [pointing to a wall of books in his dining room]. There's nothing but baseball books there, and that's only one of my libraries.

MARTIN: Of all the professional team sports, there's a much higher proportion of women fans in baseball.

BRIAN: Because they've played it. My wife doesn't understand hockey because she's never played it, but she understands baseball because she played on a women's softball team.

MARTIN: My mother once came to one of my games when I was playing juvenile baseball, and she arrived in the fifth inning of a 0–0 tie—I was pitching—and said, "Oh, good, I haven't missed anything."

SEAN: Is there anything in particular you want to focus on for your next broadcast?

LOUIS: Olerud's plummet is a story. [After flirting with the .400 mark for the first four months of the season, Olerud's average was now down to .374.]

203

BRIAN: Tommy Hutton said you can tell Olerud is tired because his doubles production is down. I want to know why.

SEAN: I'm noticing with Olerud that more managers are pinching in the right and left fielders, cutting off the gaps. They're giving him the lines.

LOUIS: Yep. A lot of his doubles went to left centre. They began moving the left fielder in the gap. Olerud was taking that little slice line drive to left centre and they were just pocketing it, easy. Olerud rarely pulls the ball. Rick Cerone is now an advance scout for the Yankees. He told Tom Cheek on the air, "I've spotted a few things with Olerud. I think we can stop him." The first game, Olerud goes 4-for-4.

SEAN: This would be an interesting trivia question. How many players have led the major leagues in spring training batting average and during the regular season in the same year?

LOUIS: How about this one. Name the only player to pinch-hit for Maris, Yastrzemski and Ted Williams? The key is the only man to ever pinch-hit for Ted Williams: Carroll Hardy—an outfielder. Williams figures the Red Sox had a game won and went into the dressing room and got undressed. Then the other team came back and tied it up, and it was Williams's time at bat. The manager sent out this kid Carroll Hardy. He did it for Maris in Cleveland before he went to New York and became a big star. I don't know the Yaz situation.

SEAN: How's this for something you never heard before: a quadruple play. I read about it in a collection of essays by Thomas Boswell. It almost happened in a Cuban League game about ten years ago. The bases are loaded, no outs, and there's a deep fly ball to centre field.

It's just like Devo's catch in the 1992 World Series—an incredible play. One out. The centre fielder throws to second before the runner gets back to the base. Two outs. Then the second baseman throws to first and gets *that* guy before he gets back to the bag. Triple play. But the runner on third had tagged up and scored before the last out at first. The opposing team appealed the play, saying he left the bag too soon. The appeal was denied, but if it had been successful, there would have been four legal outs and the run would not have counted. As it was, one team got a triple play and still gave up a run.

LOUIS: I never heard that one before.

=== 12 ===

Travels at SkyDome (3)

Years ago, when they were building the CN Tower, that tall whachamacallit beside the SkyDome, David Garrick was standing on the space deck when he watched in horror as a long piece of plywood blew off from the tallest part of the tallest freestanding building in the world and sailed down, down, down in a rocking to-and-fro motion to the city below. To Garrick's immense relief—that was when he was president of the CN Tower—the plywood landed on King Street West, on the streetcar tracks in front of the Royal Alexandra Theatre. "That's when I thought, there is a God," Garrick remembered. Then he watched as a station wagon stopped and the driver got out, picked up the plywood, walked around the rear of the vehicle, pushed the plywood in the window and drove off. "Maybe he thought there was a God, too," Garrick said. "Maybe he was a carpenter."

Garrick told the story as we stood in one of the SkyBoxes at the SkyDome, watching Frank Grespan's conversion crew prepare the floor of the SkyDome for a rock concert. It was early in September, and the Blue Jays were playing in California. Some of Grespan's workers were on the floor of the SkyDome, on their hands and knees, unzipping strips of artificial turf. Others were grinding the football grid lines

206

from the field. Much of the floor already was reduced to bare concrete; only the south end remained that bright ersatz green. Other workers were lowering the large rack of metal scaffolding that hangs high above what is centre field for baseball. The scaffolding would be rolled over toward second base, then raised up again over where the concert stage would be.

Garrick had long since left the CN Tower to take up duties as SkyDome's vice-president of corporate affairs, which makes him SkyDome's number-one flack. He was on a roll. "We're going to beat Madison Square Garden this year," he said. "We expect to hold 245 events at SkyDome this year. We'll be the most-used box office attraction in North America." He meant biggest attraction, not biggest gross. "Other places gross more than us because they have more seats. This year, the Colorado Rockies will beat us because they have more seats. Their stadium has eighty thousand seats. It took us nineteen games to hit a million. Colorado did it in seventeen games. They'll probably beat our record season attendance this year."

Garrick is a SkyDome official, not a Blue Jay official, though he appreciates that the Blue Jays are his best customers. The Blue Jays signed a twenty-year contract with SkyDome in 1989, but Garrick would not reveal the terms or the annual rent, saying it is not public information. All he could admit to was, yes, compared with most other major-league teams, the Blue Jays pay a whomping-high fee to play baseball at the SkyDome. Nearly a third of baseball's major-league teams own the stadiums they play in, which means they don't pay any rent at all. Most of the other two-thirds have sweet deals with the cities that own the stadiums.

"Take Cleveland," Garrick said. "They're drawing about eight thousand a game, and paying 5 to 6 percent in rent. We're drawing fifty thousand, and paying the same percentage...." Garrick stopped here, and abruptly cranked his public relations transmission into reverse. "Those aren't the right figures," he said, "because we don't give that out." Got that? Okay. He continued, "On paper, they're paying us really good

207

rent, but one of the reasons they're able to pay us a really good rent is because they've got a really good facility. There's never a rainout, and that's important for fans coming from outside of Toronto. The SkyDome's attendance breaks down to a third, a third and a third—a third from Metro Toronto, a third from fifty miles away, a third from beyond fifty miles. So if you're from Rochester and planning to come to Toronto for the weekend, you've no hesitation buying tickets for Friday night, Saturday and Sunday. You know there won't be any rainouts."

Got that? Okay.

"We work well together," Garrick said. "We do all the preparations to get the field ready, except for the bases and the dirt. The Blue Jays do the bases and the dirt at home plate and the mound." The texture of dirt varies. It is firm, almost hard, on the mound. The dirt at home plate is softer, so the batters can wedge themselves in comfortably. The softest dirt is around the bases, where runners are cushioned when they slide into the bags. "It used to take the conversion crew forty-eight hours to complete its job," Garrick said. "Now they've got it down to nine, ten hours."

We were in one of the SkyBoxes on 300 Level, the same level that contains the baseball and football press boxes. There are 161 SkyBoxes, some of which are double-sized. The out-field boxes lease for $100,000 a year, the ones beyond first base and third base go for $150,000, and the SkyBoxes behind home plate from home to first and home to third go for $225,000. They all have ten open seats in front, inside the sta-dium, with the box itself behind sliding glass doors. The SkyBox we were in had a microwave oven, stand-up bar, couches and chairs, paintings on the walls, a dishwasher, an ice machine and a washroom. The corporations and individuals who lease the boxes must buy sixteen tickets for every Blue Jay home game, which adds another $25,000 a year. For events other than baseball, the occupants need only buy one ticket, and they can sublet their boxes to other people. No one is allowed to stay in the boxes overnight. Guards patrolling the SkyDome discreetly check the SkyBoxes late in the evening to make sure no one is bedding down for the night.

"In the summer, business people make deals on the golf course during the day and in the boxes at night," Garrick said. Paul Godfrey, *Toronto Sun* president and chief executive officer, the man more responsible than anyone else for bringing major league baseball to Toronto in 1977, agreed with Garrick's comment, though he said business shoptalk during a game was more "foreplay" than consummation. Nevertheless, as a means of rubbing shoulders with Toronto's corporate élite, the boxes are hard to beat. As Godfrey said, "The banks are here. The insurance companies. The oil companies. We're not talking small money."

The *Sun* got its box because it was part of the thirty-company consortium that "donated" $5 million each to the building of the SkyDome. Each consortium member received a box for its "generosity." As for the box holders not in the consortium, Godfrey speculates that many have come to regret signing ten-year leases in 1989 that included the tenth year's payment up front, an amount that would be forfeited if the company opted out. "A lot of companies leased these boxes when times were good in the late eighties. I would venture to guess that many of them would not do it again in the nineties. How do they get their money's worth? I don't think they do. As a business decision, I don't think there's a logical return. Take $225,000 plus sixteen tickets a game plus the cost of catering, divide it by eighty-one, and that is a very expensive way of entertaining." Okay, here goes: If each of the minimum sixteen people consumes $20 worth of food and drink, plus the cost of the box itself, it works out to about $3,500 for each home game, give or take a tip and bag of peanuts. And this does not include furniture and decor, which SkyBox occupants must provide themselves. All they get are three bare walls and sliding glass doors. Godfrey said the *Sun* spent at least $60,000 furnishing and decorating its box.

It is also not the best place to watch a baseball game. There are too many distractions. And ice cubes rattling in highball glasses do not make for baseball sounds. Godfrey's own sons prefer to sit in the stands. The Blue Jays provide a special SkyBox for officials with visiting teams, but most of them prefer to watch the game from seats behind the visitors' dugout. Peter Gzowski, the writer and host of CBC's "Morningside," after spending an evening watching the Blue Jays from the Imperial Oil SkyBox, was not impressed. The next morning he faxed a note to Martin to say, "Maybe it was the surroundings ("Can I get you another helping of the beef Wellington, Mr. Gzowski?"), but it sure wasn't a *baseball* experience."

Garrick led the way around the circular corridor of 300 Level, walking by large mounted photographs of various events held at the SkyDome. One of the blown-up colour photographs showed wrestler Hulk Hogan in midhowl, the featured performer in what was the biggest single event ever held at the SkyDome. The "Wrestlemania" of April 1, 1990, attracted 67,500 patrons to the SkyDome. Other events have included "Disney on Ice," when special ice-making facilities are installed; polo, when special earth is brought in to accommodate the polo ponies; as well as soccer, basketball, rib cook-offs, truck races, cricket and Madonna.

Suddenly, whoosh, down an elevator, and we were at 000 Level again. Garrick took us to Central Control, a serious, glassed-in cubicle in the basement that has the look and feel of a Star Trek base station. Garrick calls it "the hub of the SkyDome." Here attendants monitor video screens that allow them to scan nearly every inch of the SkyDome, day or night. At the time, there were thirty-seven cameras spread through the SkyDome, and they were planning on adding three more to bring the number of cameras to an even forty. Usually, two people in Central Control monitor the entire building, and on the overnight shift only one is needed. A separate bank of screens in a corner of the room monitors every elevator in the building, including SkyDome Hotel. The monitors are in colour, and they show whether the elevators are open or closed, which makes one instinctively look for a joystick, as if it were a giant Nintendo game.

Whoosh, back up to 300 Level, where Garrick entered The Founders Club, an elegant, dark-wooded eatery and drinkery named after the thirty members of the consortium formed to get SkyDome built. There are pictures of the consortium members on the walls, among them Arden Hayes of Imperial Oil and Douglas Creighton, formerly of the *Sun*. The Founders Club is on two levels, and anyone can join for $950 a year. There is a closed-circuit television, with Blue Jay games and other sporting events around the world shown on a pull-down screen. Occasionally, members are treated to lectures from visiting speakers, which have included Beeston and Gillick of the Blue Jays. The motif is art deco, softly lighted, and the washroom has two hammered-brass sinks, each worth $4,500. In the upstairs level there is a lounge and private dining room, capable of holding twenty people, with soft beige leather chairs, the leather imported from Italy. On the menu for that night was smoked Atlantic salmon ($9.50), corn chowder ($7.75), swordfish ($13.25), lobster ravioli ($16.95). A shipment of Cabernet Sauvignon from the Napa Valley, made by the obscure but highly rated Ridge Winery, was being unpacked for a special California evening scheduled for the weekend.

Garrick carried with him a heavy ring of keys, which he used to enter the SkyBoxes. He tried some of his keys on the door to the Blue Jays' box, number 337, but they did not work. The Blue Jays are on a different system from the rest of the SkyDome because they do not want unlimited access to their private digs, which might contain crucial info on the latest phenom they are preparing to deal for. (Late in 1992, when Martin found himself unaccredited for the World Series, he called Beeston and asked if he could watch the game from the Blue Jays' private box. Beeston said, "No." Pausing only for a breath, Beeston then told him, "Am I being equivocal?" Another pause, and Martin heard Beeston's hee-hee-hee naughty-boy laugh, but he did not relent.)

Walking clockwise along the 300 Level corridor, Garrick came to the roof control room. For such an important room, it is surprisingly small and cramped. For a one-thirty after-noon game, the roof control people arrive at ten-thirty in the morning; for a seven thirty-five evening start, they arrive at three-thirty. First order of business is to call the weather bureau to determine if any storms are moving in or, if the sky looks menacing, whether the bad stuff will bypass Toronto. Garrick prefers the roof open. "We'll get $2 more a person when the roof is open on a hot, sunny day than on a cold Friday night when the roof is closed," he said.

It is not just that people might buy an extra beer or Big Mac; operating with the roof open provides all sorts of economies, including the cost of lighting, heating and air-conditioning the place, all of which is controlled from the roof control room. When the roof is closed, and no game or batting practice on, minimum lighting is used, which gives the inside of the SkyDome a subdued, dawn or dusk effect. To prepare for action on the field, the lights are turned on slowly, so as to prevent a costly surge of electricity. "Hydro is our most expensive single cost, about $2 million a year," Garrick explained. "So we stagger the lights. There are 750 lights, and they're high-powered. Because we're charged by our peak demand, whatever day of the month we use our most power we pay that rate for the whole month. So we turn on a dozen, wait half an hour, then turn on another dozen. It's much cheaper to do gradually."

The official in charge of the roof control room is Scot Muncaster, who has been overseeing the opening and closing since the SkyDome opened. When the decision is made to open or close the roof, the call goes out to the "roof rats," a team of three workers whose job is to walk the rails to make sure nothing is obstructing the tracks, which could cause the "earthquake effect" Rod Robbie mentioned. To open or close the roof, the operator in charge must punch in a code to get the go-ahead from the computer, then it is a matter of punching the proper buttons, which are quarter-sized and in colours of amber, green and red. They control the three mov-ing panels.

"One thing to worry about is if one panel gets going faster than the others, which could cause twisting," Garrick said. "If this happens, even if it's only a couple of inches, the process stops automatically, then one panel catches up to the other. It's all computerized." The controls in the roof control room are duplicated in a boxcar-shaped hut tucked under the girders high on 500 Level, just under the roof. "You can drive the roof up there, too," Garrick said. "And if something goes wrong, if there's a major power failure, we can put high-pressure air hoses on, and that'll move it, too."

We walked up a series of steps until we were on 500 Level, then Garrick came to a door at the north end of the building that opened onto a bright, early-September morning, all blue and white, like the light on a Greek island. It was a chance for Garrick to light up a cigarette, now that he was out of the no-smoking SkyDome. We sat on the edge of the abutment that holds the railway tracks on which the panels of the roof are carried.

"When the SkyDome was ready to open, the city wanted us to spend $1 million to educate the people of Toronto on how to get in and out of the SkyDome efficiently. With the dome right downtown, they expected horrific traffic jams. We decided the easiest way to educate the people was to buy up the Toronto Transit Commission and provide free rides to anyone with a Blue Jay ticket. We did that for a month, and it cost us $600,000 for about twenty events at SkyDome. The rest of the $1 million we spent on newspaper ads explaining how to get here, and how to get home again. The traffic catastrophe never happened. At the beginning, 56 percent of people going to the SkyDome used public transit, now it's down to 27 percent. People found it was no hassle at all. They could be out of the stadium in ten minutes. SkyDome has turned out to be the fastest-emptying stadium in North America."

Having finished his cigarette, we re-entered the SkyDome, found our way down the stairs to 300 Level, then took the elevator to 100 Level. Somewhere in the bowels of SkyDome, Garrick opened one more door and we were inside a fitness club, with a pool, five squash courts, weight room, whirlpool, sauna, a locker room with mahogany lockers, and a licensed lounge. It is open from six in the morning to ten at night. Like The Founders Club, anyone can join, for $895 a year—$995 if you wish to play squash.

Walking along 100 Level, Garrick said, "Not much here was left to chance. We did a study and found women take two minutes longer on average in the washrooms than men, so we installed more women's washrooms than the building code required...."

Martin wanted to know how the washroom study was done.

"Early on, we paid a guy to stand in the corridors with a stopwatch, timing the women when they went in the washrooms."

Baseball, more than any other sport, is a game of rituals. Batting practice begins at the same time every day, varying only for afternoon games and evening games. The home team always bats first. The players bat in the same three- or four-man groupings and take turns in the same order for the same fifteen-minute intervals. When their time in the cage draws to a close, they wind down in the same way, facing four pitches each, then three, two, one more and out. Fistfights have erupted when a player bats out or order, or asks for one more pitch.

We had our own game rituals. One was after the field was closed to the media at six forty-five on a game night, when we would walk outside, across from Gate 9, sit on the same concrete stump and smoke precisely two cigarettes. Another ritual was at three o'clock in the afternoon, when we would go to the same front-row window at Café on the Green, the SkyDome Hotel's restaurant on 300 Level overlooking left centre field. There we would have two cups of coffee, making notes, kibitzing about the day during early batting practice.

By the end of the 1993 regular season we were veterans of the café, listening to stories from the waiters, waitresses, the bartender and SkyDome-struck tourists gawking at the view of the inside of SkyDome, astonished that they could actually sit down and order something.

It is the same view occupants of the seventy hotel rooms facing the field see, except they must pay upwards of $925 a night. When the American League Championship Series began—Chicago White Sox versus Toronto Blue Jays—the seats we were on in Café on the Green would cost $150 apiece come game time, $190 apiece for the World Series. That was if there were any seats available, which there were not when we met Jocelyne Collett of SkyDome Hotel's public relations department, and Ray Thompson, the manager of the hotel. It was the final week of the regular season.

They were as unlikely a duo as the earnest Jerry and affable Tom in the radio booth. Thompson is polite, stiff-lipped and rather humourless, a man who could be a credible stand-in for actor Leslie Nielsen if Nielsen ever plays the role of a hotel manager. Collett has the personality of a glass of 7-Up—fizz, fizz, fizz all day long. She showed us a clipping from *Eye*, a local entertainment listings newspaper that has a gossip section with a line from her saying, "I put bodies in beds." She *loved* that one. "There have been so many love affairs in this building, I call it the LoveDome," Collett told us. "Buy me a glass of white wine and I could tell you some stories," she said. We tried to take her up on the offer many times over the next few weeks, which included the playoffs and postgame parties when the wine was complimentary. She kept saying she could tell us some stories, but she never did. We didn't care about attribution, we insisted, we just wanted the dirt, but we never got anywhere. Oh, maybe somewhere. One afternoon in her office she presented us with yellow-and-blue pin-on buttons, each the circumference of a baseball, that say, "Do it at the Dome."

There has been a wink-wink, nudge-nudge aura of naughtiness from the beginning at SkyDome Hotel, which, whether designed or serendipitous, has provided welcome publicity in the competitive field of putting bodies in beds.

Collett was happy to discuss one famous scandal, the one Thompson dryly referred to as "the incident of May fifteenth." That was the day in 1990 when Alison Gordon—that baseball-writer-turned-mystery-novelist again—noticed through her binoculars a couple having sex in one of the field-view hotel rooms just west of the JumboTron. Gordon has an astonishing knack of being in the right place at the right time. Two years later, in 1992, she was lined up at Gate 15. The people at SkyDome had arranged for a special whoop-de-do to honour the 15-millionth customer at SkyDome. The prize would be various knick-knacks and one day's interest on $15 million, an amount that came to nearly $3,000. The deal was, the fifteenth person at Gate 15 would be the 15-millionth fan. SkyDome and Blue Jay officials stood by, waiting. They could see a fine-looking older man, obviously a dedicated and loyal Blue Jays fan, at the right turnstile at the right gate and fifteen fans away from glory. At the last moment someone shouted, "Hey, Harry!" The man stepped out of the line, revealing—

"Holy shit!" Beeston exclaimed. "It's Alison Gordon!"

Anyway, "the incident" happened in the seventh inning, during a pitching change. As Gordon explained in a column in the *Star*:

> He was corpulent, hairy and nude. She was blonde, buxom and wrapped none too securely in a towel. They were both old enough to know better and sat in armchairs pulled up to the window.
>
> It was, after all, a very dull game. But when the couple blatantly began to alleviate their boredom during a seventh-inning pitching change, the definition of an indecent act under the Criminal Code of Canada became more than a theoretical question.

Gordon was at the game as a fan, with her husband, Paul Bennett, a criminal lawyer. When she told Bennett what was happening in the hotel window, Bennett took a look, confirmed it, then walked down the aisle a few rows to consult with some lawyer colleagues who worked for the Crown. He handed them the binoculars, they took a gander and it was their considered opinion that there was, indeed, a criminal act in progress.

Being a good reporter, Gordon did not step there. She hunted down one of Fred Wootton's extra-duty coppers and told him what she had just witnessed. "You're kidding," he said. The policeman reported this to his superior, who borrowed Gordon's binoculars for another look. "They probably don't realize they can be seen," he said, intently studying the action, just to be sure. It was one of those exceptional moments—like when Wootton escorted Morgana off the field—when a policeman's lot is not an unhappy one. Gordon intrepidly tracked down Paul Beeston for a reaction. "We thought we might have some problems with drunks who wouldn't be able to control themselves," Beeston told her. When he recovered his composure, he said, "I never suspected in my wildest dreams that someone would be doing it right in front of the window. Something has to be done about this without delay. We are running family entertainment. What if it happened on Cap Day with twenty thousand kids out there?"

After more calls, Gordon discovered that the anonymous amorous couple in the room at SkyDome Hotel were not the only sexual miscreants at the World's Greatest Entertainment Centre who thought the windows were made of one-way glass. Six weeks earlier, a quiet fellow was contentedly masturbating in his chair by the window, watching the game below, when there was a knock on the door and in swooped a delegation of armed policemen in what surely must have been the ultimate manifestation of the man's worst paranoid teenage fantasies.

Collett and Thompson hastily drew up a waiver for hotel guests to sign that contained a new subsection, Clause 2(e): "The guest acknowledges that the room and its occupants are on public view and shall accordingly not carry on any activity which is not normally appropriate to be carried on in public (whether or not it constitutes a violation of the law or the rights of others). This includes (but is not limited to) being in a state of partial or complete undress."

Gordon's column on the hotel-room tryst made headlines around the world. Collett and Thompson at first were embarrassed, but that was before they realized what a public relations and advertising bonanza they had stumbled upon. It was so rich, so fraught with intrigue, so blessedly un-Canadian. Soon, Collett and Thompson began getting calls, and requests for reservations, from Europe, Asia and Australia. Late-night television host Arsenio Hall did a shtick on the incident in which he said most husbands after a session of lovemaking would be content with a gratifying *Uh!*—but how would you like to be rewarded with fifty thousand fans outside your window doing The Wave? Anyone who did not know about the world's first retractable domed stadium knew about it now.

(Late in the 1993 season, in a moment of idle curiosity, Sean scanned the hotel rooms with his binoculars. Despite Collett's assurances that there had been no more salacious occurrences in three full seasons, Sean noticed the unmistakable urgencies of horizontal jogging in a darkened room above the top left corner of the JumboTron. He did not feel any sense of moral indignation, and he entertained no thought at all of reporting the incident to the police. This time the couple was under the sheets, and Sean thought it was refreshing, considering the woeful state of the Blue Jays' middle relief corps, that someone other than a visiting baseball player was scoring in the seventh inning.)

Collett and Thompson still have Roberto Alomar as their most famous tenant. Rance Mulliniks, Candy Maldonado, Juan Guzman, Devon White and David Cone all stayed at SkyDome Hotel in 1992, as did Rickey Henderson in 1993. Collett has to walk a fine line with Alomar, trying to keep unsolicited groupies from going door-to-door in search of his room in the middle of the night. Alomar was a handful. Collett had to talk him out of having an engraved "RA" attached to his door.

"I could tell you some stories," she said.

On the long padded blue bench in the Blue Jay dugout, while the pennant race was as exciting as it ever gets in mid-September, Martin was chatting with Sudden Sam McDowell, the team's employee assistance program director, otherwise known as the team psychologist.

In a fifteen-year career spent mostly with the Cleveland Indians, starting in the early 1960s, McDowell was the Nolan Ryan of his day, leading the league in strikeouts five times by virtue of his wicked fastball, which gave him his nickname. Unfortunately, he also had Ryan's wildness, walking a lot of batters, plonking more than a few and sending his catchers scurrying after blistering one-hoppers.

His job with the Blue Jays was dealing with substance abuse and anything else that affected the mind and brain, such as a six-game hitless streak. He was the guy who came up with the idea for the "We can, We are, We will—3 for 3 in 1992" T-shirts some of the players wore throughout their first championship season. (The slogan didn't scan and didn't rhyme, but it obviously must have provided some inspiration.)

Martin sometimes sat beside McDowell in the top row of the press box, jotting notes on what the man had to say about cocaine, pot, booze, endorphins and how the first three screw up the body's ability to produce the fourth, which is the body's natural way of making itself feel good. Martin told Sam about Kris Kristofferson abruptly quitting a ten-year daily marijuana habit, then rediscovering what it was like to go through a day without that constant sky-is-falling paranoia. "I don't believe that," McDowell said in his deep baritone. "Anyone who smoked pot for ten years, regularly, wouldn't drop his paranoia that quickly, if at all." He went on to say that all drugs, taken excessively, including alcohol, but especially cocaine and its derivative crack, impede the body's ability to produce endorphins. Crack is the worst because it permanently impedes the production of endorphins, which explains why youngsters exposed early in life to crack come

219

to accept paranoia as a natural state of being a person in today's world.

Another season of Tony Robbins–style motivational speeches must have taken their toll, however, for when Martin turned on his tape recorder that day in the dugout, McDowell seemed to have run out of insights, or perhaps he had become bored with the whole thing as the days dwindled down to a precious few. At the end of the session, Martin's insight into the mind of a baseball player had been enhanced imperceptibly, if at all. "Maybe it's battle fatigue," he told Sean. "That, or clichés are contagious." He turned his tape over to Sean to see what he could make of it, then wandered away, shaking his head. Sean took the tape home and made a transcript, with annotations.

MARTIN: How do you get these guys motivated, Sam? How do you motivate a team of world champions?

SUDDEN: First, I don't necessarily believe you motivate anybody else. Individuals motivate themselves, especially at the professional level up here. They motivate themselves pretty well. My interest is helping them produce as much as they can, help them overcome roadblocks that are continually put in place, when they might not be producing the way they can.

(SEAN: Sounds like he just rented *Bull Durham*.)

MARTIN: What is a roadblock, an individual or a team thing?

SUDDEN: They can be exterior and have nothing to do with the game. Or something they have seen on television, or something they have heard, a doubt creeping in. A myriad of things. There are so many ballplayers on this earth who know how to play baseball and do it fairly well, but when you start talking about the major-league level, you're talking about something far beyond the realm of what an individual is trained to do. We are talking about the psychic, the emotions, physical strength. And when you do that the slightest thing can really set you off. So most of the individuals, because of the training they have had at high school and the college level, escalate the ability to handle situations coming at them through the minor-league system. Most of them are able to handle it, so they are just refining things—primarily concentration, focus, self-confidence....

(SEAN: What in hell is he talking about?)

MARTIN: Is there any emphasis on focusing away from the distractions of the pennant race, things like scoreboarding?

(SEAN: What in hell are *we* talking about?)

SUDDEN: I really don't believe, especially here in Toronto, that is very much of a factor at all. The only thing that matters is what they do on the field today—what they do at each at-bat, with each pitch. It's like going from here to British Columbia without a road map. You may ultimately get there, but it may take you three weeks or a month or what have you. Whereas if you have a road map to follow, you are going to get there in as quick a time as you possibly can, with no damage to your car. It's the same with an athlete, he's got to focus on his road map.

MARTIN: As for talking to the players now, is it primarily offence—hitting?

SUDDEN: It's neither. I don't get into specifics. I get into generalities...

(SEAN: You can say that again.)

SUDDEN: ...and educational systems. What people don't understand is that my schedule was set for me back in the last week of spring training. Each time I come to town we have, on average, at

221

least one team meeting. We just deal with some forms of education. It can be preventative, in that we discuss certain situations that may come up in the future—how to prevent them, how to recognize when they are coming, what to do about them....

(SEAN: Yeeeaaaggghh!)

SUDDEN: I'm a firm believer in teaching the individual how to fish, so he can handle himself...

MARTIN: How to fish?

(SEAN: I hope he doesn't say what I think he's going to say.)

SUDDEN: How to fish, rather than just give him a meal. A little Biblical philosophy.

(SEAN: Sweet Jesus, no.)

MARTIN: Do you use any mantra?

(SEAN: Now you're encouraging him.)

SUDDEN: Huh?

MARTIN: Mantras? Mental exercises?

SUDDEN: We have mental exercises.

MARTIN: Well, Sam, this time of year in a close pennant race, who is it toughest on—hitters or pitchers?

(The tape is silent for a time, save for the clink-boink-crack of batting practice in the distance.)

MARTIN: Is that a stupid question?

(SEAN: Say what?)

SUDDEN: No, it's a valid question. It depends on the specific circumstances that particular day, or that particular team, or with the individual. It can change day to day, or it can change in a game, from inning to inning. I don't necessarily believe that there is such a thing as it's tougher time now as opposed to opening day, or any other day, because what we condition the ballplayers, or help the ballplayers condition themselves for, is that every single pitch and every single game is extremely important to them. The way they are going to be successful is what they do on this pitch....

(Sean remembers Martin saying that at one point he was gazing around SkyDome, watching the crowd trickle in, wondering whatever happened to Marilyn Watson. Marilyn and Martin were engaged when he was in his early twenties, still at university. Two months before the wedding she told him she had bought her dress. He got cold feet and called off the wedding. She got married on the exact day, in the same church, but to somebody else. Martin wondered what life would be like now if he had married Marilyn Watson.)

SUDDEN: We have a system that the meetings we have in spring training are connected to the meetings we have now.
MARTIN: Huh? Oh, a continuum.
SUDDEN: Yes, a continuum.
MARTIN: That's great, Sam.

(Here the interview ended. Before Martin left, he told McDowell one of his favourite sayings, by Napoleon: "Once you start to take Vienna, take Vienna." "Why did you tell him that?" Sean wanted to know. "I thought Sam might be able to use it some day," Martin said.)

In the office next to Pat Gillick on 300 Level sits his assistant, Gord Ash, Gillick's heir apparent. Gillick had been insisting throughout the 1993 season that he would retire from the Blue Jays after the 1994 season, though Beeston kept saying he would believe it when it happens. Whatever, should Ash succeed Gillick, it would be the final triumph of the running-off-to-the-circus workers—all the way from part-time ticket seller to the new guy who pulls the trigger on the big trades, the major acquisitions.

223

Ash is short, stocky and balding, and—were it really a circus—he would be the perfect candidate for the clown with the bulbous red nose, flapping feet and baggy pants. This is not to suggest he is anything but a very serious executive, intent on learning as much about baseball as he can, as quickly as possible. If he does succeed Gillick, Ash will be stepping into a pair of the biggest shoes in major league baseball.

When he moved into the executive offices in 1984, Ash faced the greatest challenge of his career. He also faced the risk of being Peter Principled, rising to the level of his own incompetence. Gillick, after all, had pitched in the minors for five years, then was a scout for a dozen more. Besides Gillick, one of Ash's predecessors was Bobby Mattick, who started a brief career with the Chicago Cubs as a shortstop in 1938. (Mattick's father played for the crosstown White Sox in 1912.) Mattick had forty-five years' experience as a baseball man when he joined the Blue Jays in 1978. Ash had no baseball background whatsoever, other than playing work-your-way-up in the fields of Toronto and watching the odd Triple A game at old Maple Leaf Stadium. He played football and hockey, but he never played any organized baseball. When he joined the executive ranks of the Blue Jays, one of his jobs was to supervise scouts who spent their lives putting dollar signs on the muscle of sandlot ballplayers. Ash had to compensate for his lack of visceral baseball knowledge with raw intelligence, patience and hard work. Unlike Gillick and Mattick, who could scout prospects personally if they chose to, Ash had to be a listener. If he tried to fake it with the scouts he would be eaten alive.

"For the first four or five years the scouts would get together—Bobby Mattick, Al LaMacchia—and I would listen to them talk, and watch games with them. They observe games much differently than a fan does. They are not looking for results. That was the biggest obstacle for me to overcome. I had to look at performance, how the pitcher is releasing the ball, how the batter is setting up in the box, what the outfielders are doing. Too many times a pitcher makes a great

224

pitch, a guy gets a base hit and somebody says the pitcher has 'failed.' I still think the most amazing thing is for a scout to go to a high school game, look at a kid and say five years down the line he'd be a major-league player. That I wouldn't be comfortable doing. When I look back to my twenties, when I thought I was a knowledgeable fan, it seems pretty naïve."

After graduating from York University with a history and sociology degree in 1974, Ash, now forty-two, wanted to be a teacher. "I was one of those weird people who liked school. I liked the atmosphere. I wanted to be a teacher, maybe do some coaching on the side." Teaching prospects were bleak in the mid-1970s, so Ash got a job as an administrative clerk for the Canadian Imperial Bank of Commerce, starting at $8,000 a year. He worked as a teller, then in the foreign exchange department, then loans and mortgages, then administration. Being a quick study, within nine months he was appointed manager of a CIBC branch. After a time, he got restless.

When a friend who had been working in the Blue Jay ticket office said he could make $20 a game for a few hours' work, then watch the game for nothing after the second inning, Ash jumped at it. He continued working at the bank, but when the Blue Jays were playing at home he would head for the stadium at five o'clock to sell tickets. George Holm was in charge of the ticket operation, so at the end of the first season Ash told him that if any full-time work came up to let him know. In January, 1978, Holm called Ash to say there was a full-time job as a mail-order clerk. "It took me about two minutes to decide," Ash said. "I was ready for change. I had a naïve view that it would be great working around baseball, down at the ballpark, but it wasn't a heckuva lot different from what I was doing at the bank."

Later that year, Ash got his first real baseball job, supervising the grounds crew. He had to hire batboys, ballboys, order supplies and familiarize himself with the arcane matters of baseball dirt, artificial turf and things like the "Diamond Dust" used when the field is wet and sticky. "A lot of it was hit and miss, but it was mainly common sense. If I didn't know, I wasn't afraid to ask someone who did. It always amazes me when people are afraid to ask. It's like they don't want to know, so they don't ask."

The busier he got with the trees of baseball, the less he was able to sit back and enjoy the forest. He was not able to watch as many games as when he was a part-time ticket seller, but he was learning. Most of the knowledgeable baseball people were Americans, and not just the Pat Gillicks, Bobby Matticks and the scouts. George Holm had come to Toronto from Cincinnati, where he had worked at the Reds' new ballpark. There was also Peter Bavasi, the flamboyant hustler who directed the original Blue Jays, who was the son of Buzzie Bavasi of the San Diego Padres. Ash became aware that for Americans, baseball is a game that is bred in the bone, as hockey is for Canadians. (National Hockey League teams in the United States need their Canadians as much as major-league baseball teams in Canada need their Americans.)

When he was a boy, Ash's favourite team was the San Francisco Giants, his favourite player Willie Mays. In 1984, when he became a baseball executive, he went to Buffalo to represent the Blue Jays at an old-timers game and met Willie Mays in the flesh. It was a baseball epiphany for Ash, who used to think of Mays as larger than life—not only a Giant, but a giant. "He wasn't a small man, but he wasn't really big, about five-eleven [actually 5'10½", 170 pounds]. It was the same when I met Hank Aaron. I realized my boyhood heroes were ordinary guys. That started demystifying some of the game."

That was when he began seeing professional baseball players as life-sized, mortal, with the same fears and foibles as himself. Some he liked, some he didn't, most were just— baseball players. Apart from extraordinary skills, they were much like anyone else, including Gord Ash. "The players are always very critical of what they call 'greenflies,' the autograph hunters. It's a clubhouse term. What's interesting is that when you bring in a big entertainer—Tom Selleck was here three years ago, researching the *Mr. Baseball* movie—the players reacted to him just the way fans act to the players. They wanted autographs, they wanted photographs with him. They couldn't get enough of him. They became greenflies."

When Ash moved into baseball operations in 1984, his responsibilities were the minor leagues, setting up spring training, setting up instructional leagues. He got to travel more. After four seasons he became more involved with the major-league operation of the franchise—working with Gillick, doing contracts, player evaluations, working with scouts. Perhaps because of his lack of early baseball experience, Ash looked for new ways to evaluate talent. Over the past five years he has become deeply interested in the inchoate field of athletic psychological testing.

"You learn a lot from psychological testing. You learn what motivates a player. Some players you have to beat over the head, others you have to pat on the back. We're trying to eliminate the mistakes, which is an extension of what baseball is, a game of eliminating mistakes. We sign 250 players in the minor leagues and our success rate [at getting them to the majors] has been five to ten percent. We want to jack that up to fifteen percent."

The idea jelled three years ago, at the time the Blue Jays traded Fred McGriff and Tony Fernandez to San Diego for Joe Carter and Roberto Alomar. "We felt we had been physically talented for a number of years," Ash said. "We were physically talented in 1984, the year Detroit got off to that 35–5 start. Near the end of the season we got to within three games of them, then we fell out. Same thing in 1987, when we lost seven consecutive games to end the schedule. Physically we *were* there. Mentally, it just wasn't clicking. We felt we needed to do something to change the make-up of the club. We knew Alomar and Carter were quality people. And we got Devon White. Things started to click. It helps that a guy like Alomar comes from a real baseball family. He has a terrific instinct for the game. You can't teach a guy to be looking to third base when he's fielding a grounder, just in case the runner rounds the bag too far. That instinct is natural to a guy like Alomar."

Baseball is not the only sport where can't-miss prospects miss and never-will-make-its make it, but it seems to have an inordinate proportion of players who combine skill with character to forge long, lucrative careers, causing scouts to shake their heads. In his book *Dollar Sign on the Muscle*, Kevin Kerrane details a few from the 1981 draft. Mark McGwire, who became one of the top sluggers in the game, was drafted 200th—and he was drafted as a *pitcher*. Lenny Dykstra, who was tearing up the National League in 1993—and would come very close to single-handedly winning the World Series for the Philadelphia Phillies—was picked 316th. Another baseball book, *Men at Work*, written by political commentator George F. Will, describes the gems that can be found deep in the draft. Will explains: "Baseball is so difficult, and its particular skills require so much honing, and the honing requires so much character, that the baseball draft is a highly unscientific, uncertain plunge. Other players picked in the late rounds who turned out to be good investments include Andre Dawson (11th round), Roger Clemens (12), Jack Clark (13), Dave Parker (14), Jose Canseco (15), Mark Langston (15), Frank Viola (16), Kent Hrbek (17), Bret Saberhagen (19), Don Mattingly (19), Ryne Sandberg (20), Bob Boone (20), Paul Molitor (28) and Keith Hernandez (42)."

"In our draft we don't ever bypass a guy with talent," Ash said. "But if there's two people side by side on the draft board and they have a like physical talent, we're going to side with the guy with a little better character."

One of the best examples of this for the Blue Jays—besides Molitor, whose skills were honed mainly by the Milwaukee Brewers—is catcher Pat Borders. When Ash met him, Borders had nearly given up on baseball, after spilling his guts trying to make it to the majors. That was in 1984 in Florence, when Borders played in the South Atlantic League. He was a first baseman, then he tried third, then the outfield. He had started in Medicine Hat, moved up to Florence, then went to Kinston in the Carolinas, back to Florence, up to Knoxville, down to Dunedin, back to Knoxville....

"By 1986, Borders was nearly out of baseball, when he finally decided to give catching a try. He'd catch in games, and he'd catch in the bullpen. He worked six hours a day just blocking balls. Talk about perseverance! Last spring we asked Pat to speak to our minor-leaguers about sticking with it, not giving up."

Ash commissioned Tim Hewes of the Orwellian-sounding Institute of Sport and Athletic Motivation in California to tackle the job of psychological evaluation of potential major-leaguers. "We're building a database, trying to find what traits the ideal major-league player would have," Ash said. "We don't know what the model is yet. Mental toughness? Leadership? Coachability? Maybe there isn't an answer, but we don't want to leave it to chance. We are going to need seven or eight years of data to find that out. Then we can go into the draft and look for those kind of people. What we are trying to do is marry the physical with the mental. Baseball is a very mental game."

Special exercises and drills in handling arguments, beanball incidents, ejections, and media relations refine your understanding of the professional job.
                              —Brochure for the Academy of Professional
                                                  Baseball Umpiring

Jim Evans is the owner and operator of the Academy of Professional Baseball Umpiring. He is also an umpire in the American League, has been since 1971, when he was twenty-three years old. He became a crew chief in 1980. Since that time he has umpired in three World Series, six league championships and two All-Star games. He makes a good living, upwards of $200,000 a year, with most of the winter off.

We caught up to Evans on a rainy, foggy day in June, at the Hilton Hotel in Toronto. It was Father's Day, but Evans's family was far away in Colorado. "Every game is a road game," Martin intoned, beginning one of his long questions. "This is Father's Day. Your family's down in Colorado. You wake up on a rainy, foggy morning in downtown Toronto—"

"Oh, man," Evans broke in, repeating the preamble to the question in a mocking, singsong voice. "You guys have a way with words."

He is not a man to be trifled with, by players, managers or interviewers. The fact is, *he* has a way with words, and he is seldom bested in any confrontation. That comes with years of the arrogance of umpiring, and, in Evans's singular case, by having won a debating scholarship to the University of Texas, where he studied political science and law.

"Why don't you come and see me November 1, when I'm with my family and everybody else is getting up at six o'clock in the morning to be at work at eight. I'm not lonely. I'm staying in a nice hotel. I'm travelling around the country to some of the finest cities in the world. My family can join me any time I choose for them to join me."

The night before, the Blue Jays defeated the Boston Red Sox 9–4 for their fifth straight win, though they were still two games out of first place. Dave Stewart started, held the Bosox runless for eight innings, then Mike Greenwell hit a two-run home run, Boston added two more, so Mark Eichhorn had to be brought in to get the last out. The ongoing story at the time was John Olerud's hit streak, which had been extended to twenty-four games the night before. He still had a long way to go to reach Joe DiMaggio's fifty-six-game streak, but Olerud was approaching the halfway mark of one of the great records of baseball. He was also hitting over .400, which was another ongoing Olerud story in the season of 1993.

We wanted an umpire's perspective on this. "Suppose you're behind the plate, calling balls and strikes, and Olerud's up for his last at-bat and he's on this torrid streak and he hasn't had a hit?" Sean asked.

Evans was ready for it. "I don't read newspapers, so I don't know about these streaks," he said. "You guys create all that. You create the tension. I don't let any of that into my work." At this point Evans picked up a cushion from the couch he was sitting on and held it out in front of him to demonstrate the strike zone. "Now, either the ball is here [indicating part of the cushion], or it's here [indicating an area off the cushion]. How can I say [he speaks *sotto voce*], 'Hey, John Olerud has a streak going, so I'm not going to call this a strike today, I'm going to make sure he gets his pitch.'" Evans slapped the cushion back on the couch and said, "You guys create all this."

Sean wound up and tried again, this time with a question about rookies and veterans, or ordinary stars and superstars. "Some writers have said that when George Brett lays off—"

Evans barged in again, anticipating the rest of the question.

"I would love to sit down with one of those writers and tell them how full of BS they are. You don't say, 'Here's a guy been in the league twenty years, so I'm going to give him a break.' No way! Umpires don't think that way. And don't give me that garbage about an umpire not calling a strike on Ted Williams because he didn't swing at a ball and he's got great eyes. That's baloney! Read his book. You'll find that Williams had the strike zone *charted*. When the pitch was low and inside, he hit .296. If it was up, middle of the plate, above the waist, he hit .348. He took a lot of strikes. But with a one-strike count he would not be as selective as he was with no strikes. And he would swing at pitches with two strikes that he wouldn't swing at with one strike."

Martin could not resist. "Williams used to say he could see his bat hitting the ball. From where you stand behind the plate, can you see the bat hitting the ball?"

Martin felt like ducking after asking that, but Evans replied, "Occasionally."

"You can see the bat hitting the ball?"

Oops, that was going too far.

"My job is not to say [that singsong voice again], 'Okay, bat swings, hits ball. Hey, press box—The Bat Has Hit The Ball.' I mean, who cares? It's not my job. My job is to call the ones he *doesn't* swing at."

No matter what he says, Evans does watch the batters,

and he does admire the way some hitters swing the bat, especially John Olerud. "He has a beautiful swing, and he's in a groove right now. What you guys fail to realize is that Olerud will go into a slump. Nobody can sustain that kind of swing and meet the ball like he's meeting it right now. He has found a very good groove. And don't get on him when he doesn't. Don't start writing bad things about him, that he's lost his swing. My job isn't to stand there and admire a player's swing. I like to see players succeed, but sometimes I have to be the bearer of bad news."

Evans's umpiring school is one of three recognized by major league baseball. It is a five-week course, held in January. Anyone who aspires to be a major-league umpire must attend one of the three schools. The top students at the three schools then move on to the Umpire Development Program, which is an administrative branch of major league baseball. The five-week course costs about $2,000, including accommodation. For those who do make it to the majors, the minimum pay is $60,000 a year, and they earn more if they umpire postseason games.

"Umpiring is also a great part-time job for amateurs," Evans said. "Nobody leaves my program a loser. You're going to learn more skills in a month than you could learn in thirty years on your own. Some might go on to professional baseball, most of the others might go back home and improve the umpiring in their local areas. They might make $1,500 umpiring sandlot games back home. That's a pretty good part-time job."

The umpires' room at the SkyDome is on 000 Level, right next to the visitors' dressing room. To get to the field they actually have to walk through the visitors' dugout. That is where we caught up with Evans next, as he was preparing to work the final game of the four-game Boston–Toronto series.

"This is a beautiful facility," he said, meaning the SkyDome, but he also said that the umpires' room itself is the best in the major leagues. The Blue Jays provide a chef, Stan

Stanchseon, who prepares food just for the umpires. The umps don't have to beg for scraps from the players' dressing rooms, as they do at some other stadiums in the league. As for the SkyDome as a baseball stadium, he said, "I have nothing but a plus, plus, plus for this place."

Part of the preparations for a game involves preparing a bucket of mud to rub on the baseballs. It is the home-plate umpire's duty to rub the mud into the balls, five dozen for each game. It takes about twenty minutes. The mud is "New Jersey Mud," and it comes from the banks of a tributary of the Delaware River. It is a lovely bit of baseball tradition and folklore. "That's the best mud found," Evans said. "They don't use it in the minor leagues. In the minors they go off to the parking lot or wherever, find some mud and rub it on the balls." The purpose is to take the shine and newness off the balls, and it gives the pitcher a better grip. "It started back in the 1930s. The third-base coach for the Philadelphia Athletics is the guy who originally came up with the mud." Evans's crew mixes the mud in a white plastic container, like a Tupperware jar. The umps used to use large coffee cans, but they abandoned that when rust from the cans became part of the mixture. The mixture is a sloppy mess, which has the consistency of chocolate syrup. When the new balls have been rubbed with the mud, they still look white to anyone in the stands, but they are several shades darker, as if they had been used for a few innings of sandlot ball. In a game, each new ball lasts about two or three outs, then it is removed from play, destined for batting practice.

For the game that afternoon, the home-plate umpire was Ted Hendry, which meant Evans was free to ramble on about umpiring and how the press hardly ever gets anything right and occasionally resorting again to that singsong voice when a question did not meet his exacting specifications.

At the end of the session Sean asked what a player has to say to be automatically tossed. "He has to say the magic words," Evans said. "The words themselves get you ejected. They don't even need inflections."

"And what are the magic words?" Martin wanted to know.

"'Motherfucker' and 'cocksucker,'" Evans answered, "preceded by the pronoun 'you.'"

In the game against the Red Sox that afternoon, Evans was at second base. The umpires rotate clockwise around the diamond from game to game; the day before, Evans was at third, next time he would be at first. While waiting for the game to start, we sat with George Holm, director of stadium and ticket operations. It was a hot, humid afternoon, and the roof was closed. Holm said they were expecting rain. It was the same the Friday before, when there was a 70 percent chance of rain, but the rain blew away. Trouble was, Holm had sent the roof crew home at five o'clock that afternoon, so the roof stayed closed, and it was even hotter and stickier inside than it was this Sunday. The roof can't be opened during a game—baseball rules, not the mechanics of the dome— it can only be closed, and most times Holm makes the decision himself. If it's tricky, he consults Bob Nicholson, the Blue Jays' vice-president of business. If it's trickier still, Holm consults Beeston.

Late in August we returned to the umpires' room, before a game between the Cleveland Indians and the Blue Jays. The American League East race was a squeaker, with the Blue Jays clinging to first by a game. This time the crew chief was Joe Brinkman, who was still embroiled in an ugly feud with the Blue Jays that went back several years to remarks former catcher Ernie Whitt had made about Brinkman in a book.

Brinkman was eating a pregame meal of fried eggs, toast and back bacon. It was a hot, breezy day, the wind blowing gently from left to right. This time the roof was open.

Like Evans, Brinkman runs an umpires' school. Sean asked him about the qualifications needed for someone to be a professional umpire. He wanted to know about the intangibles, beyond the basic physical skills. "It's a lot of gut feeling, being around a guy for five weeks, seeing what he does under stressful conditions, and what he does *off* the field. The big thing, you've got to be an extrovert. You've got to go out and really take charge of the situation. You're going to get yelled at, the house comes down on you, and you've got to be able to maintain your composure."

"Like Ron Luciano [the former umpire who wrote several books on umpiring, and is about as extroverted as a person can be]?"

"No, no, no," Brinkman said. "I like Ronnie personally, but he turned umpiring into show business for himself. He could have been very good for umpires, because he was known to the press and the public. If he had been very pro-umpire he would have been excellent for us, but he went the other way and turned everything into a joke."

As for the Ernie Whitt controversy, and the feud, Brinkman conceded it was still an issue. Earlier in the month, at Yankee Stadium, Brinkman had ejected Roberto Alomar for what was an obvious display of bad manners. After he called a third strike on Alomar, Alomar stood in the batter's box and motioned with his bat that the ball was inside. Then he argued with Brinkman, which is a flagrant no-no. Still, Brinkman did not eject him. Only when Alomar trudged back toward the dugout, then threw his bat, did he get the heave-ho. Brinkman said Alomar also had uttered the magic words.

Back in June, Richie Phillips, legal counsel for the umpires' union, arranged a meeting at the SkyDome between Gillick, Beeston and Brinkman. Nothing was resolved, however, and Brinkman believes it has more to do with Gillick than with Cito Gaston, who many believe harbours ill feeling toward Brinkman going back to the 1985 season. "Gillick's still pissed off because I gave a guy two bases instead of one in New York in 1987, and he thinks that's why the Blue Jays didn't win the pennant. Gaston doesn't even remember the incident."

"Is it difficult for you coming to Toronto?" Sean asked. "Is this the type of situation that would be hard on an inexperienced umpire?"

235

"If something like this happened early in your career it could run you out," Brinkman said. "It could make you go home. You'd call your wife and say, 'I'm not going to put up with this the rest of my life.'"

We asked about some of the wacky calls, like the time in the Metrodome in Minneapolis when the ball went through a hole in the Teflon roof and one side argued vociferously that it should be a home run. "That's covered under Rule 901(c)," Brinkman explained. "This means anything not covered by the rule book, the umpire's got a right to rule on it. It's the same with some fan interference calls," he said. He was referring, specifically, to an incident at Yankee Stadium when a fan ran onto the field and touched the ball, a routine infield grounder. "When the fan came on the field the ball was fair," Brinkman said. "What would have happened if the fan hadn't touched it, or if the ball hadn't hit the fan? Would the ball have gone to the second baseman? Would he have thrown him out at first base? We're going to give him the out because of spectator interference, but it could also be a Rule 901(c)."

What about those yelling, stomping confrontations between managers and umpires? Do you sometimes sense it's being staged, to rev up a team?

"That can happen," Brinkman said. "Sometimes a manager comes out and says, 'Look, I'm going to jump around a little to get this thing going.' Hub Kittle would say, I'm going to wave my arms, I'm going to kick a little dirt, maybe slap my hat on the ground, and when you've had enough just let me know and I'll leave.' Nestor Chylak once told me, 'You know when you've arrived in this game, Joe, when they yell at you nice.' It's the difference between someone saying, 'Joe, wasn't that just a little outside?' and another one saying, 'That motherfucking pitch was outside, Joe.'"

Sean asked, "Where would you put Cito Gaston? Would he be in the 'motherfucking outside' category?"

Brinkman said, "Probably."

PART TWO
GAME DAY

As the CBS camera zooms in on a closed and brightly lighted SkyDome, the television audience hears announcer Pat O'Brien say, "Surely you've heard that ooold saying abut playin' 'em one game at a time. Well, tonight, folks, this is that one game."

SATURDAY, OCTOBER 23, 1993

7:48 P.M.

S ean, Martin and Beth Hansen, a photographer from San Francisco, are watching Dave Stewart through a break in the partition separating the bullpen from the circular basement runway at 000 Level. Stewart will be the starting pitcher for Game Six of the World Series in twenty-four minutes. Hansen is taking pictures for the official World Series coffee-table book which, when the 1993 World Series is over, will be titled *A Series to Remember*. Stewart is ten feet away from us, but it might as well have been a mile. He is waiting to take his warm-up pitches, sitting on a blue park bench behind the pitcher's mound in the bullpen, his feet dangling like a child's. There is privacy there, behind the blue padded outfield fence shielding Stewart from the rest of the stadium and the television cameras that soon will carry his glowering presence across Canada, across North America and around the world—in living rooms, bedrooms, rec rooms, bars.

Stewart is a big man—six feet two inches, 200 pounds—but by major-league standards that is not huge. Stewart is big in terms of mass and power, and yet, when he speaks, his voice is high-pitched, almost squeaky. He also has small ears, which makes his head and neck look bigger. Stewart does not notice us watching him; or if he does, he does not pay us any attention. Just before we leave—Hansen has snapped off several frames—Stewart turns his head to his right and looks directly at us. There are thin red rims around his pupils, though they do not look bloodshot, more like lasers circled by infrared haloes. It is a look of such stoical menace that instinctively we feel like stepping back a couple of paces. It is hard to believe that this is the same man who, during the travel day before Game Six of the American League Championship Series in Chicago (which he started and won), stayed in Toronto to hand out Thanksgiving dinners to the homeless. Three months later, remembering that scene, we asked each other if we still believed Stewart's eyes were red rimmed. We did. That fleeting eye contact in the basement of the SkyDome is one of two images from that evening that remain as fresh in our minds as the moment we experienced them.

8:01 P.M.
"Ready to go up?" Bam Bam asks.

"Okay," says Sean. He gathers his notepad, tape recorder and binoculars from his seat in the first row of the auxiliary press box, directly behind the Blue Jay bullpen beyond left field. Bam Bam leads the way. He has made this journey hundreds of times; he can do it without thinking. He walks with Sean from the auxiliary press box in left field across the concourse of 100 Level where thousands of fans are taking their seats to watch what they hope will be sports history—a World Series win in Toronto. The Blue Jays lead Philadelphia three games to two. The fact is, sports history will be made no matter what happens; tonight or tomorrow night, the final game of a World Series will be decided in Canada. ("On Canadian soil" we would like to say, but purists might disagree.) Bam Bam and Sean enter an elevator on 100 Level.

239

"Five hundred," Bam Bam tells the attendant.

For tonight's game, the big deal for Bam Bam (a.k.a. Myles Patterson) is nitro.

"Nitro?" Sean asks.

"Nitroglycerine," Bam Bam replies, smiling. Normally, Bam Bam sets off six rounds of fireworks for a regular-season home run, thirty-two for a win. He has upped it to eight for a World Series home run. For tonight's game, he has ninety-four should the Blue Jays win, including the nitro. To set up the extra charges he needed the help of his assistant, Gord Mills, whom Bam Bam calls "Boom Boom." They have been there since five o'clock in the afternoon. To co-ordinate the added firepower he has brought in a $35,000 computer imported from California, the same system he used when he was a hired gun for China at the fireworks equivalent of the World Series in Montreal earlier in 1993. He won the silver medal, edged out by a pyrotechnic team from Spain. Bam Bam has shown Sean a two-page sheet of technical instructions he has for the game. The last line, after the sequence for setting off the ninety-four Series-winning blasts, read: "It's official—we're a dynasty."

After exiting the elevator, Bam Bam navigates the 500-Level concourse, weaving through hundreds more fans until he comes to a door, which he opens with a key. They walk up several flights of stairs, the complimentary Chicken McNuggets and goo dinner swirling in Sean's stomach. They climb and climb, higher than any fan is permitted to go. They go through another door and hear the swell of the crowd again. Far below they can see the field. They stand on a concrete perch looking down at the highest-priced seats in SkyDome. Behind them is the concrete rut where the bogies travel when the roof is opening or closing. Tonight, under the order of American League president Bobby Brown, the roof is closed. If it was a warm, dry summer night, they would be looking into open air and, if the night air was clear, they would be able to see Buffalo across Lake Ontario.

They continue up, on a long, suspended, rainbow staircase with latticework, waist-level metal railings. They are now above the lights. Far below, the swirl of bright green, the white lines, the milling crowd, the military honour guards, the World Series bunting and the makeshift banners (Next Stop, Yonge Street). How many of the 44,649 souls who braved the snow, sleet and cold to watch the first major-league game in Toronto on April 7, 1977, are here tonight? Sean and Martin are. Sean was eleven. They stayed until the last pitch on those freeze-your-ass metal benches, when they were rewarded with a glint of sunshine that pierced through the clouds over the lake. They both remember watching a fellow standing in the third-base stands whip off his straw boater expecting to catch his first major-league foul, then watching as the ball rippped through his hat and bounced away. Wonder if he's here tonight?

The view from on high is magnificent, what God's perspective would be if the Almighty were watching a baseball game (which is a clever thing to say, but in reality God would probably prefer to sit behind the dugout between third and home, chewing an ice cream bar). You can appreciate the geometry of baseball, how greatly the outfield dwarfs the infield, how fastballs really zip from mound to plate. "When Mark Eichhorn's on," Bam Bam says, "his breaking stuff crosses the plate on a diagonal."

Naturally, it is not a place for anyone with a fear of heights. Sean is not particularly squeamish, though he still feels that odd sensation many people get when approaching the edge of any great precipice—a little voice in the back of the mind that says, "Jump." Martin, in that black Irish way of his, had remarked once about what a spectacular setting for a suicide this would be. This was the same man who still talked excitedly about the existential clarity he experienced when, while working for *The Globe and Mail* in the early 1970s, he interviewed the crane operator atop the CN Tower while it was under construction. Thinking it would be a way to overcome his fear of heights, Martin had gone as high as he could by elevator, then walked outside to a metal ladder and

241

climbed fifteen rungs, hand over hand, out into the open air to a trapdoor under the crane. It was the middle of winter, with high-altitude gusts of up to a hundred kilometres an hour that flapped at his parka as if it were a spinnaker. Once inside, Martin rocked back and forth as the crane swayed in the wind, knowing all the while that everything would have to be done in reverse on the way down. He talked about it in an "I'd never do that again in a million years" tone, but the frequency and vigour of the telling, and the careful attention to detail, always made Sean suspicious. Sean agreed there was a certain panache to having the moment of one's death telecast live by CBS to 100 million Americans and viewers in Sri Lanka, Japan and the Netherlands, but it was an abstract appreciation. And since Martin's prescription of antidepressant pills was running out, Sean had quickly volunteered when Bam Bam offered us a look-see.

The crowd is atypically boisterous ten minutes before the first pitch. Placid at the best of times, the fans at SkyDome have been even more difficult to stir than usual throughout most of the 1993 pennant race and postseason. It is a blasé attitude Torontonians have only previously read about regarding hockey fans in Edmonton and Montreal, an assumption of success. They seem to have forgotten how remarkable all this is, to be in a World Series for the second year in a row. The Phillies have been around since the late nineteenth century, and they have only won the World Series once. Fans in Chicago and Boston have been praying for a moment like this for seventy-five years. Blue Jay fans have acted as if a second trip to the World Series was merely a starting point. How quickly they've forgotten the improbable twists and turns that have taken the Jays to the brink of a repeat championship. So many "What ifs?" What if Pat Borders had touched the wild pitch that went rolling into the Blue Jay dugout in the fifth inning of Game Two of the 1992 ALCS, which would have allowed the Oakland Athletics to break a runless tie on their way to a 2–0 series lead? What if Dennis Eckersley had not blown a four-run lead late in Game Four? What if the Atlanta

242

Braves had held on to either of the eighth-inning leads they held in Games Two and Three of the 1992 World Series? What if Mike Timlin had bobbled Otis Nixon's bunt for the final out in Game Six?

Even in the past two weeks there have been so many close calls. Dave Stewart getting out of a no-out, bases-loaded jam in the sixth inning of Game Two of the 1993 ALCS against the Chicago White Sox, a game in which the Blue Jays would only score three runs. Duane Ward's dead-fish fastball down the middle of the plate to Bo Jackson, who represented the tying run, in the ninth inning of Game Five. Lenny Dykstra's fatal last-second hesitation on Rickey Henderson's bloop single to centre in the eighth inning of that torrential Game Four three nights earlier. If he dives and snares it—a play he has made a few times in the World Series—Mitch Williams would have survived the eighth with a three-run lead and in all likelihood it would have been the Blue Jays coming to SkyDome needing two wins in a row. So many things that had to go exactly right for the Blue Jays to get where they are tonight, but here the fans are, waiting until Game Six of the World Series to get as excited as Philadelphia fans were on Labour Day. Philadelphia fans, even after the suffering they endured in Game Four, have a better sense of what a World Series is all about. To paraphrase what George F. Will said about the slider (and what Charles de Gaulle said about Bordeaux wine), for Philadelphia fans the World Series is like sex—when it's good, it's terrific; and when it's bad, it's still pretty good.

8:12 P.M.
Lenny Dykstra leads off for the Phillies, a wad of tobacco the size of a lacrosse ball wedged in his cheek. Dave Stewart stares down at him from the mound, the same stare we had encountered less than an hour ago, only this time even more menacing when shaded by the bill of his cap under the lights.

Whack! Before we barely realize the sixth game has started, Stewart gets a called strike on the dangerous Dykstra,

243

which is a signal that Stewart intends to come right at the Phillies tonight. Nothing fancy. Next a ninety-two-mile-an-hour zipper to the outside corner, another called strike. Next, a breaking ball that seems to loop clean over Dykstra's bat, the way a cat jumps over your arm when you brush through its legs.

Strike three.

Next up for the Phillies is Mariano Duncan, normally a middle infielder. Because the game is being played in an American League stadium, the designated hitter rule applies. In all his years in professional baseball, in the majors and minors, Duncan has never been a designated hitter, which is true for most of the Phillies. In this series, however, it is a blessing, as the Phillies are suffering many aches and pains. Stewart feeds him a ball, then a called strike, another ball, two fouls, then Duncan slices one to right field where Joe Carter chases it down for the second out.

The designated hitter rule has been in force twenty years, but to listen to the purists, one would think it was approved by a show of hands before Opening Day last April, the sole purpose of which was to ruin the stately game of baseball by not allowing pitchers to strike out in front of everybody and make damn fools of themselves. Contrary to popular belief, the DH rule was not the first serious change to the basic intricacies of this very intricate game, which was invented by Alexander Cartwright in 1845. They played something like baseball before that, an offspring of the English game of rounders, but Cartwright—a New York fireman who became a surveyor—was the genius who decided that the distance between bases should be ninety feet.

No one is sure why he chose ninety feet. (To be niggly about it, the distance is actually 88 feet 7 inches, since the 90 feet represents the distance to the back of the bag.) Baseball historians have suggested it is because 90 feet from base to base, times four, equals 360 feet, the number of degrees in a circle. More likely, Cartwright simply lucked on to the perfect distance. And it is the perfect distance. In 1845 and 1993, a batter who hits an ordinary infield grounder is thrown out by a step at first base. If the batter hits it deep to the infielders, or if the infielders are slow in reacting, or if the ball takes one of those weird AstroTurf high hops, the batter makes it by a step at first base. The result of this happenstance perfection is that baseball thinks everything about itself is perfect and must remain unalterable, preserved in amber, freeze-frozen for all time. Forget that when Cartwright invented baseball, runners were declared out if they got "plugged" by the ball, which meant conked by the ball as they were running from base to base. Forget, too, that back then pitches had to be delivered underhand, batters could request certain pitches, umpires wore silk top hats, players did not wear gloves and home plate used to be square instead of five-sided.

There have been other changes, which have been around long enough for the purists to accept them as if they had been walked down from a mountaintop by Moses wearing a baseball cap and chewing tobacco. In 1901 the National League decided to make the first two foul balls strikes. The American League adopted this rule in 1903. The first night game was played in 1935, Philadelphia Phillies versus Cincinnati Reds at Crosley Field in Cincinnati, prompting early purists to predict the ruination of baseball. In 1947 Jackie Robinson became the first black this century to play in the majors, at which point the purists threw up their hands and said, "That's it. Baseball will never be the same." In 1958 Walter O'Malley yanked the Dodgers out of Brooklyn, transported them to Los Angeles, and the purists wept and shrieked and said baseball would never be the same again. In 1965 baseball was played for the first time on artificial grass at the Astrodome in Houston, whereupon the purists began their incessant chant of "blue skies, green grass." And, of course, they moaned that baseball would never be the same again.

If there is a legitimate beef about the DH, it is that too few teams use it intelligently. Since it began, most teams have selected an aging, flawed, slowed-down player whose defensive skills have atrophied—usually an erstwhile superstar with

245

a box-office appeal—and made him the designated hitter. The exceptions? Kansas City Royals, who used Hal McRae as a full-time DH, with spectacular results. McRae made the DH a full-time, fence-busting, offensive, glamour position. For the other teams, the manager would look down the bench, cough and say, "Er, Michael, would you mind hitting for the pitcher this game?"

The Blue Jays, being as modern as modern can be, got great mileage in 1992 and 1993 using Dave Winfield and Paul Molitor as designated hitters, allowing them to step into the batter's box with some swagger and declare with heroic defiance, as Cliff Johnson used to say, "My position is home plate." Before the 1993 World Series, however, the fuss over the DH rule had taken on another dimension. Cito Gaston complained that unless something is done—either the DH rule is dropped, or applied equally in both leagues—someone is going to get seriously hurt. He first became aware of this in spring training, when American and National League teams regularly play each other, using whatever rule applies in the home park. Gaston kept watching young pitchers coming to the plate who had never swung a bat in anger, not even in Little League. Suddenly they were confronting a major-league pitcher, with ninety-plus speed, coming at them with forkballs, sliders and twitching fastballs. Gaston did not think it was fair. "There is no doubt in my mind it favours the National League team," Gaston said. "All they have to do is add a hitter to their lineup, while we have to take someone out."

Up steps John Kruk, the Phillies' long-haired, pot-bellied first baseman, who once inspired an indignant woman fan at Veterans Stadium to remark, "I'm shocked. You're a professional athlete and you smoke!" To which Kruk replied, "Lady, I'm not an athlete. I'm a baseball player."

Stewart walks Kruk on six pitches.

The top of the first ends when Dave Hollins, the third left-handed batter to face Stewart, pulls a shallow fly to right field, which Carter snags easily on the run, then continues in that galomphing trot of his across the infield to the Blue Jay dugout.

The noise rises to an early and unexpected crescendo as Rickey Henderson walks—saunters—to the plate for the Blue Jays as Nick Poulakis in the audio booth flicks on Rickey's song, "Baby, I'm a Star," by Prince. Two pitches later, Henderson is trudging back to the bench after having looped a fly to centre field where Dykstra picks it out of the air.

Devon White walks, which brings Paul Molitor to the plate. On the first pitch he cracks a liner to the opposite field, which bounces on the warning track just short of the outfield wall, then ricochets up above the fence. The hit scores White, and Molitor makes it all the way around to third for a triple. Watching from the high platform with Bam Bam, Sean has an interesting overhead view of Molitor running the bases. From up there, it looks like he is on a slot-racing track, the way he cuts the bases so tightly. It looked like a double, for sure—but a triple? All season, Martin has been collecting what he calls "Molitorites," and Sean knows this will be another one for his collection. The way Molitor turns singles into doubles, doubles into triples, the way he hits to the opposite field with a runner on, the way he does everything he does with such skill and savvy. He plays every *moment* of the game, even when he is sitting on the bench, looking and thinking. As Molitor dusts himself off at third, the noise in the SkyDome is deafening.

Joe Carter pulls his first pitch deep to left where Milt Thompson waits for it on the orange warning track, knowing he hasn't a hope in hell of catching Molitor at the plate. Blue Jays 2, Phillies 0.

John Olerud accepts two balls, then doubles to left centre, which brings Phillies pitching coach Johnny Podres to the mound. Podres wants an avuncular chat with his starter, Terry Mulholland, a tall string bean with a magician's goatee. After Olerud's effortless double, Mulholland looks shaken, as if the rabbit he expected to pull from his hat turned out to be a grenade. Things are not working out the way Podres and the

Phillies had expected, especially with the lefty Mulholland on the mound for this important game. It is an elementary truth in baseball that a hitter has an advantage when he is facing a pitcher throwing the opposite way to which he is hitting; thus, a left-handed batter sees the ball better, and, more importantly, longer, when it is coming from a right-handed pitcher. The ball also flies into him, toward him, and does not threaten to buzz by his ear enroute to the catcher's mitt. For someone like Olerud, ever aware of his life-threatening aneurism, it is no small matter. Olerud is a natural left-handed batter, not a switch-hitter, and when he faced lefties in 1993 he hit .291. Against righties, he hit .396.

In Game Five, Curt Schilling, a right-hander, pitched masterfully against the Blue Jays, shutting them down and shutting them out. If the Phillies can win Game Six and force a seventh game, the Blue Jays will start young Pat Hentgen, who won more games than any other Blue Jay starter, but tailed off at the end of the schedule. Hentgen also performed much better on the road than at home, and Game Seven would be at the SkyDome, this time against another lefty, Danny Jackson.

Podres walks back to the Phillies dugout, thinking he has calmed his pitcher enough to get out of the inning alive. Olerud's double defied the odds, to be sure, but Podres knows Roberto Alomar is up next, and Alomar is the best example of a Blue Jay hitter who is far better against righties than lefties (.359 to .241). An argument can be made that Alomar should abandon switch-hitting, and take on all pitchers from the left side. In baseball these days, if a player *can* switch-hit, he does, whether it does him any good or not. Podres barely has time to sit back down on the Phillies' bench when Roberto Alomar drives a single by a diving Kevin Stocker at shortstop, scoring Olerud from second. Tony Fernandez flies out to Dykstra in centre, but for the Blue Jays and the fans it has been a satisfying inning. The Blue Jays look pleased with themselves as they gather their stuff and run onto the field.

PHILADELPHIA	0 – – – – – – – –
TORONTO	3 – – – – – – – –

Between innings Sean scans SkyDome with his binoculars, holding them carefully, lest they fall over the railing and kill Devon White thirty-one storeys below. He had the same thought a few minutes earlier while having a smoke, wondering what he would do if a lit cigarette fell in gentle swirls onto White's hat and started a fire on his head. What to do? Yell out a warning? Thank Bam Bam for the tour and slink away? He remembers a cameraman up there who told him, "If I dropped one lens cover from up here, we'd not be allowed back again."

Sean focuses on the main press box behind home plate, 300 Level, specifically on the aisle seat on the second tier at the east end of the press box, where he sat most games during the season. It was assigned to Murray Chass of the *New York Times*, one of the best in the business. At the west end in the first row beside Howard Starkman, Dave Perkins of the *Star*, Larry Millson of the *Globe* and the rest of the regular-season beat writers are sitting in their usual seats. In the football press box, which is also on 300 Level but closer to the left-field foul pole, Sean spies the seat assigned to Roger Angell of *The New Yorker*. It is empty. When we read Angell's annual World Series essay a few weeks later, we find out to our astonishment that he watched the last game at home in New York—on television. How could he have missed this? The most elegant baseball writer alive, a man who was so good he never inspired envy among his peers for being able to make a living writing three stories a year (albeit long ones) was watching the end of such an unpredictable and dramatic World Series on TV? Every baseball writer has stories of disillusionment to tell after getting closer to the game than they may have liked. This was one of ours. Angell's prose had been flat the last few years—it always seemed flat when he wrote about the Blue Jays—but he had earned the right to a few rough outings at the keyboard. Besides, most baseball writers

249

on their very best days are not on the same planet as Angell on a "flat" day.

This was something altogether different. Sean had introduced himself to Angell and had a brief chat with him amidst the roving scrums on the field prior to one of the playoff games at SkyDome. Martin, a fan of Angell, and a huge fan of Angell's late stepfather, E. B. White, did not get to meet him. When asked what he thought of SkyDome, Angell told Sean, "It's a great stadium, I just wish they would play a different game in it than baseball. It dwarfs the game."

Fair comment. Regardless of his opinions, it is always nice to meet a writer who is as witty in person as he is in print. Sean pointed Angell out to Martin during one of the numbingly banal postgame interview-room sessions. Martin, who had never seen Roger Angell, said, "He doesn't look like Roger Angell." Sean knew what he meant. Martin thought Angell looked like a local TV Ontario host named Elwy Yost, or in more accessible terms, perhaps Elmer Fudd with a square salt-and-pepper moustache. Still, the man can write like an angel, and he is a great watcher and listener. One of his better lines in the last few years came in his 1992 World Series *New Yorker* essay, when he wrote about Devon White's catch in Game Three. When Angell asked White about his place in baseball history, White told him that his only wish was for people to ask, when he was out of the game, "Did you ever see Devon White play centre field?"

In the top of the second, Stewart faces Darren Daulton, the catcher, one of those baseball players who throws one way and bats another. In Daulton's case, he throws right and bats left. Rickey Henderson throws left and bats right. They are a strange breed, and can probably pat their heads and rub their tummies at the same time. Daulton was smashed up in the same late-night, post-bachelor-party car crash that almost killed Lenny Dykstra a few years back. The media thought this enhanced the legacy of the Phillies as lovable rogues, as compared to the "Team Briefcase" Blue Jays. But, as

Canadian Press writer Ken Becker pointed out to Sean before the game, the Phillies are almost exclusively a team of white rogues. The only non-white front-line player, including the pitchers and the coaches, is Latin second baseman Mariano Duncan. Wonder if a team of black rogues would have been considered so lovable by the national press? Whatever, Stewart has no difficulty with Daulton, getting him to fly out to left.

Next is Jim Eisenreich, the only player in the history of major league baseball to have Tourette's syndrome, an affliction that affects the nervous system, causing some victims to twitch and jerk and scream obscenities. Eisenreich controls his malady with medication. "Most players get themselves up for a game," he explained in a pregame interview. "I get myself down." Eisenreich flies out to left field, then Stewart induces Milt Thompson to ground out, third to first. As Stewart walks off the mound he still has not allowed a hit.

Leading off the bottom of the second is Ed Sprague, the Blue Jays' third baseman, the man who replaced Kelly Gruber. Back in spring training everyone knew Sprague could handle the bat, but there were grave doubts he could replace Gruber defensively. He became a special project in Florida, and one of the coaches who worked most closely with him was Bob Bailor. He had Sprague fielding grounders on his knees, to improve his glove action. Other times, practising on the half-diamond beyond the left-field stands at Grant Field, Gene Tenace would pitch to Bailor, who would hit sharp grounders to Sprague, then shout out the name of an imaginary player running to first, whether he was fast, slow or medium. If it was a fast runner, Sprague would bare-hand the ball and sweep the throw to first. If he was slow, he could use his glove, then plant himself to make the throw.

Before the game, by the batting cage, Bailor talked about grooming Sprague for third. "We knew Eddie wouldn't be as good defensively as Gruber, but we wanted his bat in the line-up." The irony is that Sprague had improved so much by season's end that he had become a defensive third baseman, so much so that during the discussions over what to do with

251

Molitor when the DH wasn't allowed in the National League park, there was concern over losing Sprague's glove at third.

"Eddie deserves all the credit for that," Bailor said. "There were days we were going to lay off him, not have him work out, because we thought he needed a rest. But he would come looking for us, asking for more. He'd take hundreds of ground balls, and he kept it up during the season. We were trying to quicken up his first step. We experimented with him taking the ball flat-footed, then had him creeping in a little—whatever he felt best with. Playing third, that first step is the important one. Brooks Robinson was never fast, but with that first step, that anticipatory step, he was lightning quick." An old story about Brooks Robinson's anticipation had him in league with the devil, who stood behind him whenever he was in the field. "Pssst, Brooks," the devil would whisper, "ball's comin' to your left." And as the batter launched into his swing, Brooks would ease a step to his left. Then, "Pssst, Brooks, next one's comin' right at your eyes...."

"Eddie's never going to have the range of Gruber. Kelly was blessed with that and Eddie isn't. But on AstroTurf you need to know positioning, and Eddie studies the charts, looks in on every pitch to see what's being thrown. The other thing, we worked on his arm. That was one of the questions going into spring training, his arm accuracy. But his arm's been terrific. Right now, I'd say Eddie's become an above-average third baseman."

Sprague goes after Mulholland's first pitch, sending it into the glove of Dykstra in centre. Pat Borders singles to centre, Henderson pops to second, Devon White strikes out and the inning is over.

| PHILADELPHIA | 0 0 | – | – – – | – – – |
| TORONTO | 3 0 | – | – – – | – – – |

While Bam Bam and Boom Boom monitor the start of the third inning on a tiny black-and-white television set perched

252

on one of the steps, Sean makes his way back down to 100
Level and the auxiliary press box behind the Blue Jay bullpen.
Watching a baseball game from the top of a thirty-one-storey
building is interesting, for an inning, but it is too much like
watching a game on television with only one camera covering the action. You want to spit peanut shells, listen to the
chatter—there will be a no-hit pool in the auxiliary press box
if Stewart holds the Phillies hitless for three innings—and
down among the players and fans and fellow scribes, you
might be able to yank a ball out of the air.

Martin's favourite foul-ball story involves his friend
Becker, who is in the football press box. Becker had grown
up in the Bronx, but was a dedicated Boston Red Sox fan,
specifically a Carl Yastrzemski fan. He even named his dog
Yaz. On a rainy August night at Exhibition Stadium in 1983,
during Yastrzemski's last appearance in Toronto, Becker sat
behind home plate. When Yastrzemski stepped to the plate
for his last at-bat he sent a foul ball spinning over the backstop. The ball bounced off the concession stand, bounced
down an aisle and landed in Becker's lap. Someone suggested
he take the ball to the Boston clubhouse and get it autographed. "No need to," Becker said. "I'll know."

Before the game, Becker had taken Sean aside and told
him that if it looked like the Jays were going to win, he
would give him his coveted clubhouse pass, which was only
accredited to journalists who were writing for the next day.
(Our plea that we needed a pass more because we were writing for eternity did not go over well with Howard Starkman
in the media relations office.) Becker had always taken a
paternal interest in Sean when he was growing up, even giving him his first job in journalism typing minor-league hockey scores into the Canadian Press computer and zapping them
across the country. Problem was, Becker was on vacation
when Sean started and no one else had bothered to teach him
the complicated series of computer commands Canadian Press
used. On his first night, all the editors and reporters were too
busy to show Sean the ropes, so he stared helplessly at his

253

computer until three in the morning and quit the next day. Becker had been none too pleased at the time, so Sean appreciated the gesture of friendship and told him he would love to take him up on it.

Kevin Stocker keeps his bat on his shoulder for the first four pitches from Stewart, two balls and two strikes, before lifting a lazy fly ball to centre that White pockets with as much casualness as if he were shagging fungoes during batting practice.

Morandini takes a ball then sends the second pitch to the same spot. Two quick outs, and still no hits given up by Stewart.

Next up is Dykstra. Though he struck out on three pitches to start the game, he is the one guy Stewart wants no part of in this game. Stewart walks him on four pitches.

Duncan takes a ball and a strike from Stewart, drives a hard foul into the third-base stands, then strikes out swinging. Stewart is rolling, but he has started behind in the count to every batter but Duncan, a mildly troubling sign.

In the bottom of the third, Mulholland and Molitor have an interesting game of cat and mouse. Molitor takes a ball just low and inside. Then Mulholland throws a pitch to almost the same spot, but an inch closer toward the plate. Home-plate umpire Dana DeMuth calls it a strike. Mulholland realized he did not have his best stuff in the first, so he is working every inch of the plate to try to gain an advantage and gauge DeMuth's strike zone. Mulholland tries it again, low and inside, except this time he misses the black by a couple of inches for ball two. Molitor dribbles the next pitch to the left side foul, then finds the pitch he is waiting for, low and down the middle, except he gets under it slightly and flies out to left. Molitor files the at-bat away in his memory bank.

Carter grounds out to Kruk on the second pitch after taking another low-and-inside strike.

Olerud has been watching Mulholland from the on-deck circle and likes what he sees. Many of Olerud's doubles during the season came on low strikes. He fouls off the first two pitches, showing an aggressiveness early in the count that was missing before 1993. In high school and college ball, Olerud was so good he could watch a few strikes to see what kind of stuff the pitcher had and still have time to hit a gapper to the wall. He found in his first three years in the majors that he could not do that anymore. Batting coach Larry Hisle, having crunched Olerud's 1992 at-bats in his personal computer, found that Olerud was an excellent first-pitch hitter, on the rare occasions when he swung at one. Hisle told Olerud repeatedly in spring training to be more aggressive, to go after those first pitches.

Mulholland wastes the third pitch way high, then coaxes Olerud into a line-drive out to shallow left, which Milt Thompson almost loses in the lights and grabs on his knees. The amazing thing about Olerud's at-bat is that every swing, the two fouls and the fly out, had exactly the same level motion and upwards follow-through It is so consistent he looks like a wind-up doll with an invisible string in the back repeating the same motion again and again.

| PHILADELPHIA | 0 0 0 | – – – | – – – |
| TORONTO | 3 0 0 | – – – | – – – |

At the start of the fourth inning, Martin scans the Blue Jays' bench with the binoculars. He finds Rich Hacker, the third-base coach who was nearly killed in a car accident during the All-Star break in July. Hacker has recovered enough to throw out the first pitch in one of the playoff games between Toronto and Chicago. His official toss bounced once in front of catcher Pat Borders, but both teams gave Hacker warm applause, which was touching to hear. Tonight he is in uniform, though his duties as third-base coach are being performed by Nick Leyva,who once managed the Phillies. He is staying in a room at the SkyDome Hotel. Even from across the field Martin can make out Hacker's penetrating blue eyes as he watches the game from the dugout bench, sitting down from Gaston.

Hacker had talked to Martin about what it was like recovering from the accident, and how it had affected his memory. One of his duties as third-base coach was to compile charts of the hitting tendencies of all the visiting players. "The biggest thing was the ballplayers on the other teams," he said. "I didn't forget the names of the Blue Jays, because they would send me reports when I was in hospital and I was able to keep up. I certainly never forgot Nick Leyva, who's a good friend of mine." Watching a game against the Baltimore Orioles, he knew the second baseman—medium-sized guy, light, been around the league for a while. He knew what he could do, knew his strengths and limitations, his tendencies, but he could not remember his name: Harold Reynolds. Same with Wade Boggs, who now was playing for the Yankees. "And there's this big guy, black, plays first base for Detroit, hits a ton of RBIs. He pronounces his name funny." He meant, of course, Cecil Fielder (who pronounces Cecil to rhyme with vessel).

Martin's mother had suffered a mild stroke that week and when he met her in hospital she couldn't talk, but she could spell. Asked what time it was, she said, "*T-h-r-e-e*." Asked if she was hungry, she said that morning she had "*E-g-g-s*." She was ninety-two. She enjoyed playing bridge and bingo, and she also liked crosswords and find-a-word puzzles, so the stroke somehow had zeroed in on a minute speck of the brain and reduced her working vocabulary from words to letters. She was living in a retirement home called Cobblestone Lodge and when Martin asked if she wanted to go home, she answered, "*C-o-b-b-l-e-s-t-o-n-e*." The brain works in curious ways. That summer, Martin had been to Montana to spend a week with Ferguson Jenkins, Canada's only Hall-of-Fame player who was working as a roving pitching instructor for the Cincinnati Reds. As with many professional athletes, Jenkins possesses an uncanny, detailed memory, one described as "eidetic," or "photographic." It is a highly efficient memory, but also highly selective. From ten, fifteen years ago, Jenkins could remember the weather, the inning, the count, what pitch he threw to the number-three man in the order, but he could not remember if he was married that season.

Hacker said he was talking to Blue Jays coach Bob Bailor about the Boston lineup and couldn't remember the name of Carlos Quintana, who played first base. He knew what he could do, knew who he was and what he looked like (six feet two inches, 195 pounds), but try as he might he could not nudge the player's name into his brain. He thought he made a breakthrough, however, when he came up with Luis Rivera. Rivera played shortstop for the Red Sox, and he is a much smaller man than Quintana, but the name sounded similar, had the same number of syllables and the surname ended on a vowel. "I must be getting better," Hacker said. "I was close."

Beside Hacker is Jack Morris, in full uniform, complete with jacket for his pitching arm, which he blew out late in the season, saving Cito Gaston from an unpleasant decision and saving Morris from the wrath of the fans who have not forgotten his atrocious 1992 postseason. He had created a bit of a stink at season's end by making comments to the press about the Jays being a team lacking character, saying there were unnamed players he would "not want to go to war with." A popular story exchanged among the press corps had it that Morris, after his regular early exit from a game was hastened somewhat by indifferent fielding from his team-mates, had muttered, "seven all-stars, my ass" before heading to the showers. Before the first game of the ALCS he was singing the same tune, plus the usual "You can't relate to what I'm saying. I pitched in two World Series in a row" stuff to Sean and a small group of reporters. When Rosie DiManno of the *Star* asked him if he would rather be healthy, pitching and getting booed again instead of riding the bench, Morris's answer was typically acerbic. "If what you're asking me is, would I rather go out and fail than not go out at all, no, I would not rather go out and fail. I don't want to fail. But you can't take the boos personally. They don't know me."

It was sad seeing Morris get bombed game after game in 1993. He is such a competitor. His ten-inning shutout in

257

Game Seven of the 1991 World Series was one of the gutsiest high-stakes performances in the history of the game. Now, suddenly, his arm was not doing what his brain was telling it to, and there was nothing he could do about it. There was talk about him tipping off his pitches with his delivery, but Morris, to his credit, was having none of that. He had heard the same talk a few years earlier when he was struggling a bit. The difference then was that even if the batters knew what was coming, more often than not they still could not hit it.

But in sport, unlike the arts, inspiration and will are not always enough. A musician like ex-Beatle Paul McCartney can go fifteen years without producing anything of merit and still find a record company that will let him record drivel like the 1993 *Off the Wall* album, in which songs like "Biker Like an Icon" bore as much resemblance to "Let It Be" as the Jack Morris of the 1991 World Series bore to the Jack Morris of the 1992 World Series. It is sad to hear such a familiar voice making such unpleasant sounds, but the sounds keep coming.

In baseball, however, talent can erode over months rather than years, and when it goes, so does the player. For modest talents like Candy Maldonado, the fall can be brutish and short. For greater talents, like Morris, it is often a gentler slope, but it is still a slope—downward, unrelenting and impossible to predict. No one knows why Nolan Ryan was able to do what he did for so many years any more than they know why Bill Caudill lost six inches off his fastball from one year to the next. It is a mystery to the best minds in the game, including the players. The players push negative externals from the mind, or use them as motivation, as Morris did in 1993 by pasting above his locker a local newspaper story that said he was finished. Ignore it, rage against it, but never believe it.

What makes sport so poignant is that there will come a time in virtually every player's career when it will not matter what he believes anymore—someone will take him aside and say, "Jack, you're going down." If Jack has the heart to ask why, he will be told, "Because you're not good enough."

It happened to Willie Mays and he could not believe it. He went to the New York Mets instead and hit .211 with six homers before hanging it up in 1973. It happened to Babe Ruth and he could not believe it. He went to the National League and hit .181 in seventy-two at-bats before packing it in in 1935. It happened to Bert Blyleven in the spring of 1993 when, after twenty-two years in the majors, he could not make the cut on the worst team in the American League. After Minnesota told him he wasn't good enough, something he probably had not heard since he was three or four, if ever, Blyleven went home to Anaheim, California. Two months into the season he would still get into his car at three o'clock in the afternoon as he had always done on a game day, drive a few miles to Anaheim Stadium where he had pitched some of his best seasons for the Angels, do a couple of laps of the empty park, then go home.

Morris was released after the World Series. Perhaps right now he is having a fine comeback season somewhere else. Perhaps he has packed it in and gone back to his ranch in Montana to play soft-toss with his kids. Either way, the Jack Morris of Game Seven of the 1991 World Series is gone forever and there is nothing he can do about it. Just wanting it badly enough will not do. Maybe Jack Morris would pitch into his eighties if his abilities allowed him to, but he can't. Baseball won't let him. There is a minimum standard that every player, no matter how many hits they had in the past, must meet. They can play as long and as often as their heart compels them to; they just can't do it in the majors. It is baseball's way of saying, "We want to remember you at your best. When we hear your name, we want to hear 'Let It Be' ringing in our ears."

Before the start of the fourth, a no-hitter pool is organized in the auxiliary press box. It is a season-long ritual that takes place every time either starting pitcher tosses three hitless innings to start the game. We each put in two dollars and pick numbers from a hat to indicate which Philadelphia players will be our candidates to break up the no-hitter. If you

draw zero you can win the $20 pot only if the pitcher main-
tains the no-hitter over nine innings. Sean draws Milt
Thompson, Martin draws Mickey Morandini.

Kruk taps one back to Stewart on a 2–1 pitch, then Hollins
pops out to Sprague in foul territory on the first pitch. Two
quick outs. Stewart has retired eleven batters without allowing a hit.

   With Daulton, however, he begins to falter, the first indi-
cation he may be tiring. He is missing the plate more frequently, starting off with balls outside or low. Stewart recovers
with two called strikes, low and away. After two fouls and a
ball to run the count full, Daulton hits a looper to short left
field for the first Philadelphia hit (so much for Thompson and
Morandini). The ball takes so long to come down that
Daulton is able to hustle into second. It is the kind of play
teams losing by three runs and facing elimination have to try
for.

   After Stewart starts Eisenreich off with two balls, Borders
jogs out to the mound. If it were Stottlemyre on the mound,
he would be trying to calm him down. Because it is Stewart,
Borders is only trying to break up the bad rhythm. It doesn't
work. Stewart throws another ball. Eisenreich takes strike one
down the middle then fouls one off, which means Daulton
can now run off the crack of the bat on a full-count swing,
which he does as Eisenreich hits an RBI single over Tony
Fernandez's head. If he hadn't been running on the pitch,
Daulton would not have scored.

   Stewart falls behind Thompson 2 and 0, but gets lucky as
Thompson fouls what would have been ball four before he
grounds out to Alomar to end the inning. Stewart has not
thrown a complete game in 1993, and it looks like he will
need help tonight.

   In the bottom of the fourth, Alomar leads off with a
ringing double off the left-field wall. It misses the top of the
fence by three feet. Alomar shakes his head as he stands on
second base. Alomar, who had never hit more than nine

home runs in a season before 1993, fancied himself more of a power hitter this year and accomplished that rare feat of raising his home-run total to 17 while raising his average to .326. Sean winces whenever he sees a replay of Alomar's famous ninth-inning homer against Dennis Eckersley to tie the fourth game of the 1992 ALCS. Alomar raised his hands in triumph immediately after the swing and began a slow home-run trot, but the ball just barely cleared the right-field fence. How embarrassing it would have been if he had danced around the bases while a warning-track fly ball was being tossed back to the infield.

After a groundout by Fernandez that moves Alomar to third, Sprague hits a fly ball deep to right field to drive in Alomar and nullify the Philadelphia run a few minutes earlier. Borders singles, then Henderson hits a check-swing dribbler to Mulholland on what would have been ball four to end the inning. It does not look like Mulholland will be around much longer, either.

PHILADELPHIA	0 0 0	— —	— — —
TORONTO	3 0 0	— —	— — —

In the Blue Jay bullpen, John Sullivan is standing by a soiled Plexiglas window facing the field, behind the two mounds. It is too early for the relievers to be warming up, so they sit on an elevated bench adjacent to the bullpen, where they rest their elbows on the outfield wall and spit sunflower seeds on the wooden floor. In a packed SkyDome in the middle of the sixth game of the World Series, Sullivan is alone with his thoughts. He is a grown man, rather portly now, squeezed into a young man's double-knit baseball uniform, his cleats crossed at the ankles as he leans against the window watching the game. He is only fifty-two, but he looks ten years older, his Irish pug face creased by experience. Riding the buses, eating hotel food, staying up late as a player and manager and coach for more than three decades have taken their toll. He needs medical attention for some of his worn-out parts, but he abhors hospitals, hates needles and knives. Sitting in the dugout before the game, Sully shuddered at the mere mention of hospitals and surgery. Whatever Blue Jay executives do to make themselves look so much younger than their age, coaches must do in reverse. Detroit Tiger manager Sparky Anderson, fifty-nine, has one of those timeless faces that looks like it was scraped off Mount Rushmore. Sullivan's face looks like it belongs on the wall of an Irish bar in Boston, where patrons could hoist steins of beer at last call and sing a wobbly version of "Danny Boy."

Sullivan announced at the beginning of the year that he would retire when the 1993 season ends, so tonight's game could be his last. It would certainly be over tomorrow, if the Series goes seven games. Roy Railey, the octogenarian bullpen security guard who rides to work every day on his 1925 one-speed Eaton Glider, told Sean three hours before the start of Game Six, "Sully talked to me the other day about his retirement. I told him, 'Sully, my kids are older than you.'"

Sullivan played parts of five years in the majors in Detroit, New York and Philadelphia. He was a catcher. Most of his career happened in smaller places: Erie, Durham, Birmingham, Knoxville, Syracuse, Vancouver, San Diego, Rochester, Omaha and Jacksonville. His best baseball season as a player was 1965, with Detroit, when he played in eighty-six games, hit two home runs and posted a batting average of .267. Sullivan once aspired to be a manager, and he was a good one, compiling an impressive won–loss record over six minor-league seasons (434 wins, 288 losses, five first-place finishes). He got as high as Blue Jays bench coach when Gaston was out for a stretch in 1992 with a bad back and Gene Tenace was at the helm. But by his own admission his temper often got the best of him, so he settled for the relative anonymity of the bullpen. And the bullpen coach is as anonymous as anyone can be who regularly does his job in front of fifty thousand people. Milt Dunnell, the graceful columnist for *The Toronto Star*—he is thirty years older than Sullivan and still writes a three-times-a-week column—had some fun asking various Blue Jays if they knew

Sullivan's uniform number. Nobody did, not even Cito Gaston. "It's 9, right?" Gaston told Dunnell. "No, no, it can't be 9, that's Olerud. It's 5, that's what it is." Sullivan's uniform number is 8.

Before the final home game of the 1993 season, against the Yankees—the Blue Jays would have clinched the American East that day if they had won, but the Yankees won 7–3—Sullivan was presented with his framed number-eight jersey and an all-terrain vehicle that looked like an adult scooter. B. J. Birdie drove it in looping circles around the field then parked it in front of the Blue Jay dugout where he hopped off and gestured to Sullivan to try it out. It was as if the grandfatherly Sullivan was being coaxed onto a crowded dance floor to do the Mashed Potato. Sully looked at the new machine, seemed rather pleased, but declined to take it for a spin. When the applause died down, the crowd turned its attention elsewhere, and Sully walked across the outfield toward the bullpen, opened the door, then pulled it shut behind him.

The day before Game Six, the big story involved another Blue Jay coach, Larry Hisle, the gentle man we got to know in Florida. There was a story in the *Sun* by Bob Elliott saying Hisle was finished as a Blue Jay. The timing for everyone but Elliott and the *Sun* was atrocious. Just when the Blue Jays were on the verge of winning their second World Series, this time in their own backyard—a championship that would have been the crowning touch to Hisle's tough baseball career—the man learns he is being fired. And for what? As the hitting coach in 1993, he surely had something to do with three Blue Jays—Olerud, Molitor and Alomar—finishing one, two, three in hitting in the American League. Overall, the Jays finished behind only Philadelphia and Detroit in runs scored.

Hisle awoke early that Friday morning, dressed and walked down the street to buy a *Sun* so he could analyse the stats on Philadelphia starter Terry Mulholland. When he got back home, he flipped to the sports section and at the top of one page was the Elliott story, under the headline Hisle Out

263

As Jays Coach.

"I was shocked," Hisle said as he fielded questions the next afternoon by the batting cage at the SkyDome. "It was like being hit by a sledgehammer, a thirty-pound sledgehammer. No subtlety to it at all."

Earlier, sitting in the makeshift patio by the interview room on 000 Level, Martin sat with his friend Becker of Canadian Press. They had been in the newspaper game all their lives, but Martin had gotten close to Hisle, really liked the man, and heard himself saying to Becker that he wished the story could have been held until after the World Series. "What difference would it have made?" he asked. Becker looked across at Martin as if he had turned into a marshmallow. He would have no part of that. "It's a hell of a story," Becker said, and he was right.

Typically, Hisle accepted the verdict, even though it had appeared in a morning tabloid. He knew Elliott, knew the way he worked, knew his reputation for accuracy. Cito Gaston had called him the day the article appeared, but he gave Hisle no reassurance that he had heard differently. Later, at a pregame media session, Gaston would not confirm or deny that Hisle was out. "I'm still under the assumption the article is accurate," Hisle said before Game Six. "I'm probably no longer a Toronto Blue Jay. This has been a difficult day. I'm going to make some calls as soon as this is over. I truly believe I have something to offer. I'm going to turn this negative into a positive. I love this game. I love being around the players." There were tears in his eyes when he said this, but that is the way it is with Larry Hisle.

Someone asked Hisle if it might be because he is too popular.

"I hope that wouldn't be true," he answered. "I hope it wouldn't be the reason for my dismissal. All I know is for some reason the people making the decisions are not pleased with me."

Hisle had always been the most accessible of the Blue Jay coaching staff, always ready to explain the art of hitting, no matter what pressures he was under. Even when he was too busy to talk and was trying to dodge an interview, he dodged politely, usually with profuse apologies. ("I…I'm sorry, but I…I promised Butler I would…") Hisle is one of those people of whom it can accurately be said that he is gracious to a fault.

A few months earlier, in the midst of a killer schedule, when the team had returned from a dismal road trip and was struggling to hang on to first place, Hisle took us to a boardroom under the stands where he spent more than two hours discussing the study of hitting, and explaining his specially designed and constantly updated computer program. "All these areas I have down here are very important," he said, indicating a line of tiny letters and numbers trailing across the bottom of the screen. "The take, the pitch, the speed, the count. The count to me is real, real, real critical."

The light on the computer screen faded, then the screen went blank. "Oh, damn, battery's dead," Hisle said. He carried the machine to the other side of the table and plugged it into an outlet on the wall. Several minutes later, the screen blanked out again, and he plugged it into another outlet. As he had said in spring training, Hisle confessed he was still having difficulty organizing the vast amount of information in his little laptop. It seemed odd that an organization that spent more than $51 million in player salaries in 1993 would not pay a computer geek a few thousand dollars to help Hisle out. Probably Hisle never asked. Time management is not his strong point.

The news of Hisle's apparent dismissal, still unconfirmed and undenied, puzzled the broadcast crew of CBS during Game Six. One of their cameras caught Hisle sitting in the Blue Jay dugout, stoically watching the game as the Blue Jays were winning 4–1, looking like he was sitting on a bucket in a field. That was when announcer Tim McCarver told the television audience, "If you're going to fire a guy like Larry Hisle, nobody's job is safe."

Stocker taps a soft liner to Fernandez to open the fifth, then Morandini hits what looks like a routine grounder between first and second—Blue Jay fans have come to regard *anything* in Alomar's territory as a routine grounder—but Alomar misjudges the bounce and the ball sails over his glove—E4, the last thing Stewart wants with Lenny Dykstra up next.

But Stewart is no Dave Stieb. Instead of glowering at his teammate, or grabbing at his jock, Stewart appears unfazed. The appearance is not deceiving. Though Stewart's much-discussed stare on the mound makes him look like he is perpetually on the verge of committing an indictable offence, it is a controlled rage, a rage that he summons up hours before he is to pitch and releases on the walk from the dugout to the showers when his day is done. Morris would give Thoreauesque sermons after each drubbing about the inner calm that comes from seeing beyond the immediacy of a baseball game, but everyone knew it was mostly a pose. Morris agonized over what was happening to him and there was often a bitter edge to his words.

Stewart was different. After giving up three homers and seven runs in a start the day before the All-Star break in July, the man was all aglow because his son, Adrian, had flown in from California and they were going to see Niagara Falls for the first time. In late August, on a day Sean was to meet Stewart for a lengthy interview, Sean approached hesitantly, not knowing what mood Stewart would be in after giving up six walks and four runs in a loss to Seattle the night before. When Sean began in an earnest tone, promising not to ask about the previous night's performance, Stewart laughed. "Sheeit," he said. "I don't think about that stuff." Then he pulled out a chair by his locker and gestured for Sean to take a seat, the first and last time in 1993 that any player showed either Sean or Martin that small courtesy.

This was the kind of man Gord Ash had in mind when he talked about "character ballplayers." Stewart was the prototype. Not only did he and Molitor contribute more of their time and energy to charity than any other player on the team, he has the kind of presence on the mound that scouts drool over. In the classic book on scouting, *Dollar Sign on the Muscle* by Kevin Kerrane, forty-year St. Louis Cardinal scout George Kissell talks about the proper *walk* to and from the dugout a major-league pitcher should possess, the kind of walk Stewart makes every inning—crisp and authoritative. "You have to stride to the mound like you mean business," Kissell said to one prospect who sauntered too much for his liking. "You're the boss."

Following the Alomar error, Stewart serves two balls to Dykstra before inducing a pop fly to centre for what should have been the third out of the inning. Then Ed Sprague bobbles Mariano Duncan's grounder for another error, putting runners on first and third and bringing the tying run to the plate. A walk to Kruk loads the bases. Though he has yet to give up a hit in the inning, Stewart has thrown a lot of pitches, and seems to be fading, but he knows Gaston is going to let him work out of the jam. Whatever Gaston's faults as a manager may be, pulling starting pitchers too early is certainly not one of them. Gaston has said in the past that he would rather go with a guy one pitch too long than have him looking over his shoulder into the dugout whenever he gets into trouble. In the most crucial at-bat of the game so far, Dave Hollins hits a first-pitch grounder to Olerud to end the inning.

In the bottom of the fifth, a Devon White fly to centre is followed by a second-deck, line-drive home run by Paul Molitor. The first chants of "MVP" began as Molitor stepped to the plate, and with the game seemingly well in hand, the chorus grows louder. The usually cautious fans should know better. Was it not enough of a jinx that City Hall announced the victory parade route for the second year in a row before the World Series was over? Remember Bruce Hurst? He was the Boston Red Sox starting pitcher who was announced as the Most Valuable Player in the 1986 World Series after a two-run Boston eleventh in Game Six, only to have the award annulled by Bill Buckner's egregious E3 in the bottom of the eleventh—Mookie Wilson's grounder dribbled between Buckner's legs—to lose the game and ultimately the Series.

The next two batters go quietly, with Carter grounding out to third on the first pitch, and Olerud lining out to centre.

PHILADELPHIA	0 0 0	0 –	– – –
TORONTO	3 0 0	1 1 –	– – –

At the end of the fifth, as usual, the grounds crew makes its mad dash from the outfield fence like college students tumbling out of a telephone booth. The Blue Jays' marketing department dubs them "fastest grounds crew in the world," and who can say it isn't? It is another of those because-we-say-so monikers, like SkyDome's claim to be "the world's greatest entertainment centre." They are fast, though—replacing all the bases, raking the dirt, stomping on the mound, redrawing the baselines, then scampering back across the outfield in about sixty seconds.

This time, Chuck Macaluso, the itinerant klutz, manages to perform his duties without falling down or leaving a zigzag trail of chalk on the field. Macaluso's postseason had been typical. The day before the first game of the World Series he had been catching fellow grounds-crew member Paul Eagan during an impromptu batting practice. Eagan is the earnest fifty-year-old with degrees in philosophy and theology who attends to his duties on the pitching mound as if it were a sacred trust. One of Eagan's pitches got by Macaluso, ricocheted off a steel bar at the back of the batting cage and conked him where his right eye meets his temple. Trainer Tommy Craig drove him to Mount Sinai Hospital where doctors found that the cornea of his right eye had been scratched. Macaluso got a clean bill of health before the opening game, just in time to knock over one of Craig's children while sprinting along 000 Level on some vital errand. At least, he thought it was one of Craig's kids; another member of the grounds crew thought it was Pat Borders's son.

With the Blue Jays in the World Series, Paul Eagan's quest for his personal lifetime pitching nirvana went into overdrive. Before Game Three of the ALCS he showed Sean his time card for the week leading up to the first ALCS game at SkyDome: twenty-nine hours, virtually all of it spent sixty feet six inches from home plate. Officials from Major League Baseball measure the slope of every mound once during the season to make sure it meets their standards. The slope has to start six inches from the rubber and decline precisely one inch per foot. It is measured again before the first game of the World Series, something Eagan had been preparing for since the Jays clinched the American League East with a week to go in the regular season.

"I'm a perfectionist," Eagan said. "When the pitchers from other teams come up to me and say they like the mound, I want to keep making it better. I met David Cone this year in a hallway and he said, unprompted, that this was the best mound of any he had pitched from. That meant a lot to me. He's pitched in both leagues. But if everyone on the crew was like me, nothing would ever get done. I'm pretty obsessive."

Later that same day, less than two hours before Pat Hentgen was to throw the first SkyDome pitch of the ALCS, Sean bumped into Eagan again behind the batting cage while George Bell was taking his cuts. Eagan was in a wistful mood, like an artist who has painted the last brush stroke on the most inspired creation of his life. "Yes, that mound is in the best shape it's ever been," said Eagan, unprompted. "It's almost a shame anyone has to use it tonight. Yesterday [the day Macaluso got pinged] I threw from it for the first time. It's ironic—I spend more time on it than anyone in the world, but I never pitched from it before. Chicago was late for BP, so I threw for about an hour. That's the first time I've ever pitched in front of five dozen photographers."

The next day Eagan rushed up to Sean, dizzy with excitement. One of the coaches had asked him if he was

269

interested in throwing early batting practice to Darnell Coles and a few other non-starters on Sunday morning before Game Five, which would start at four o'clock. "All good things come to those who wait," Eagan said, as if he had been canonized. But, like that day in Presque Isle, Maine, in 1959, when he attended that all-comers Boston Red Sox tryout camp, Paul Eagan's moment never came. Coles and the other non-starters either changed their minds, forgot, or had better things to do. Eagan waited, and waited, walking the sidelines, adjusting the bunting on the front rows, sometimes sitting by the dugout, popping a ball into his glove like Steve McQueen in *The Great Escape*. As for Coles and the other non-starters, Eagan shrugged and said, "They walked right by me and didn't say boo."

Two months after the season ended, Sean received a Christmas card from Eagan in which he said a newspaper from his home province of New Brunswick had asked him to write some thoughts about his experiences as a member of the Blue Jay grounds crew. Eagan sent the newspaper sixty pages.

In the top of the sixth, the crowd begins to enjoy that "Where's the party?" feeling. The federal election would be held on Monday, Canada would have a new prime minister, but for the fans at the SkyDome the only PM that matters tonight is Paul Molitor. And the way Stewart is pitching—the Phillies have managed only two hits so far—it looks like many Torontonians will be up all night celebrating again this year. Uptown the Maple Leafs are on their way to their ninth straight victory to start the 1993–94 hockey season, a National Hockey League record.

The first batter Stewart faces is Darren Daulton, who scored the Phillies' only run. He flies out to White, who glides to the spot where he knows the ball will fall, then cups it in his glove as if it is a sparrow that had dropped from the sky. The way Devo catches these things, it could have been a Ming vase, and it would have survived without a scratch. It is

270

an easy inning for Stewart. Eisenreich goes down second to first, Alomar making a deft move to his right, backhanding the grounder, then flipping it to Olerud, making a tricky play look easy as pie. Milt Thompson goes after the first pitch and sends a high pop-up to Sprague, who catches it west of third base. Nine pitches is all it took.

In the bottom of the sixth, this time facing Roger Mason, a right-hander, Alomar comes to bat and positions himself on the left side, where he is more comfortable and more effective. During the season he hit .241 from the right side, .359 from the left, making a good argument that he is a natural left-handed hitter and should stay there against all pitching. On the first pitch, Alomar golfs one to right centre for his twelfth postseason base hit.

There is a television monitor in the front row of the auxiliary press box and CBS flashes a remarkable graphic on the screen. It lists the top five players and their career postseason batting averages, each with at least a hundred at-bats:

1.	Roberto Alomar	.376
2.	Paul Molitor	.365
3.	Lou Gehrig	.361
4.	Thurman Munson	.357
5.	Devon White	.344

This is no small-potatoes statistic. Major-league postseasons go back a long time. And *three* Blue Jays in the all-time top five? With Lou Gehrig! And they are thinking of firing Larry Hisle?

(There *are* small-potatoes statistics in the World Series. In the official handout to the media for Game Six, we are told, "The only other time that opposing World Series managers have had the respective surname initials F [Fregosi] and G [Gaston] was in 1980 with the Phillies' G [Dallas Green] defeating the Royals' F [Jim Frey] in six games.")

With Alomar dancing off first, Fernandez strikes out, Sprague flies out to left and Borders pops up to Kruk at first.

PHILADELPHIA	0 0 0	1 0 0	– – –
TORONTO	3 0 0	1 1 0	– – –

Martin leaves the auxiliary press box at the end of the sixth, intending to head up to 300 Level to visit Poulakis and the others in the audio booth. On his way, he stops in at the medical station on 100 Level.

Dr. Noah Forman is having an easy time of it in his medical station—no sprained fingers, no broken noises, no foulball abrasions. Forman is watching the game on a television monitor hanging from the ceiling. He is a talkative, streetsmart guy who works as an emergency physician at North York General Hospital. It had been a busy season, again, in his medical station, the busiest at the SkyDome.

The most dramatic incident happened at one of the last home games of the season when a sixteen-year-old girl "died" at the SkyDome. It was in the fourth inning of a game against the Boston Red Sox. She was with her father, a St. Catharines dentist, and in the fourth inning he gave her $6 and asked her to buy some doughnuts and something to drink. The girl walked up the aisle and while she was standing in line to buy the doughnuts she collapsed, stricken by a heart attack, though she had no history of heart problems. An AmbuCart was called, the paramedics brought her to Dr. Forman's station and, as the doctor recalls, she presented as VSA, emergency-room shorthand for "vital signs absent." She was dead.

Forman quickly applied fibrillators, "zapped" her a few times, and the patient responded; he got a blip on the flatlined graph. An ambulance took her to Sick Children's Hospital in Toronto, with Dr. Forman riding in the back beside the young woman, whose heart now was beating. He stayed at the hospital with her for twenty minutes, then went back to the SkyDome. She survived the attack and by the end of the next day was back home in St. Catharines. When he heard of Forman's heroics, George Holm, director of stadium and ticket operations, was not surprised. "I'd rather have a heart attack here than at a hospital," he said.

Dave Stewart walks out for the top of the seventh as purposefully as he had for the other six, *like he means business*. At the same time, Sean decides he will go to the football press box to get Becker's clubhouse pass during the seventh-inning stretch so he can witness the victory celebration firsthand. Within the clubhouse, Jeff Ross's assistant, Kevin Malloy, is putting plastic sheets over each player's cubicle to protect their suits, Italian shoes and fan mail from the spray of chilled Freixenet Spanish champagne, cases of which are being wheeled into the clubhouse. New "1993 World Series Champions" caps and T-shirts are also being brought in.

Kevin Stocker, another Phillies lefty, digs in at the plate. Who knows what all contributes to that Big Inning, but Stocker's at-bat—ten pitches in all—begins to wear down Stewart.

After fouling off four pitches, Stocker reaches base on a well-earned walk. Morandini takes two strikes, hits a foul, gets a ball, hits another foul, then connects for a single, sending Stocker to third. The Phillies bench suddenly looks much less sullen as Dykstra, the dreaded Lenny Dykstra, walks to the plate like a street tough out to settle matters personally with the entire north end gang. Gaston has seen something in Stewart's delivery that makes him uncomfortable. He phones John Sullivan in the Blue Jays' bullpen. Relievers Al Leiter and Danny Cox, a lefty and a righty, rouse themselves from their wooden perches behind the left-field fence and clunk, clunk, clunk down the stairs to Sully's little private den.

From directly below the auxiliary press box, the *whomp!* of cleanly caught fastballs sounds like heavy boxes dropping from a high roof. During the regular season, when we were in the main press box behind home plate, we could not hear or see the relievers warming up, but we did have an indirect way of finding out when they were almost ready to come in. The first dozen or so pitches, the ones that merely got the kinks out of the arm, would be delivered in a gentle arc, the peak of which could be seen cresting over the bullpen wall.

273

When the pitchers were throwing at game speed, the trajectory flattened, and we could not see the ball over the fence anymore.

Dykstra takes two balls, then Galen Cisco, the pitching coach, calls time and strides to the mound to have a talk with Stewart. By now the decision has been made; the Blue Jays are biding time so the relievers can get warm. Dykstra fouls off the next pitch, then takes another ball, bringing the count to 3–1, which for as long as people have played baseball has been known as "the hitter's pitch." With runners at first and third, the last thing Stewart wants to do is walk Dykstra, loading the bases with no outs.

Well, almost the last thing.

Crack! Dykstra sends the next pitch, a fastball, soaring high to right field, all the way into the second deck. Stewart leaves, having thrown 120 pitches, and Danny Cox takes over, the Jays' lead suddenly cut to 5–4. Up in the audio booth Matt Carnovale asks Nick Poulakis, "Do you want 'Haywire?'" He meant the music for Cox, which is played as a relief pitcher walks from the bullpen to the mound. "No, no," Poulakis tells him. "It's 'Livewire.'" Poulakis looks a little rough for wear. Several games earlier, when he was driving home from the SkyDome, he got stuck in traffic on Front Street and some toughs walked by and pounded on the roof of his car. He exchanged words with them, whereupon one of the toughs walked back, unleashed a roundhouse fist through the driver's side window and connected with Poulakis's right eye, leaving a bloody and bruised shiner. What miffed Poulakis most was that the guy probably was one of the fans he was trying so hard to entertain at the stadium that evening. "He's probably sitting down there tonight," he said, working the keyboard to produce another *Charrrge!*

Someone in the back of the audio booth asks where the party would be after the game. The night before it was at Windows, with free eats and free beer. Tonight it will be on the ramps, between sections 105 and 108, north of the outfield. There will be eats, beer, music, dancing—and if the

Blue Jays win it might go on all night. Debbie Alleyne, pro-duction co-ordinator of JumboTron, is ready to party. She is wearing a snappy United States Naval Academy blazer with brass buttons. "It's my neighbour's," she says. "I gave her a bottle of Glenfiddich if she let me wear it tonight."

Mariano Duncan singles to centre. John Kruk strikes out on a checked swing. Next up is Dave Hollins, a switch-hitter, but Cox seems more concerned about Duncan on first. Doesn't matter, as Duncan steals second on a close Borders-to-Fernandez throw. Hollins then singles over second, bring-ing in Duncan, a nicely orchestrated run that ties the game 5–5.

Cox stays in to face Daulton, and the first serious second-guessing of Gaston begins, this time before a world audience. Why Cox? Why not Leiter? More calls to and from the dugout and the bullpen. Now Todd Stottlemyre gets up and starts warming up on the mound beside Leiter. Why Stottlemyre? Questions, questions. Leiter is ready, so why not bring him in to face the left-handed-hitting Daulton? Why bother having Leiter warm up if you are not going to bring him in? Baseball is such a wonderfully querulous game.

Al Widmar, the Blue Jays' former pitching coach who is now Pat Gillick's special assistant, has a theory on why Stottlemyre, who has undeniable pitching talent, keeps falling short of his potential. There are few pitchers more competi-tive than Stottlemyre; when a brushed-back, knocked-down or plonked batter looks like he is about to charge the mound, Stottlemyre's instinct is to charge the batter. He has all the tools, except, in tough situations, he tends not to use all of them. "He becomes a two-pitch pitcher," Widmar told Martin one evening when they sat together in the press box. "That makes it easier for the batter to guess. Juan Guzman sometimes does that, too, but not as much." Widmar, sixty-eight, pitched for the St. Louis Browns in the late 1940s. One of his ears was thickly bandaged, covering the surgery he had had for another skin cancer. Farmers often get these basal-cell carcinomas on their face and neck from hours working directly in the sun; baseball players tend to get them on their ears from hours of exposure on baked diamonds. The bill of the baseball cap shields a player's face, makes the nose less vulnerable to direct sunlight, but the ears are constantly exposed, and over many hot seasons the impact is cumulative and lesions erupt.

Daulton walks, which brings Eisenreich to the plate, another lefty. He smashes the ball into the ground and it shoots up high over the mound—up, up—allowing Eisenreich to reach first safely, loading the bases.

Cox gets the hook, Leiter comes in—*Why didn't he bring Leiter in earlier?*—and manager Jim Fregosi of the Phillies counters by sending in Pete Incaviglia, a right-handed hitter, to pinch-hit for Milt Thompson. The stocky Incaviglia pounds the first pitch deep to White in centre, a sacrific RBI that brings in Hollins for the go-ahead run. In the Blue Jay clubhouse, Malloy wheels the Freixenet back to the stockroom, then frantically tears down the clear plastic sheets at the players' cubicles.

Stocker comes to the plate for the second time in the inning and Leiter strikes him out. In all, a good performance by Leiter—he got out the two hitters he faced, on his twenty-eighth birthday, no less—but it is an entirely different game now. A hush falls over the SkyDome.

For the seventh-inning stretch, the wholesome Fitness Ontario cheerleaders run onto the sidelines for their "Okay! Blue Jays!" routine. This time Bam Bam is allowed to ignite his rhythmical airbursts once again, just like old times. "Okay! [*Bam! Bam!*] Blue Jays! [*Bam! Bam!*]..." During this exchange, Bam Bam, connected to Poulakis on a headset, smiles as he hears Nick do his street version of the popular "Okay! Blue Jays!" song. Most of it is unprintable, and it does *not* end with "Let's play ball!"

In the bottom of the seventh, Henderson faces Roger Mason and flies out to left. White strikes out on a high fastball, then Molitor flies out to centre. The seventh inning finally ends. Altogether, the seventh inning took forty mintues to play, but to use a football term, the time of possession was nearly all Philadelphia's—thirty-two minutes for the Phillies, eight for the Blue Jays.

| PHILADELPHIA | 0 0 0 | 1 0 0 | 5 – – |
| TORONTO | 3 0 0 | 1 1 0 | 0 – – |

The selections by *The Sporting News* of the 1993 managers of the year were announced prior to the World Series. The newspaper selected John Oates of the Baltimore Orioles in the American League, Bobby Cox of the Atlanta Braves in the National League. Curious selections, as both their teams had been eliminated, the Orioles after a surprising late-season swoon at a time when the Blue Jays seemed vincible. From all accounts, Cito Gaston did not even make the short list in the American League.

Martin was with Darnell Coles by the batting cage during an off-day workout at the SkyDome and he asked him, "What does Gaston have to do before he is recognized as one of the best managers in major-league baseball?" Coles said, "To be manager of the year, maybe he has to go from last to first."

Maybe that's it. Maybe Gaston has been winning too much: four division titles in five years, two AL pennants, a World Series championship and another pending. Maybe it is because Gaston started winning as soon as he was appointed interim manager early in the 1989 season. Under manager Jimy Williams, the Blue Jays that year got off to a 12–24 start; after Gaston took over on May 15, the Blue Jays compiled a 77–49 record to finish in first place by two games. An astonishing turnaround, which should have merited Gason serious consideration as manager of the year for 1989.

There was a game late in September when the Blue Jays were losing 7–5 to the Boston Red Sox in the bottom of the tenth inning. The catcher, Randy Knorr, was due up. What remained of the crowd of 50,532 at the SkyDome wondered who Gaston would select to pinch-hit for the weak-hitting

277

backup catcher. As Turner Ward walked to the plate to face relief pitcher Ken Ryan, a loud, angry voice from the field seats behind first base shouted, "Bring out Delgado, stupid!"

The voice meant Carlos Delgado, the young Puerto Rican catcher brought up from the minors at the end of the season, but the insult clearly was directed at Gaston. No matter that the Blue Jays had recovered heroically from a six-game losing streak, when their lead in the American League East had dwindled to nothing. No matter that the Blue Jays had won six in a row, outscoring their opponents 47–16, had a five-game cushion atop the East and were sailing once again into postseason competition.

"Bring out Delgado, stupid!"

In another locale, in another time, one might be tempted to suspect something racist here. Gaston, in fact, *does* suspect racism. He has mentioned it in casual conversations to several beat writers. More probably, it is something Canadian, as in: How can one of our guys be this good?

Baseball is so many things. At a majestic level, it could well be mankind's ultimate way to choreograph and dignify our most basic activities—running, hitting, throwing, catching (spitting, scratching, hawking). On a less majestic level, baseball is the most competitively snobbish team sport in the world. It is a game made for second-guessing, which is the fun of it, but the manager always takes the tomato in the face. Why is it that everyone thinks he or she has a marvellous sense of humour, and everyone thinks he or she can manage a professional baseball team?

"I don't know why Cito's not manager of the year," said Gene Tenace, the Blue Jays' bench coach, who sees and studies Gaston as much as anyone else on the team, from the dugout to the front office. Tenace sits beside Gaston during the games, shares baseball strategy, knows how the man's brain works. "All successful managers know how to handle ten people—the pitching staff. Cito's good at that, too, but his real strength is handling all twenty-five players on the team. He played the game, so he knows the mental aspect of baseball. He instils confidence. A lot of managers break down players mentally, and they can destroy a player. Cito knows how to handle personalities, individuals. He has a feeling for people. The players know it, and they respect him for that."

For Paul Molitor, Gaston is the perfect choice to manage a team as good as the Blue Jays, which is not as easy as home hecklers like to think. Many good teams, possible World Series winners, have blown apart in a snarl of bruised egos and personality collisions. "This is a team with a wonderful atmosphere, and it's *because* of the manager," Molitor said. "Cito Gaston has the knack of keeping everyone happy, and, in return, everybody is anxious, even willing, to go to the wall for him."

The baseball season is long, 162 games. Add to this spring training, the playoffs and World Series, and a major-league team can play more than 200 games in a season. The demands of baseball's long haul require a different manager than in any other sport. There is no need of Knute Rockne inspiration or Vince Lombardi exhortation. Baseball players are not expected to level cross-body blocks, slam opposing forwards into the boards, or score the winning goal on a broken ankle. They perform best when they perform consistently, on an even keel, their mental and physical games clicking together. In a book called *The Mental Game of Baseball*, authors H. A. Dorfman and Karl Kuehl present exercises and techniques for gearing down, relaxing and arranging mental priorities so one can be in the proper frame of mind to play the game of baseball. Among them are "The Two Rules of Life," designed expressly for hitters in the midst of a slump.

Rule number one: Don't sweat the small stuff.

Rule number two: It's all small stuff.

Consider the Delgado–Ward example in the game against the Red Sox. It is typical of Gaston's style that he would go to Ward, who had been with the team all year. Gaston also faced choices as to who would be on the postseason roster. This was a good time to see what Ward could do as a pinch-hitter in a game-winning situation, a test of fire. Ward failed,

279

and Ward did not make the postseason roster.

The closest Gaston comes to showing up a player is illustrated by an incident involving shortstop Manny Lee in 1992 in a game early in the season against Boston. Lee had been unenthusiastic about laying down a bunt, so Gaston ordered him to lay one down when he had two strikes. When you bunt the third strike foul, you're out, which is what happened to Lee that night. Gaston kept him in the game but pulled him in extra innings for pinch-hitter Alfredo Griffin. He also benched Lee for two games, after which Lee played some of the best baseball of his career.

In the clubhouse after the workout, Martin found Pat Borders sitting at his cubicle and asked him what he thought of Gaston as the manager of a team of all-stars, World Series champions. "Cito's a players' manager," Borders said. "To handle a team with this many high-profile players is really tough. Cito's got a knack of knowing who he can get on, and who he shouldn't get on. He doesn't believe in team meetings, but he'll take groups—the pitchers, the catchers, the infielders—and sometimes really let them have it. He also knows when to ease off. After we lost six in a row off that West Coast trip, all he said was, 'We'll get 'em next time, fellas.' He never shows anybody up, never embarrasses us. We respect what he says. And we respect him physically, too. I mean, he's not a small guy in stature. He could come up and say, 'Let's go outside and I'll kick your butt.' He doesn't but he could. We'd *listen*."

One Blue Jay fan, Professor Joseph Green of York University—he sits at most games behind the home plate screen, toward the visitors' dugout—has an interesting perspective on the managing abilities of Gaston. Professor Green is director of arts and media administration in the Faculty of Administrative Studies, which means his job is to understand and explain managers. As the former dean of fine arts, he also appreciates the peculiar high-wire act of management and entertainment. And he is no baseball innocent, having grown up in Philadelphia where he was a loyal fan of the Phillies.

Professor Green sees Gaston as "very stable, unflappable, in control of himself." Like Molitor, he regards Gaston as the perfect choice to manage a team of exceptional talent. Managing a great team, one with high expectations, can be more difficult than managing a mediocre team. It is like managing a world-renowned opera company: massaging the egos, creating harmony, achieving maximum performance from dissonant parts. "I was impressed by the way Cito handled himself at the All-Star Game in Baltimore, when he faced all that abuse. The way he conducted himself then, it really helped the team. Baseball players are like artists. They are easily humiliated. In spite of the bravado, they are very vulnerable. In the Chicago series, when Bo Jackson was taken out for the sixth game, you could see he was really *hurt*. Cito's strength as a manager is that he sees that vulnerability."

Professor Green believes baseball players are unlike other athletes in team sports in that, one by one, as they step into the batter's box, they step into the spotlight. A pitcher, of course, is always the centre of attention, but on a baseball team, the entire starting lineup comes to bat, one by one, to take centre stage. Each player, in turn, must stand and deliver the soliloquy that carries the play.

After the off-day workout before the World Series, Martin walked with Gaston along 000 Level when he was heading back to his office after a media session in the interview room. "Just what *do* you have to do to be manager of the year?" he asked. Cito entered the door to the clubhouse, and as it closed behind him he said, "I don't know, but I'm not going to worry about it much."

"What about Oates being picked top manager in the American League?"

"Good for him," Gaston said. "Guess it means they got to hire Oatesy back now."

As Leiter finishes his warm-up tosses before the start of the eighth, Sean is making his way out of the 100-Level "Puffers" designated smoking area behind the auxiliary press box. It is a concrete box, with all the ambience of a holding cell. This late in the game the air is so thick with carcinogenic haze that it is difficult to see more than a few feet in any direction. This is fine by Sean, who is actively trying to avoid Ed, a radio journalist from upstate New York. Ed had seemed an amiable sort at the beginning of the ALCS, full of good cheer and chatter. By the end of the ALCS, Ed was causing Sean to think about an old Indian saying: "Don't speak unless you can improve the silence." Ed liked to tell Sean about his days as a helicopter gunner during the Vietnam War, when he smoked filterless Salems while shooting at the North Vietnamese. "When Charlie was shooting up our ass, we wouldn't worry about high nicotine counts—we worried about high lead counts," he said. During Game Four of the ALCS he would scream out, "I can't believe they got another hit, there's only one out!" whenever a Chicago player reached base safely. This was a humorous reference to all the two-out hits Chicago and Toronto got in the first three games. Martin tried to break up the monotony once by telling Ed the joke public address announcer Murray Eldon had told, the one about his job being vital because without him all the players would come to the plate at the same time. Ed frowned. "I don't get it," he said. Then he told Martin how pleased he was with the radio script he had just written on his laptop. "Would you like to read it?" he asked. By the eighth inning of Game Six of the World Series, Sean wished Charlie had been a better shot.

Leiter starts strongly, striking out Morandini on four pitches. But then Dykstra steps up again. If it were a regular-season game, Leiter might have been inclined to plonk him as retribution for Dykstra's upper-deck three-run homer. Instead, he walks Dykstra on four pitches, Dykstra's second walk of the game. None of them were close. (Dykstra has been playing so well, an opposing manager might be tempted to walk him with first base occupied, as was done once by Baltimore manager Earl Weaver during George Brett's .390 season.)

Dykstra is already the consensus MVP choice for Philadelphia because of his four home runs and sparkling defence. Now he is dancing off first, daring Leiter to pick him off. After two balls high to Mariano Duncan, Leiter gets a visit from Galen Cisco, as Mike Timlin and Tony Castillo are throwing in the bullpen. Whatever Cisco says, it has no effect, as Leiter misses again, his seventh consecutive ball, which runs the count to 3–0. Duncan keeps his bat on his shoulder for the next two pitches, both called strikes, then realizes he has to earn his way on. This seems to fluster him, and he pops up meekly to Alomar for the second out of the inning.

With Kruk at the plate, Dykstra takes matters into his own hands, breaking for second on Leiter's second pitch. He gets such a good jump that Borders does not even attempt a throw. Before Dykstra has a chance to steal third and home as well, Kruk hits a broken-bat bouncer to Sprague, who fires a crisp throw on the run to Olerud for the third out.

Though the Blue Jays are down by a run, the crowd in the SkyDome is boisterous. They know that Roger Mason is beginning his third inning in relief, and will almost certainly not finish the game. Will Fregosi dare bring in Mitch Williams? The prospect of seeing "Wild Thing" again is enough to hearten a SkyDome crowd that is notoriously glum and quiet whenever their Blue Jays fall behind.

After Carter gets under Mason's third pitch and lifts it to left for the first out, pear-shaped reliever David West comes in to face John Olerud, more cause for rejoicing among the locals. In two World Series before 1993, West had accomplished something of a rare feat by never recording an out despite ample opportunity. He maintained his perfect record in Game One of the 1993 World Series, giving up hits to both batters he faced. He finally recorded his first World Series out in Game Four, that monsoon affair at Veterans Stadium, giving up three hits and two runs in one inning, which lowered his 1993 World Series earned run average from infinity to a merely embarrassing 27.00. Whether overcome by cockiness or relief, West walks Olerud on five pitches, then is taken out of the game.

283

So, too, is Olerud, who is replaced by pinch runner Alfredo Griffin. If the Blue Jays come back and win this one, Olerud's astonishing season is now over. The fans do not seem to appreciate this as Olerud walks off the field, so intent are they on following the machinations that might lead to a game-tying run in the bottom of the eighth.

Olerud has fascinated Martin all season, as well as the season before when he first started hanging around the SkyDome asking questions. This phenomenally talented, fundamentally decent young man first took a run at Joe DiMaggio's fifty-six-game hit streak, then persisted into August on a pace to become the first hitter since Ted Williams to hit over .400 over a full season. But it was Olerud himself, Olerud the man, that was fascinating. He was shy, quiet—utterly devoid of strut and style—yet for most of the 1993 baseball season he calmly withstood the scrums and cameras and TV lights. In an interview with Radio Canada, he ended by thanking the interviewer by saying, "Merci."

What was refreshing about Olerud was that in a sport crowded with self-obsessed jerks, he emerged as one of the most likeable athletes competing today. In spring training, Cito Gaston summed it up when he said Olerud is "the type of man you hope your son will grow up to be." Despite the constant comparisons to Ted Williams, Olerud the man is the antithesis of "The Splendid Splinter." And his boyhood hitting model was George Brett. Apart from hitting from the left side, having excellent eyes and being tall and lanky, Olerud as a personality is a foil to Williams. After a game in 1949, Lou Stringer, a backup second baseman for the Boston Red Sox, complimented Williams on looking great at the plate, to which Williams replied, "I'm the best goddamn hitter in the world, kid, and you better believe it, the best goddamn hitter who ever lived!" Lay a compliment like that on Olerud and he would probably—blush.

Whenever Olerud came to bat Martin trained his binoculars on him, studying his swing. Each time Olerud comes to bat he takes one, two stiff, level swings before he steps in the

284

box. Once in the box, as he watches the pitcher, he takes measured half-swings: 1, 2, 3, 4... There is a metronomic rhythm to these swings. Depending on the pitcher, he might take only two of these half-swings, or as many as seven, but that's it. During an at-bat against Bobby Witt of the Oakland Athletics, Olerud got to seven of these half-swings and when there was still no pitch he called time and stepped out of the box.

When the pitch is about to fly, Olerud drops his bat about an inch and gently taps it on his uniform at the left collarbone. He does this for every pitch, twenty to twenty-five times a game. In the clubhouse after a game there is always a small pine-tar stain on his uniform where he taps his bat. The secret to his success? The universe in a grain of sand? Martin asked him about it after a game and Olerud said it is "an unconscious habit, a little timing movement." The little tap has been part of his at-bat routine going back to Pony League and Little League and probably to the days when he used to take batting practice against a tennis ball to overcome any fear of inside pitches.

Olerud's presence on the 1993 Blue Jays, though he is barely twenty-five, had a noticeable impact. As if by osmosis, Olerud's fundamental decency—not to mention his ability— had a contagious effect on his teammates. Even hard-nosed beat writers had to admit that the 1993 edition of the Blue Jays was the best ever in terms of character and maturity, as opposed to, say, the Blue Jays of the George Bell era. A high compliment indeed, considering the baseball writers know that many players refer to them as "pond scum." According to David Halberstam's *Summer of '49*, when Ted Williams noticed a writer on the team bus he would say, "There must be a writer on the bus. It smells like shit."

When Olerud was hitting .435, he told an assembled scrum by the batting cage that he hits balls "where they aren't." Someone reminded Olerud that Wee Willie Keeler used to say he hit them "where they ain't." Olerud listened politely, then said, "I know." No strut, no guile, an invulnerable ego. Before

285

Game Three there was much speculation about how to get Molitor into the game with the DH outlawed in Philadelphia. One afternoon when Olerud was playing bridge in the clubhouse with Sprague, Carter and Molitor, Molitor mentioned that Gaston had not made a decision, but he suspected Gaston would sit Olerud and play Molitor at first. "That's what I would do," Olerud said.

The other card players were dumbstruck in admiration. Molitor later said, "It's strange that in today's game of egos and personalities that that would happen, but he said it and he meant it."

When the teams returned to the SkyDome for the rest of the World Series, Olerud sat on the dais in the interview room on 000 Level—during the season the room is used for indoor batting practice—and answered questions. Someone at the back of the room asked Olerud if his ego had suffered from having been benched in Philadelphia. Sitting respectfully behind the microphone, wearing his plastic batting helmet, Olerud looked genuinely puzzled.

He said, "What do you mean?"

Still in the bottom of the eighth, the Phillies bring in reliever Larry Andersen, the forty-year-old right-hander, who is greeted by Nick Poulakis's booming "We Will Rock You" ("There's mud on your face, you're a big disgrace..."). For Andersen, nothing could be further from the truth. He is that rarity among Phillies: a clean-cut, decent fellow, and a member in good standing at David Fisher's Bible study sessions. As he did all season, Fisher conducted his Sunday-morning meeting in the green room under the left-field stands before Game Two of the World Series. Attendance for the Philadelphia service was sparse, but Andersen was there.

Sean had been talking to Fisher in the Blue Jay dugout a few days earlier, finding him as sombre and serious as on the summer afternoon they met for coffee in the restaurant on Danforth Avenue. During the conversation, Darnell Coles breezed by, full of piss and vinegar as usual. He gave Fisher a pat on the back. "Hey there, Mr. Excitement," Coles said. "How's it goin', man?" When Coles breezed away, Fisher turned to Sean and said, "He always calls me that. Kind of ironic, isn't it?"

Alomar digs in to face Andersen, fouling off the first three pitches into the stands. The tension mounts. Ball one, high. A breaking ball runs outside to even the count at 2–2. When Andersen throws in his sixth pitch for another ball, this one outside, he looks frustrated. He stomps the mound in disgust. Manager Fregosi is red faced in anger, the arteries in his neck bulging as he shouts from the dugout at home-plate umpire Dana DeMuth. Arguing balls and strikes is verboten, but the noise in the SkyDome is so loud that Fregosi's shouts are drowned out, so he is not ejected. The battle between Andersen and Alomar continues, as Alomar fouls off two more pitches, then drives a one-hopper to Kruk for what looks like a certain double play. Griffin was running on the pitch, however, and he scampers safely into second, keeping the inning alive.

Next up is Fernandez, who has already set a World Series record for shortstops with nine RBIs and is looking for a clean single to make double digits. He dribbles the first pitch to Kruk for what appears to be the third out, but DeMuth says the ball nicked Fernandez's foot after he hit it and rules it a foul strike. Andersen goes back to the mound, quickly falls behind Fernandez with two balls, then throws so wildly two pitches later that he hits Fernandez on the inside of his left thigh, putting runners at first and second.

Ed Sprague is having a terrible series, one hit in fifteen tries, for an .077 average. But after getting within a strike of ending the inning, Sprague refuses to let the third strike by him. He fouls off three good pitches, then watches a ball come in low to run the count full. With the runners going to the pitch, Andersen delivers ball four outside. Now the bases are loaded.

With 1992 World Series MVP Pat Borders up, reliever Mitch Williams is standing on the bullpen mound, warmed and ready to be brought in. He looks as nervous as Atlanta closer Jeff Reardon had looked in the bullpen in the eleventh inning during Game Six of the 1992 World Series after having blown saves in games two and three. One could hardly blame Williams for thinking, "Please, not me." But probably not. He probably wants a chance to redeem himself. Fregosi stays with a fading Andersen, who rewards him by inducing an infield pop-up to end the inning.

Three outs to Game Seven.

| PHILADELPHIA | 0 0 0 | 1 0 0 | 5 0 – |
| TORONTO | 3 0 0 | 1 1 0 | 0 0 – |

The scalpers were aggressively at work before all the postseason games, but a turf war erupted when the World Series games started. Outside the SkyDome, the scalpers known as the "French Connection"—they are from Montreal—encountered a group of dudes from Detroit trying to sell World Series tickets on the sidewalk. Martin and Sean are sitting on their favourite curb outside Gate 9 for their usual pregame meditation when a dust-up happened along the street. A young man, bare chested, was scuffling with another young man wearing a Detroit Pistons jacket. The shirtless guy connected with a right to the face and the other guy went down, then jumped up flailing at his assailant with what looked like a golfing iron. It turned out to be a shiny belt, with a thick buckle at the end that was being twisted in circles. The bare-chested Québécois deked away from the weapon and decked the other fellow again. The guy in the Pistons jacket walked away, climbed into an idling Cadillac and drove off.

We mentioned this to Fred Wootton, who did not give it a priority at tonight's game. He was more concerned with the crowd control that would be needed if the Blue Jays should win. He had extra off-duty coppers stationed on the different levels of SkyDome, and he had a plan that would have them down by the field from the seventh inning on. There was also a contingent of police on horseback stationed in a lane across the city for the party that would erupt on Yonge Street. Wootton was determined to avoid a repeat of the turf tearing, warning-track stealing that happened after the 1992 championship, when the SkyDome television audience ran onto the field. He was having fun, though. At an earlier game he found five young men on 000 Level, which they reached by using an elevator at the SkyDome Hotel. They told Wootton they wanted to watch batting practice, but he suspected they were stowaways who would sneak up the aisles and watch the game from one of the concourses. Wootton marched the boys to a uniformed policeman, telling them they probably would be charged with trespassing and fined. "They were nervous as hell," Wootton said. "I knew they would be given a reprimand and escorted out of the stadium, which is what happened. But before they got turfed out, I told them, 'You got a break today, fellas.'"

Top of the ninth now, and Griffin is staying in at third base while Sprague moves over to first for the first time in 1993. Gaston makes another move almost as rare by bringing in stopper Duane Ward in an non-save situation. Ward had forty-five saves to lead the American League in 1993, but he had only two wins. Ward has been a good-luck charm in the postseason the past two years, getting credit for the comeback wins in the fourth game of the 1992 ALCS and the second and third games of the 1992 World Series. This time, luck has nothing to do with it. Gaston knows that the Philadelphia bullpen is almost empty. He hopes he can get to the bottom of the ninth down by one run, with the top of the order going against Mitch Williams.

Ward, unlike Andersen the previous inning, is a fast worker, taking little time between pitches. Seven pitches later, the inning is over. Elapsed time: two minutes, twenty-nine seconds.

As soon as Mitch Williams is announced to start the ninth, Kevin Malloy starts reassembling the cases of champagne in the players' lounge of the Blue Jay clubhouse. Brad Bujold, head of the grounds crew, is not as optimistic. If Philadelphia wins, his job is to escort the Phillies players to the interview room immediately following the last out. He is sitting in a motorized cart on 000 Level, catching peaks of the action on a television monitor.

Williams looks tense. He may be scared for his life, as he had received death threats following Game Four and stayed awake until dawn in his house with a loaded revolver in his hand. However serious the threats were, he knows that if he gives up two runs this inning, his life will never be the same again. At this level of the game, any mistake is colossal, and never forgotten. After blowing the big lead in Game Four three nights earlier, Williams said he was not going to kill himself just because he lost a World Series game. It was an unsolicited comment that would normally have been filed in the postgame cliché bin—if not for California Angels' reliever Donnie Moore. Several years after giving up a two-run homer to Boston's Dave Henderson in 1986, when he was one strike away from taking the Angels to their first World Series, Moore *did* kill himself. Friends said Moore never recovered from the home-run pitch to Dave Henderson.

Rickey Henderson leads off. As happened throughout his two months with the Jays in August and September, Henderson has been getting near-unanimous bad press in the postseason. In the playoff series against Chicago, he hit only .120. Entering the bottom of the ninth, his batting average in the World Series is .227. There was talk before the Series shifted to Philadelphia that Henderson should be benched so that Molitor could get in the game in left field. Pat Gillick, in another curious example of weird timing, said in a radio interview just before the ALCS that if he could do it over again, he would not have traded for Henderson. Funny thing, though, Henderson kept scoring runs—nine in the first eleven 1993 postseason games, behind only White and Molitor. Somehow, he was maintaining the same run-scoring pace as he did during the end of the regular season, when he hit .215 for the Jays but scored 37 runs in 44 games. Henderson's batting average bears no relation to his ability to score runs. His on-base percentage is a more reliable indicator of his effectiveness, but there is also a smoke-and-mirrors effect that defies analysis. It is the same as Joe Carter's ability to knock in runs. Carter can be hitting over .300, or he can be hitting in the low .200s, but year after year after year he produces more than 100 RBIs.

A fraction of a second before Williams delivers the first pitch, while he is in his peekaboo windup, Henderson raises his right arm to call for time. DeMuth gives it to him, and Henderson backs out of the box. Williams, like reliever Al (The Mad Hungarian) Hrabosky of the St. Louis Cardinals and Kansas City Royals in the 1970s, does not look toward home until he is about to release the ball. Henderson knows this. He also knows that even if the umpire does not grant his request for time, there is a good chance Williams's first pitch would be a ball. The impact of Henderson's deliberate mind game on the already frazzled Williams cannot be underestimated. As a result, with Henderson, DeMuth and catcher Darren Daulton all running for cover, Williams jerks his left arm violently as he is making his falling-down delivery, holds on to the ball and nearly falls on his face on the mound. His composure shattered, Williams's next four pitches all miss, only one coming close to the mark, and Henderson begins his wiggly-ass saunter to first.

Henderson's influence does not end there. Obviously, he is a threat to steal. And Williams, with his high leg kick and erratic aim, is terrible at holding on runners. To compensate, he compacts his delivery greatly into what is called a "slide step," losing speed and accuracy as a result. A pitcher whose only weapon is speed is now throwing lukewarm sliders and so-so fastballs. After a strike to White, Williams throws twice to first, the second time forcing Henderson to dive to the bag. Henderson usually has at least one foot on the turf when he is on first, but when Williams throws ball one to White, Henderson has both feet planted in the dirt near the bag.

291

After throwing ball two high to White, Williams again throws to first to keep Henderson close. The sequence then goes foul strike, foul strike, throw to first, foul strike, foul strike, throw to first, ball three. If Williams throws one more ball, two of the best base-stealers in the game are on first and second with no outs. As he had done all season, creating jams then getting serious, Williams throws his first good pitch of the ninth, a slider down and away, which White hits meekly to left field for the first out.

Next up is Molitor. He could not help but think what fun it would be to win a World Series with a home run. But before 1993, Molitor had never hit more than nineteen home runs in a season. This time he knows that another fly-ball out will kill Toronto's momentum, bringing them an out away from a Game Seven crapshoot. Instead, he chooses to wait on Williams's third pitch as long as he can, then, with his quick wrists he muscles a looping single over second base. His swing is so economical, and the trajectory of the hit so tight, Henderson has to stop at second.

Next up: Joe Carter. Carter, a notorious streak hitter, is slumping, going hitless in his previous seven at-bats. His last hit was at the beginning of the fateful eighth inning in the downpour of Game Four. But that was before Williams had entered the game. Carter has never had a base hit off Williams in his career. Ahead in the count 2–1, Carter swings through a slider on what would have been ball three. Now the count is two balls, two strikes. "A flat-footed swing," says CBS announcer Tim McCarver. "Looked awkward, didn't it?" One more miss by Carter and the only obstacle between Williams and Game Seven would be on-deck hitter Alfredo Griffin, who had twenty hits in the regular season and has yet to step to the plate in the postseason.

Williams throws a fastball down and in that is so slow that Carter thinks it is another slider. Carter pulls it over the left-field fence for a three-run home run. The ball lands in the Toronto bullpen where it is retrieved by coach John Sullivan, who is now officially retired from baseball. Twenty feet away, in the first row of the auxiliary press box, Sean watches the ball cross the plane of the outfield wall and disappear. Martin loses it in the lights. Because it looks for a moment that the ball might land in our laps, we are standing at our table in the auxiliary press box. It is only the second time that a World Series has ended on a home run, the first being Bill Mazeroski's tie-breaker in the bottom of the ninth in Game Seven of the 1960 World Series. We remain standing in silence for what feels like a minute or two, though it is only a few seconds. Emily Dickinson once wrote describing a sensation of timelessness: it was the moment between a crash, and when a crash has been.

The Blue Jays rush out of the dugout onto the infield and pick up Carter rounding third after his gleeful jumps around the bases. Nobody jumps like Joe Carter. And he always seems to be the conspicuous cog in the game-winning machine, jumping when the Blue Jays beat the Atlanta Braves, now jumping as the Blue Jays beat the Philadelphia Phillies. Carter's jumps are like the splish-splashy jumps Gene Kelly does in *Singing in the Rain*. They are jumps of joy. It is exactly what the fans, in the SkyDome, and at home watching television, want to see. And it is what they will remember years from tonight, how Joe Carter jumped. "Touch 'em all, Joe, you'll never hit a bigger home run in your life," Tom Cheek says in the radio booth, this time finding the perfect line for a championship evening.

"That's it," Sean says to Martin as it finally dawns on him. "It's over."

There is no cheering in the press box, not even the auxiliary press box, where it might have been excusable to be a little reckless. Bam Bam's nitro-enhanced airbursts make centre field look like first light of morning at Normandy. In the audio booth an ecstatic Poulakis flicks on "Oh, What a Feeling, What a Rush!" Quietly, furtively, Martin lowers his right hand beneath his work table and spreads open his palm. Sean slaps it, a low five.

Hey!

PHILADELPHIA	0 0 0	1 0 0	5 0 0	6
TORONTO	3 0 0	1 1 0	0 0 3	8

When we come to our senses enough to make it down there ourselves, Rob Butler is on top of the dugout, having pulled his brother, mother and father out of the field-level stands. Kevin Shanahan, a.k.a. B. J. Birdie, is taking a breather on the dugout bench after having jumped all over the place for ten minutes straight. "Who hit the home run?" he asks Sean. "I blanked out. I'm getting too old for this."

Larry Hisle watched the players pile on each other at home plate, but from a distance, then he walked down the steps of the dugout to the dressing room. Days later, he would be hired back as the hitting coach, probably thanks to the Bob Elliott story in the *Sun*, which made Hisle's case embarrassingly conspicuous.

Brad Bujold is standing guard on the mound in his favourite pose—hands on hips, eyes darting about. As it turned out, it was one of his last carefree moments. A month after the season ended he was diagnosed with liver cancer. He died a few days before spring training in 1994.

At first base, Mario Coutinho is breathing easier. He was in the dugout runway and did not see Carter's blast, though he did run out onto the field with the players—not to join in the celebrations, but to tackle a fan who came within inches of Carter during his home-run jag around third. "I'm glad it's over," Coutinho says. "It all starts again next year."

Two hours later Sean and Martin have lost each other at the packed postgame party being held along the long runways between 000 Level and 300 Level. He bumps into Murray Eldon, who opens his jacket to show him the compact disc he just bought: *Croonin'* by Anne Murray.

There could have been no better sense of completion to a long season spent following the Blue Jays from Dunedin to Game Six of the World Series at SkyDome than Carter's home run. Sean knew that if he lived to be a hundred he would likely never witness firsthand such a dramatic baseball moment, not as a fan, anyway. How many people can say they were as close to Bobby Thomson's home run, or Bill Mazeroski's, as he was? He could see the seams on the ball as it passed over the outfield fence into the bullpen.

But there was still one pact Sean had made with himself before the home opener back on April 9 that he had yet to honour. He figured now was as good a time as any to follow through. He took his girlfriend, whom he had met a few weeks before spring training, and moved in with shortly after the All-Star break, for a tour of the building where he had been spending his days and nights for the past seven months. They walked up to the 100-Level concourse, sat in a field-level aisle a few rows up from the visiting dugout and watched Frank Grespan and his conversion crew tear down the baseball field for the last time in 1993. There was a victory parade the next day at SkyDome to prepare for. Grespan would be working all night.

Sean took his girlfriend back down to 000 Level to show her the bogies that the stands between first and third move on. They walked under the stands, deep into the bowels of SkyDome, until the whoops and hollers from the runways grew dim. There they hid under a steel beam, and circled the bases one last time. When they came out, Sean almost tripped over a previously unseen object. It was a National League baseball, with a scuff to the right of President William White's signature. It must have bounced under the stands during BP. It sits on Sean's desk as he writes this.

Martin took the subway to Game Six, figuring there would be a party after the game, and if the Blue Jays won the streets would be jammed with celebrators. He found the party in the runways under the stands—people shouting, singing, dancing, kissing, high-fiving. "Whoomp, there it is!" kept playing. And the chant, "Blue Jayayays!" He took his beer and sat in the field-level seats, watching the conversion crew do its job, taking down the baseball field to prepare for Sunday's reception.

295

GAME DAY

When it came time to leave at around two-thirty in the morning, he could not find a taxi at SkyDome, so he walked to Front Street, then up Avenue Road. People were riding by on the tops of cars, blowing horns, screaming, slapping palms. By the time Martin reached Bloor Street it still looked like there would be no taxis, so he walked the rest of the uphill walk and when he arrived at his apartment at Yonge Street and St. Clair Avenue it was nearly five o'clock. His black cat, Stokely, greeted him as the eastern sky was turning light over Lake Ontario. He could still hear the horns blaring from the streets eighteen storeys below. He poured himself a stiff vodka on ice, then walked through the living room where he slid open the door to the balcony, sat on his patio chair and looked out at the Toronto skyline.

What a feeling, what a rush.